LITTLE,
BROWN

LARGE
PRINT

Also by Malcolm Gladwell

Blink
The Tipping Point

OUTLIERS

The Story of Success

MALCOLM GLADWELL

LITTLE, BROWN AND COMPANY

LARGE PRINT

Little, Brown and Company
Hachette Book Group
237 Park Avenue, New York, NY 10017
Visit our Web site at www.HachetteBookGroup.com

First Large Print Edition: November 2008

The Large Print Edition is published in accord with the standards of the N.A.V.H.

Little, Brown and Company is a division of Hachette Book Group, Inc. The Little, Brown name and logo are trademarks of Hachette Book Group, Inc.

ISBN 978-0-316-02497-6
LCCN 2008934571

10 9 8 7 6 5 4 3 2 1

RRD-IN

Book designed by Meryl Levavi

Printed in the United States of America

For Daisy

Contents

PART TWO: LEGACY

Outliers

INTRODUCTION

The Roseto Mystery

"THESE PEOPLE WERE DYING OF OLD AGE. THAT'S IT."

out•li•er \\-ˌlī(-ə)r\\ *noun*
1: something that is situated away from or classed differently from a main or related body
2: a statistical observation that is markedly different in value from the others of the sample

1.

Roseto Valfortore lies one hundred miles southeast of Rome in the Apennine foothills of the Italian province of Foggia. In the style of medieval villages, the town is organized around a large central square. Facing the square is the

Palazzo Marchesale, the palace of the Saggese family, once the great landowner of those parts. An archway to one side leads to a church, the Madonna del Carmine—Our Lady of Mount Carmine. Narrow stone steps run up the hillside, flanked by closely clustered two-story stone houses with red-tile roofs.

For centuries, the *paesani* of Roseto worked in the marble quarries in the surrounding hills, or cultivated the fields in the terraced valley below, walking four and five miles down the mountain in the morning and then making the long journey back up the hill at night. Life was hard. The townsfolk were barely literate and desperately poor and without much hope for economic betterment until word reached Roseto at the end of the nineteenth century of the land of opportunity across the ocean.

In January of 1882, a group of eleven Rosetans—ten men and one boy—set sail for New York. They spent their first night in America sleeping on the floor of a tavern on Mulberry Street, in Manhattan's Little Italy. Then they ventured west, eventually finding jobs in a slate quarry ninety miles west of the city near the town of Bangor, Pennsylvania. The following year, fifteen Rosetans left Italy for America, and several members of that group ended up in Bangor as well, joining their compatriots in the slate quarry. Those immigrants, in turn, sent word back to Roseto about the promise of the New World, and soon one group of Rosetans after another packed their bags and headed for Pennsylvania, until the initial stream of immigrants became a flood. In 1894 alone, some twelve hundred Rosetans applied for passports to America, leaving entire streets of their old village abandoned.

The Rosetans began buying land on a rocky hillside connected to Bangor by a steep, rutted wagon path. They built closely clustered two-story stone houses with slate roofs on narrow streets running up and down the hillside. They built a church and called it Our Lady of Mount Carmel and named the main street, on which it stood, Garibaldi Avenue, after the great hero of Italian unification. In the beginning, they called their town New Italy. But they soon changed it to Roseto, which seemed only appropriate given that almost all of them had come from the same village in Italy.

In 1896, a dynamic young priest by the name of Father Pasquale de Nisco took over at Our Lady of Mount Carmel. De Nisco set up spiritual societies and organized festivals. He encouraged the townsfolk to clear the land and plant onions, beans, potatoes, melons, and fruit trees in the long backyards behind their houses. He gave out seeds and bulbs. The town came to life. The Rosetans began raising pigs in their backyards and growing grapes for homemade wine. Schools, a park, a convent, and a cemetery were built. Small shops and bakeries and restaurants and bars opened along Garibaldi Avenue. More than a dozen factories sprang up making blouses for the garment trade. Neighboring Bangor was largely Welsh and English, and the next town over was overwhelmingly German, which meant—given the fractious relationships between the English and Germans and Italians in those years—that Roseto stayed strictly for Rosetans. If you had wandered up and down the streets of Roseto in Pennsylvania in the first few decades after 1900, you would have heard only Italian, and not just any Italian but the precise southern Foggian dialect spoken back in the Italian Roseto. Roseto, Pennsylvania, was its own tiny, self-sufficient world—all but unknown by the society around it—and it might well have remained so but for a man named Stewart Wolf.

Wolf was a physician. He studied digestion and the stomach and taught in the medical school at the University of Oklahoma. He spent his summers on a farm in Pennsylvania, not far from Roseto—although that, of course, didn't mean much, since Roseto was so much in its own world that it was possible to live in the next town and never know much about it. "One of the times when we were up there for the summer—this would have been in the late nineteen fifties—I was invited to give a talk at the local medical society," Wolf said years later in an interview. "After the talk was over, one of the local doctors invited me to have a beer. And while we were having a drink, he said,

'You know, I've been practicing for seventeen years. I get patients from all over, and I rarely find anyone from Roseto under the age of sixty-five with heart disease.' "

Wolf was taken aback. This was the 1950s, years before the advent of cholesterol-lowering drugs and aggressive measures to prevent heart disease. Heart attacks were an epidemic in the United States. They were the leading cause of death in men under the age of sixty-five. It was impossible to be a doctor, common sense said, and not see heart disease.

Wolf decided to investigate. He enlisted the support of some of his students and colleagues from Oklahoma. They gathered together the death certificates from residents of the town, going back as many years as they could. They analyzed physicians' records. They took medical histories and constructed family genealogies. "We got busy," Wolf said. "We decided to do a preliminary study. We started in nineteen sixty-one. The mayor said, 'All my sisters are going to help you.' He had four sisters. He said, 'You can have the town council room.' I said,

'Where are you going to have council meetings?' He said, 'Well, we'll postpone them for a while.' The ladies would bring us lunch. We had little booths where we could take blood, do EKGs. We were there for four weeks. Then I talked with the authorities. They gave us the school for the summer. We invited the entire population of Roseto to be tested."

The results were astonishing. In Roseto, virtually no one under fifty-five had died of a heart attack or showed any signs of heart disease. For men over sixty-five, the death rate from heart disease in Roseto was roughly half that of the United States as a whole. The death rate from all causes in Roseto, in fact, was 30 to 35 percent lower than expected.

Wolf brought in a friend of his, a sociologist from Oklahoma named John Bruhn, to help him. "I hired medical students and sociology grad students as interviewers, and in Roseto we went house to house and talked to every person aged twenty-one and over," Bruhn remembers. This happened more than fifty years ago, but Bruhn still had a sense of amazement in his voice as he described what they found. "There was no suicide, no alcoholism, no drug addiction, and very little crime. They didn't have anyone on welfare. Then we looked at peptic ulcers. They didn't have any of those either. These people were dying of old age. That's it."

Wolf's profession had a name for a place like Roseto—a place that lay outside everyday experience, where the normal rules did not apply. Roseto was an *outlier.*

2.

Wolf's first thought was that the Rosetans must have held on to some dietary practices from the Old World that left them healthier than other Americans. But he quickly realized that wasn't true. The Rosetans were cooking with lard instead of with the much healthier olive oil they had used back in Italy. Pizza in Italy was a thin crust with salt, oil, and perhaps some tomatoes, anchovies, or onions. Pizza in Pennsylvania was bread dough plus sausage, pepperoni, salami, ham, and sometimes eggs. Sweets such as biscotti and *taralli* used to be reserved for Christmas and Easter; in Roseto they were eaten year-round. When Wolf had dieticians analyze the typical Rosetan's eating habits, they found that a whopping 41 percent of their calories came from fat. Nor was this a town where people got up at dawn to do yoga and run a brisk six miles. The Pennsylvanian Rosetans smoked heavily and many were struggling with obesity.

If diet and exercise didn't explain the findings, then what about genetics? The Rosetans were a close-knit group from the same region of Italy, and Wolf's next thought was to wonder whether they were of a particularly hardy stock that protected them from disease. So he tracked down relatives of the Rosetans who were living in other parts of the United States to see if they shared the same remarkable good health as their cousins in Pennsylvania. They didn't.

He then looked at the region where the Rosetans lived. Was it possible that there was something about living in the foothills of eastern Pennsylvania that was good for their health?

The two closest towns to Roseto were Bangor, which was just down the hill, and Nazareth, a few miles away. These were both about the same size as Roseto, and both were populated with the same kind of hardworking European immigrants. Wolf combed through both towns' medical records. For men over sixty-five, the death rates from heart disease in Nazareth and Bangor were three times that of Roseto. Another dead end.

What Wolf began to realize was that the secret of Roseto wasn't diet or exercise or genes or location. *It had to be Roseto itself.* As Bruhn and Wolf walked around the town, they figured out why. They looked at how the Rosetans visited one another, stopping to chat in Italian on the street, say, or cooking for one another in their backyards. They learned about the extended family clans that underlay the town's social structure. They saw how many homes had three generations living under one roof, and how much respect grandparents commanded. They went to mass at Our Lady of Mount Carmel and saw the unifying and calming effect of the church. They counted twenty-two separate civic organizations in a town of just under two thousand people. They picked up on the particular egalitarian ethos of the community, which discouraged the wealthy from flaunting their success and helped the unsuccessful obscure their failures.

In transplanting the *paesani* culture of southern Italy to the hills of eastern Pennsylvania, the Rosetans had created a powerful, protective social structure capable of insulating them from the pressures of the modern world. The Rosetans were healthy because of where they were *from*, because of the world they had created for themselves in their tiny little town in the hills.

"I remember going to Roseto for the first time, and you'd see three-generational family meals, all the bakeries, the people walking up and down the street, sitting on their porches talking to each other, the blouse mills where the women worked during the day, while the men worked in the slate quarries," Bruhn said. "It was magical."

When Bruhn and Wolf first presented their findings to the medical community, you can imagine the kind of skepticism they faced. They went to conferences where their peers were presenting long rows of data arrayed in complex charts and referring to this kind of gene or that kind of physiological process, and they themselves were talking instead about the mysterious and magical benefits of people stopping to talk to one another on the street and of having three generations under one roof. Living a long life, the conventional wisdom at the time said, depended to a great extent on who we were—that is, our genes. It depended on the decisions we made—on what we chose to eat, and how much we chose to exercise, and how effectively we were treated by the medical system. No one was used to thinking about health in terms of *community*.

Wolf and Bruhn had to convince the medical establishment to think about health and heart attacks in an entirely new way: they had to get them to realize that they wouldn't be able to understand why someone was healthy if all they did was think about an individual's personal choices or actions in isolation. They had to look *beyond* the individual. They had to understand the culture he or she was a part of, and who their friends and families were, and what town their families came from. They had to appreciate the idea that the values of the world we inhabit and the people we surround ourselves with have a profound effect on who we are.

In *Outliers,* I want to do for our understanding of success what Stewart Wolf did for our understanding of health.

Part One

OPPORTUNITY

CHAPTER ONE

The Matthew Effect

"FOR UNTO EVERYONE THAT HATH SHALL BE GIVEN, AND HE SHALL HAVE ABUNDANCE. BUT FROM HIM THAT HATH NOT SHALL BE TAKEN AWAY EVEN THAT WHICH HE HATH."
— MATTHEW 25:29

1.

One warm, spring day in May of 2007, the Medicine Hat Tigers and the Vancouver Giants met for the Memorial Cup hockey championships in Vancouver, British Columbia. The Tigers and the Giants were the two finest teams in the Canadian Hockey League, which in turn is the finest junior hockey league in the world. These were the future stars of the sport—seventeen-, eighteen-, and nineteen-year-olds who had been skating and shooting pucks since they were barely more than toddlers.

The game was broadcast on Canadian national television. Up and down the streets of downtown Vancouver, Memorial Cup banners hung from the lampposts. The arena was packed. A long red carpet was rolled out on the ice, and the announcer introduced the game's dignitaries. First came the premier of British Columbia, Gordon Campbell. Then, amid tumultuous applause, out walked Gordie Howe, one of the legends of the game. "Ladies and gentlemen," the announcer boomed. "Mr. Hockey!"

For the next sixty minutes, the two teams played spirited, aggressive hockey. Vancouver scored first, early in the second period, on a rebound by Mario Bliznak. Late in the second period, it was Medicine Hat's turn, as the team's scoring leader, Darren Helm, fired a quick shot past Vancouver's goalie, Tyson Sexsmith. Vancouver answered in the third period, scoring the game's deciding goal, and then, when Medicine

Hat pulled its goalie in desperation, Vancouver scored a third time.

In the aftermath of the game, the players and their families and sports reporters from across the country crammed into the winning team's locker room. The air was filled with cigar smoke and the smell of champagne and sweat-soaked hockey gear. On the wall was a hand-painted banner: "Embrace the Struggle." In the center of the room the Giants' coach, Don Hay, stood misty-eyed. "I'm just so proud of these guys," he said. "Just look around the locker room. There isn't one guy who didn't buy in wholeheartedly."

Canadian hockey is a meritocracy. Thousands of Canadian boys begin to play the sport at the "novice" level, before they are even in kindergarten. From that point on, there are leagues for every age class, and at each of those levels, the players are sifted and sorted and evaluated, with the most talented separated out and groomed for the next level. By the time players reach their midteens, the very best of the best have been channeled into an elite league known as Major Junior A, which is the top of the pyramid. And if your Major Junior A team plays for the Memorial Cup, that means you are at the very top of the top of the pyramid.

This is the way most sports pick their future stars. It's the way soccer is organized in Europe and South America, and it's the way Olympic athletes are chosen. For that matter, it is not all that different from the way the world of classical music picks its future virtuosos, or the way the world of ballet picks its future ballerinas, or the way our elite educational system picks its future scientists and intellectuals.

You can't buy your way into Major Junior A hockey. It doesn't matter who your father or mother is, or who your grandfather was, or what business your family is in. Nor does it matter if you live in the most remote corner of the most northerly province in Canada. If you have ability, the vast network of hockey scouts and talent spotters will find you, and if you are willing to work to develop that ability, the system will reward you. Success in hockey is based on *individual merit*—and both of those words are important. Players are judged on their own performance, not on anyone else's, and on the basis of their ability, not on some other arbitrary fact.

Or are they?

2.

This is a book about outliers, about men and women who do things that are out of the ordinary. Over the course of the chapters ahead, I'm going to introduce you to one kind of outlier after another: to geniuses, business tycoons, rock stars, and software programmers. We're going to uncover the secrets of a remarkable lawyer, look at what separates the very best pilots from pilots who have crashed planes, and try to figure out why Asians are so good at math. And in examining the lives of the remarkable among us—the skilled, the talented, and the driven—I will argue that there is something profoundly wrong with the way we make sense of success.

What is the question we always ask about

the successful? We want to know what they're *like*—what kind of personalities they have, or how intelligent they are, or what kind of lifestyles they have, or what special talents they might have been born with. And we assume that it is those personal qualities that explain how that individual reached the top.

In the autobiographies published every year by the billionaire/entrepreneur/rock star/celebrity, the story line is always the same: our hero is born in modest circumstances and by virtue of his own grit and talent fights his way to greatness. In the Bible, Joseph is cast out by his brothers and sold into slavery and then rises to become the pharaoh's right-hand man on the strength of his own brilliance and insight. In the famous nineteenth-century novels of Horatio Alger, young boys born into poverty rise to riches through a combination of pluck and initiative. "I think overall it's a disadvantage," Jeb Bush once said of what it meant for his business career that he was the son of an American president and the brother of an American president and the grandson of a wealthy Wall Street banker and US senator. When he ran for governor of Florida, he repeatedly referred to himself as a "self-made man," and it is a measure of how deeply we associate success with the efforts of the individual that few batted an eye at that description.

"Lift up your heads," Robert Winthrop told the crowd many years ago at the unveiling of a statue of that great hero of American independence Benjamin Franklin, "and look at the image of a man who rose from nothing, who owed nothing to parentage or patronage, who enjoyed no advantages of early education which are not open — a hundredfold open — to yourselves, who performed the most menial services in the businesses in which his early life was employed, but who lived to stand before Kings, and died to leave a name which the world will never forget."

In *Outliers,* I want to convince you that these kinds of personal explanations of success don't work. People don't rise from nothing. We do owe something to parentage and patronage. The people who stand before kings may look like they did it all by themselves. But in fact they are invariably the beneficiaries of hidden advantages and extraordinary opportunities and cultural legacies that allow them to learn and work hard and make sense of the world in ways others cannot. It makes a difference where and when we grew up. The culture we belong to and the legacies passed down by our forebears shape the patterns of our achievement in ways we cannot begin to imagine. It's not enough to ask what successful people are like, in other words. It is only by asking where they are *from* that we can unravel the logic behind who succeeds and who doesn't.

Biologists often talk about the "ecology" of an organism: the tallest oak in the forest is the tallest not just because it grew from the hardiest acorn; it is the tallest also because no other trees blocked its sunlight, the soil around it was deep and rich, no rabbit chewed through its bark as a sapling, and no lumberjack cut it down before it matured. We all know that successful people come from hardy seeds. But do we know enough about the sunlight that warmed them, the soil in which they put down the roots, and the rabbits and lumberjacks they were lucky enough to avoid? This is not a book about tall trees. It's a book about forests—and hockey is a good place to start because the explanation for who gets to the top of the hockey world is a lot more interesting and complicated than it looks. In fact, it's downright peculiar.

3.

Here is the player roster of the 2007 Medicine Hat Tigers. Take a close look and see if you can spot anything strange about it.

No.	Name	Pos.	L/R	Height	Weight	Birth Date	Hometown
9	Brennan Bosch	C	R	5'8"	173	Feb. 14, 1988	Martensville, SK
11	Scott Wasden	C	R	6'1"	188	Jan. 4, 1988	Westbank, BC
12	Colton Grant	LW	L	5'9"	177	Mar. 20, 1989	Standard, AB
14	Darren Helm	LW	L	6'	182	Jan. 21, 1987	St. Andrews, MB
15	Derek Dorsett	RW	L	5'11"	178	Dec. 20, 1986	Kindersley, SK

No.	Name	Pos.	L/R	Height	Weight	Birth Date	Hometown
16	Daine Todd	C	R	5'10"	173	Jan. 10, 1987	Red Deer, AB
17	Tyler Swystun	RW	R	5'11"	185	Jan. 15, 1988	Cochrane, AB
19	Matt Lowry	C	R	6'	186	Mar. 2, 1988	Neepawa, MB
20	Kevin Undershute	LW	L	6'	178	Apr. 12, 1987	Medicine Hat, AB
21	Jerrid Sauer	RW	R	5'10"	196	Sep. 12, 1987	Medicine Hat, AB
22	Tyler Ennis	C	L	5'9"	160	Oct. 6, 1989	Edmonton, AB
23	Jordan Hickmott	C	R	6'	183	Apr. 11, 1990	Mission, BC
25	Jakub Rumpel	RW	R	5'8"	166	Jan. 27, 1987	Hrnciarovce, SLO
28	Bretton Cameron	C	R	5'11"	168	Jan. 26, 1989	Didsbury, AB
36	Chris Stevens	LW	L	5'10"	197	Aug. 20, 1986	Dawson Creek, BC
3	Gord Baldwin	D	L	6'5"	205	Mar. 1, 1987	Winnipeg, MB
4	David Schlemko	D	L	6'1"	195	May 7, 1987	Edmonton, AB
5	Trever Glass	D	L	6'	190	Jan. 22, 1988	Cochrane, AB
10	Kris Russell	D	L	5'10"	177	May 2, 1987	Caroline, AB
18	Michael Sauer	D	R	6'3"	205	Aug. 7, 1987	Sartell, MN

No.	Name	Pos.	L/R	Height	Weight	Birth Date	Hometown
24	Mark Isherwood	D	R	6'	183	Jan. 31, 1989	Abbotsford, BC
27	Shayne Brown	D	L	6'1"	198	Feb. 20, 1989	Stony Plain, AB
29	Jordan Bendfeld	D	R	6'3"	230	Feb. 9, 1988	Leduc, AB
31	Ryan Holfeld	G	L	5'11"	166	Jun. 29, 1989	LeRoy, SK
33	Matt Keetley	G	R	6'2"	189	Apr. 27, 1986	Medicine Hat, AB

Do you see it? Don't feel bad if you don't, because for many years in the hockey world no one did. It wasn't until the mid-1980s, in fact, that a Canadian psychologist named Roger Barnsley first drew attention to the phenomenon of relative age.

Barnsley was at a Lethbridge Broncos hockey game in southern Alberta, a team that played in the same Major Junior A league as the Vancouver Giants and the Medicine Hat Tigers. He was there with his wife, Paula, and their two boys, and his wife was reading the program, when she ran across a roster list just like the one above that you just looked at.

"Roger," she said, "do you know when these young men were born?"

Barnsley said yes. "They're all between sixteen and twenty, so they'd be born in the late sixties."

"No, no," Paula went on. "What *month*."

"I thought she was crazy," Barnsley remembers. "But I looked through it, and what she was saying just jumped out at me. For some reason, there were an incredible number of January, February, and March birth dates."

Barnsley went home that night and looked up the birth dates of as many professional hockey players as he could find. He saw the same pattern. Barnsley, his wife, and a colleague, A. H. Thompson, then gathered statistics on every player in the Ontario Junior Hockey League. The story was the same. More players were born in January than in any other month, and by an overwhelming margin. The second most frequent birth month? February. The third? March. Barnsley found that there were nearly five and a half times as many Ontario Junior Hockey League players born in

January as were born in November. He looked at the all-star teams of eleven-year-olds and thirteen-year-olds—the young players selected for elite traveling squads. Same story. He looked at the composition of the National Hockey League. Same story. The more he looked, the more Barnsley came to believe that what he was seeing was not a chance occurrence but an iron law of Canadian hockey: in *any* elite group of hockey players—the very best of the best—40 percent of the players will have been born between January and March, 30 percent between April and June, 20 percent between July and September, and 10 percent between October and December.

"In all my years in psychology, I have never run into an effect this large," Barnsley says. "You don't even need to do any statistical analysis. You just look at it."

Look back at the Medicine Hat roster. Do you see it now? Seventeen out of the twenty-five players on the team were born in January, February, March, or April.

Here is the play-by-play for the first two goals

in the Memorial Cup final, only this time I've substituted the players' birthdays for their names. It no longer sounds like the championship of Canadian junior hockey. It now sounds like a strange sporting ritual for teenage boys born under the astrological signs Capricorn, Aquarius, and Pisces.

> *March 11 starts around one side of the Tigers' net, leaving the puck for his teammate January 4, who passes it to January 22, who flips it back to March 12, who shoots point-blank at the Tigers' goalie, April 27. April 27 blocks the shot, but it's rebounded by Vancouver's March 6. He shoots! Medicine Hat defensemen February 9 and February 14 dive to block the puck while January 10 looks on helplessly. March 6 scores!*

Let's go to the second period now.

> *Medicine Hat's turn. The Tigers' scoring leader, January 21, charges down the right side of the ice. He stops and circles, eluding the Vancouver defenseman February 15. January 21 then deftly passes the*

puck to his teammate December 20—wow! what's he doing out there?!—who shrugs off the onrushing defender May 17 and slides a cross-crease pass back to January 21. He shoots! Vancouver defenseman March 12 dives, trying to block the shot. Vancouver's goalie, March 19, lunges helplessly. January 21 scores! He raises his hands in triumph. His teammate May 2 jumps on his back with joy.

4.

The explanation for this is quite simple. It has nothing to do with astrology, nor is there anything magical about the first three months of the year. It's simply that in Canada the eligibility cutoff for age-class hockey is January 1. A boy who turns ten on January 2, then, could be playing alongside someone who doesn't turn ten until the end of the year—and at that age, in preadolescence, a twelve-month gap in age represents an enormous difference in physical maturity.

This being Canada, the most hockey-crazed country on earth, coaches start to select players for the traveling "rep" squad—the all-star teams—at the age of nine or ten, and of course they are more likely to view as talented the bigger and more coordinated players, who have had the benefit of critical extra months of maturity.

And what happens when a player gets chosen for a rep squad? He gets better coaching, and his teammates are better, and he plays fifty or seventy-five games a season instead of twenty games a season like those left behind in the "house" league, and he practices twice as much as, or even three times more than, he would have otherwise. In the beginning, his advantage isn't so much that he is inherently better but only that he is a little older. But by the age of thirteen or fourteen, with the benefit of better coaching and all that extra practice under his belt, he really *is* better, so he's the one more likely to make it to the Major Junior A league, and from there into the big leagues.*

---

* The way Canadians select hockey players is a beautiful example of what the sociologist Robert Merton famously called a "self-fulfilling prophecy"—a situation where "a false definition, in the beginning...

Barnsley argues that these kinds of skewed age distributions exist whenever three things happen: selection, streaming, and differentiated experience. If you make a decision about who is good and who is not good at an early age; if you separate the "talented" from the "untalented"; and if you provide the "talented" with a superior experience, then you're going to end up giving a huge advantage to that small group of people born closest to the cutoff date.

In the United States, football and basketball don't select, stream, and differentiate quite as dramatically. As a result, a child can be a bit behind physically in those sports and still play

---

evokes a new behavior which makes the original false conception come true." Canadians start with a false definition of who the best nine- and ten-year-old hockey players are. They're just picking the oldest every year. But the way they treat those "all-stars" ends up making their original false judgment look correct. As Merton puts it: "This specious validity of the self-fulfilling prophecy perpetuates a reign of error. For the prophet will cite the actual course of events as proof that he was right from the very beginning."

as much as his or her more mature peers.* But baseball does. The cutoff date for almost all nonschool baseball leagues in the United States is July 31, with the result that more major league players are born in August than in any other month. (The numbers are striking: in 2005, among Americans playing major league baseball 505 were born in August versus 313 born in July.)

European soccer, similarly, is organized like hockey and baseball—and the birth-date distributions in that sport are heavily skewed as well. In England, the eligibility date is September 1, and in the football association's premier league at one point in the 1990s, there were 288 players born between September and November and only 136 players born between June and

* A physically immature basketball player in an American city can probably play as many hours of basketball in a given year as a relatively older child because there are so many basketball courts and so many people willing to play. It's not like ice hockey, where you need a rink. Basketball is saved by its accessibility and ubiquity.

August. In international soccer, the cutoff date used to be August 1, and in one recent junior world championship tournament, 135 players were born in the three months after August 1, and just 22 were born in May, June, and July. Today the cutoff date for international junior soccer is January 1. Take a look at the roster of the 2007 Czechoslovakian National Junior soccer team, which made the Junior World Cup finals.

Here we go again:

No.	**Player**	**Birth Date**	**Position**
1	Marcel Gecov	Jan. 1, 1988	MF
2	Ludek Frydrych	Jan. 3, 1987	GK
3	Petr Janda	Jan. 5, 1987	MF
4	Jakub Dohnalek	Jan. 12, 1988	DF
5	Jakub Mares	Jan. 26, 1987	MF
6	Michal Held	Jan. 27, 1987	DF
7	Marek Strestik	Feb. 1, 1987	FW
8	Jiri Valenta	Feb. 14, 1988	MF
9	Jan Simunek	Feb. 20, 1987	DF
10	Tomas Oklestek	Feb. 21, 1987	MF
11	Lubos Kalouda	Feb. 21, 1987	MF
12	Radek Petr	Feb. 24, 1987	GK

No.	Player	Birth Date	Position
13	Ondrej Mazuch	Mar. 15, 1989	DF
14	Ondrej Kudela	Mar. 26, 1987	MF
15	Marek Suchy	Mar. 29, 1988	DF
16	Martin Fenin	Apr. 16, 1987	FW
17	Tomas Pekhart	May 26, 1989	FW
18	Lukas Kuban	Jun. 22, 1987	DF
19	Tomas Cihlar	Jun. 24, 1987	DF
20	Tomas Frystak	Aug. 18, 1987	GK
21	Tomas Micola	Sep. 26, 1988	MF

At the national team tryouts, the Czech soccer coaches might as well have told everyone born after midsummer that they should pack their bags and go home.

Hockey and soccer are just games, of course, involving a select few. But these exact same biases also show up in areas of much more consequence, like education. Parents with a child born at the end of the calendar year often think about holding their child back before the start of kindergarten: it's hard for a five-year-old to keep up with a child born many months earlier. But most parents, one suspects, think that whatever disadvantage a younger child faces in kindergarten eventually goes away. *But it doesn't.* It's just like hockey. The small initial advantage that the child born in the early part of the year has over the child born at the end of the year persists. It locks children into patterns of achievement and underachievement, encouragement and discouragement, that stretch on and on for years.

Recently, two economists—Kelly Bedard and Elizabeth Dhuey—looked at the relationship between scores on what is called the Trends in International Mathematics and Science Study, or TIMSS (math and science tests given every four years to children in many countries around the world), and month of birth. They found that among fourth graders, the oldest children scored somewhere between four and twelve percentile points better than the youngest children. That, as Dhuey explains, is a "huge effect." It means that if you take two intellectually equivalent fourth graders with birthdays at opposite ends of the cutoff date, the older student could score in the eightieth percentile, while the younger one could score in the sixty-eighth percentile. That's the difference between qualifying for a gifted program and not.

"It's just like sports," Dhuey said. "We do ability grouping early on in childhood. We have advanced reading groups and advanced math groups. So, early on, if we look at young kids, in kindergarten and first grade, the teachers are confusing maturity with ability. And they put the older kids in the advanced stream, where they learn better skills; and the next year, because they are in the higher groups, they do even better; and the next year, the same things happens, and they do even better again. The only country we don't see this going on is Denmark. They have a national policy where they have no ability grouping until the age of ten." Denmark waits to make selection decisions until maturity differences by age have evened out.

Dhuey and Bedard subsequently did the same analysis, only this time looking at college. What did they find? At four-year colleges in the United States—the highest stream of post-secondary education—students belonging to the relatively youngest group in their class are underrepresented by about 11.6 percent. That initial difference in maturity doesn't go away with time. It persists. And for thousands of students, that initial disadvantage is the difference between going to college—and having a real shot at the middle class—and not.*

"I mean, it's ridiculous," Dhuey says. "It's outlandish that our arbitrary choice of cutoff dates is causing these long-lasting effects, and no one seems to care about them."

5.

Think for a moment about what the story of hockey and early birthdays says about success.

---

* Even more social phenomena can be linked to relative age. Barnsley and two colleagues, for instance, once found that students who attempt suicide are also more likely to be born in the second half of the school year. Their explanation is that poorer school performance can lead to depression. The connection between relative age and suicide, however, isn't nearly as pronounced as the correlation between birth date and athletic success.

It tells us that our notion that it is the best and the brightest who effortlessly rise to the top is much too simplistic. Yes, the hockey players who make it to the professional level are more talented than you or me. But they also got a big head start, an opportunity that they neither deserved nor earned. And that opportunity played a critical role in their success.

The sociologist Robert Merton famously called this phenomenon the "Matthew Effect" after the New Testament verse in the Gospel of Matthew: "For unto everyone that hath shall be given, and he shall have abundance. But from him that hath not shall be taken away even that which he hath." It is those who are successful, in other words, who are most likely to be given the kinds of special opportunities that lead to further success. It's the rich who get the biggest tax breaks. It's the best students who get the best teaching and most attention. And it's the biggest nine- and ten-year-olds who get the most coaching and practice. Success is the result of what sociologists like to call "accumulative advantage." The professional hockey player starts out a little bit better than his peers. And that little difference leads to an opportunity that makes that difference a bit bigger, and that edge in turn leads to another opportunity, which makes the initially small difference bigger still—and on and on until the hockey player is a genuine outlier. But he didn't start out an outlier. He started out just a little bit better.

The second implication of the hockey example is that the systems we set up to determine who gets ahead aren't particularly efficient. We think that starting all-star leagues and gifted programs as early as possible is the best way of ensuring that no talent slips through the cracks. But take a look again at that roster for the Czech Republic soccer team. There are no players born in July, October, November, or December, and only one each in August and September. Those born in the last half of the year have all been discouraged, or overlooked, or pushed out of the sport. *The talent of essentially half of the Czech athletic population has been squandered.*

So what do you do if you're an athletic young Czech with the misfortune to have been born in the last part of the year? You *can't* play soccer. The deck is stacked against you. So maybe you could play the other sport that Czechs are obsessed with—hockey. But wait. (I think you know what's coming.) Here's the roster of the 2007 Czech junior hockey team that finished fifth at the world championships.

No.	Player	Birth Date	Position
1	David Kveton	Jan. 3, 1988	Forward
2	Jiri Suchy	Jan. 3, 1988	Defense
3	Michael Kolarz	Jan. 12, 1987	Defense
4	Jakub Vojta	Feb. 8, 1987	Defense
5	Jakub Kindl	Feb. 10, 1987	Defense
6	Michael Frolik	Feb. 17, 1989	Forward
7	Martin Hanzal	Feb. 20, 1987	Forward
8	Tomas Svoboda	Feb. 24, 1987	Forward
9	Jakub Cerny	Mar. 5, 1987	Forward
10	Tomas Kudelka	Mar. 10, 1987	Defense
11	Jaroslav Barton	Mar. 26, 1987	Defense
12	H. O. Pozivil	Apr. 22, 1987	Defense
13	Daniel Rakos	May 25, 1987	Forward
14	David Kuchejda	Jun. 12, 1987	Forward

No.	Player	Birth Date	Position
15	Vladimir Sobotka	Jul. 2, 1987	Forward
16	Jakub Kovar	Jul. 19, 1988	Goalie
17	Lukas Vantuch	Jul. 20, 1987	Forward
18	Jakub Voracek	Aug. 15, 1989	Forward
19	Tomas Pospisil	Aug. 25, 1987	Forward
20	Ondrej Pavelec	Aug. 31, 1987	Goalie
21	Tomas Kana	Nov. 29, 1987	Forward
22	Michal Repik	Dec. 31, 1988	Forward

Those born in the last quarter of the year might as well give up on hockey too.

Do you see the consequences of the way we have chosen to think about success? Because we so profoundly personalize success, we miss opportunities to lift others onto the top rung. We make rules that frustrate achievement. We prematurely write off people as failures. We are too much in awe of those who succeed and far too dismissive of those who fail. And, most of all, we become much too passive. We overlook just how large a role we all play—and by "we" I mean society—in determining who makes it and who doesn't.

If we chose to, we could acknowledge that cutoff dates matter. We could set up two or even three hockey leagues, divided up by month of birth. Let the players develop on separate tracks and then pick all-star teams. If all the Czech and Canadian athletes born at the end of the year had a fair chance, then the Czech and the Canadian national teams suddenly would have twice as many athletes to choose from.

Schools could do the same thing. Elementary and middle schools could put the January through April–born students in one class, the May through August in another class, and those born in September through December in the third class. They could let students learn with and compete against other students of the same maturity level. It would be a little bit more complicated administratively. But it wouldn't necessarily cost that much more money, and it would level the playing field for those who—through no fault of their own—have been dealt a big disadvantage by the educational system. We could easily take control of the machinery of achievement, in other words—not just in sports but, as we will see, in other more consequential areas as well. But we don't. And why? Because we cling to the idea that success is a simple function of individual merit and that the world in which we all grow up and the rules we choose to write as a society don't matter at all.

6.

Before the Memorial Cup final, Gord Wasden — the father of one of the Medicine Hat Tigers — stood by the side of the ice, talking about his son Scott. He was wearing a Medicine Hat baseball cap and a black Medicine Hat T-shirt. "When he was four and five years old," Wasden remembered, "his little brother was in a walker, and he would shove a hockey stick in his hand and they would play hockey on the floor in the kitchen, morning till night. Scott *always* had a passion for it. He played rep hockey throughout his minor-league hockey career. He always made the Triple A teams. As a first-year peewee or a first-year bantam, he always played on the [top] rep team." Wasden was clearly nervous:

his son was about to play in the biggest game of his life. "He's had to work very hard for whatever he's got. I'm very proud of him."

Those were the ingredients of success at the highest level: passion, talent, and hard work. But there was another element. When did Wasden first get the sense that his son was something special? "You know, he was always a bigger kid for his age. He was strong, and he had a knack for scoring goals at an early age. And he was always kind of a standout for his age, a captain of his team. . . ."

Bigger kid for his age? Of course he was. Scott Wasden was born on January 4, within three days of the absolute perfect birthday for an elite hockey player. He was one of the lucky ones. If the eligibility date for Canadian hockey were later in the year, he might have been watching the Memorial Cup championship from the stands instead of playing on the ice.

CHAPTER TWO

The 10,000-Hour Rule

"IN HAMBURG, WE HAD TO PLAY FOR EIGHT HOURS."

1.

The University of Michigan opened its new Computer Center in 1971, in a brand-new building on Beal Avenue in Ann Arbor, with beige-brick exterior walls and a dark-glass front. The university's enormous mainframe computers stood in the middle of a vast white room, looking, as one faculty member remembers, "like one of the last scenes in the movie *2001: A Space*

Odyssey." Off to the side were dozens of key-punch machines—what passed in those days for computer terminals. In 1971, this was state of the art. The University of Michigan had one of the most advanced computer science programs in the world, and over the course of the Computer Center's life, thousands of students passed through that white room, the most famous of whom was a gawky teenager named Bill Joy.

Joy came to the University of Michigan the year the Computer Center opened. He was sixteen. He was tall and very thin, with a mop of unruly hair. He had been voted "Most Studious Student" by his graduating class at North Farmington High School, outside Detroit, which, as he puts it, meant that he was a "no-date nerd." He had thought he might end up as biologist or a mathematician. But late in his freshman year, he stumbled across the Computer Center—and he was hooked.

From that point on, the Computer Center was his life. He programmed whenever he could. Joy got a job with a computer science professor so he could program over the summer. In 1975, he enrolled in graduate school at the University of California at Berkeley. There, he buried himself even deeper in the world of computer software. During the oral exams for his PhD, he made up a particularly complicated algorithm on the fly that, as one of his many admirers has written, "so stunned his examiners [that] one of them later compared the experience to 'Jesus confounding his elders.'"

Working in collaboration with a small group of programmers, Joy took on the task of rewriting UNIX, which was a software system developed by AT&T for mainframe computers. Joy's version was very good. It was so good, in fact, that it became—and remains—the operating system on which literally millions of computers around the world run. "If you put your Mac in that funny mode where you can see the code," Joy says, "I see things that I remember typing in twenty-five years ago." And do you know who wrote much of the software that allows you to access the Internet? Bill Joy.

After graduating from Berkeley, Joy cofounded the Silicon Valley firm Sun Microsystems, which was one of the most critical players in the computer revolution. There he rewrote another computer language—Java—and his legend grew still further. Among Silicon Valley insiders, Joy is spoken of with as much awe as someone like Bill Gates of Microsoft. He is sometimes called the Edison of the Internet. As the Yale computer scientist David Gelernter says, "Bill Joy is one of the most influential people in the modern history of computing."

The story of Bill Joy's genius has been told many times, and the lesson is always the same. Here was a world that was the purest of meritocracies. Computer programming didn't operate as an old-boy network, where you got ahead because of money or connections. It was a wide-open field in which all participants were judged solely on their talent and their accomplishments. It was a world where the best men won, and Joy was clearly one of those best men.

It would be easier to accept that version of events, however, if we hadn't just looked at hockey and soccer players. Theirs was supposed to be a pure meritocracy as well. Only it wasn't.

It was a story of how the outliers in a particular field reached their lofty status through a combination of ability, opportunity, and utterly arbitrary advantage.

Is it possible the same pattern of special opportunities operate in the real world as well? Let's go back over the story of Bill Joy and find out.

2.

For almost a generation, psychologists around the world have been engaged in a spirited debate over a question that most of us would consider to have been settled years ago. The question is this: is there such a thing as innate talent? The obvious answer is yes. Not every hockey player born in January ends up playing at the professional level. Only some do—the innately talented ones. Achievement is talent plus preparation. The problem with this view is that the closer psychologists look at the careers of the gifted, the smaller the role innate talent seems to play and the bigger the role preparation seems to play.

Exhibit A in the talent argument is a study done in the early 1990s by the psychologist K. Anders Ericsson and two colleagues at Berlin's elite Academy of Music. With the help of the Academy's professors, they divided the school's violinists into three groups. In the first group were the stars, the students with the potential to become world-class soloists. In the second were those judged to be merely "good." In the third were students who were unlikely to ever play professionally and who intended to be music teachers in the public school system. All of the violinists were then asked the same question: over the course of your entire career, ever since you first picked up the violin, how many hours have you practiced?

Everyone from all three groups started playing at roughly the same age, around five years old. In those first few years, everyone practiced roughly the same amount, about two or three hours a week. But when the students were around the age of eight, real differences started to emerge. The students who would end up the best in their class began to practice more than everyone else: six hours a week by age nine, eight hours a week by age twelve, sixteen hours a week by age fourteen, and up and up, until by the age of twenty they were practicing—that is, purposefully and single-mindedly playing their instruments with the intent to get better—well over thirty hours a week. In fact, by the age of twenty, the elite performers had each totaled ten thousand hours of practice. By contrast, the merely good students had totaled eight thousand hours, and the future music teachers had totaled just over four thousand hours.

Ericsson and his colleagues then compared amateur pianists with professional pianists. The same pattern emerged. The amateurs never practiced more than about three hours a week over the course of their childhood, and by the age of twenty they had totaled two thousand hours of practice. The professionals, on the other hand, steadily increased their practice time every year, until by the age of twenty they, like the violinists, had reached ten thousand hours.

The striking thing about Ericsson's study is that he and his colleagues couldn't find any "naturals," musicians who floated effortlessly to the top while practicing a fraction of the time their peers did. Nor could they find any "grinds," people who worked harder than everyone else, yet just didn't have what it takes to break the top ranks. Their research suggestes that once a musician has enough ability to get into a top music school, the thing that distinguishes one performer from another is how hard he or she works. That's it. And what's more, the people at the very top don't work just harder or even much harder than everyone else. They work much, *much* harder.

The idea that excellence at performing a complex task requires a critical minimum level of practice surfaces again and again in studies of expertise. In fact, researchers have settled on what they believe is the magic number for true expertise: ten thousand hours.

"The emerging picture from such studies is that ten thousand hours of practice is required to achieve the level of mastery associated with being a world-class expert—in anything," writes the neurologist Daniel Levitin. "In study after study, of composers, basketball players, fiction writers, ice skaters, concert pianists, chess players, master criminals, and what have you, this number comes up again and again. Of course, this doesn't address why some people get more out of their practice sessions than others do. But no one has yet found a case in which true world-class expertise was accomplished in less time. It seems that it takes the brain this long to assimilate all that it needs to know to achieve true mastery."

This is true even of people we think of as prodigies. Mozart, for example, famously started writing music at six. But, writes the psychologist Michael Howe in his book *Genius Explained*,

> by the standards of mature composers, Mozart's early works are not outstanding. The earliest pieces were all probably written down by his father, and perhaps improved in the process. Many of Wolfgang's childhood compositions, such as the first

> seven of his concertos for piano and orchestra, are largely arrangements of works by other composers. Of those concertos that only contain music original to Mozart, the earliest that is now regarded as a masterwork (No. 9, K. 271) was not composed until he was twenty-one: by that time Mozart had already been composing concertos for ten years.

The music critic Harold Schonberg goes further: Mozart, he argues, actually "developed late," since he didn't produce his greatest work until he had been composing for more than twenty years.

To become a chess grandmaster also seems to take about ten years. (Only the legendary Bobby Fischer got to that elite level in less than that amount of time: it took him nine years.) And what's ten years? Well, it's roughly how long it takes to put in ten thousand hours of hard practice. Ten thousand hours is the magic number of greatness.

Here is the explanation for what was so puzzling about the rosters of the Czech and Canadian national sports teams. There was practically no one on those teams born after September 1, which doesn't seem to make any sense. You'd think that there should be a fair number of Czech hockey or soccer prodigies born late in the year who are *so* talented that they eventually make their way into the top tier as young adults, despite their birth dates.

But to Ericsson and those who argue against the primacy of talent, that isn't surprising at all. That late-born prodigy doesn't get chosen for the all-star team as an eight-year-old because he's too small. So he doesn't get the extra practice. And without that extra practice, he has no chance at hitting ten thousand hours by the time the professional hockey teams start looking for players. And without ten thousand hours under his belt, there is no way he can ever master the skills necessary to play at the top level. Even Mozart—the greatest musical prodigy of all time—couldn't hit his stride until he had his ten thousand hours in. Practice isn't the thing you do once you're good. It's the thing you do that makes you good.

The other interesting thing about that ten

thousand hours, of course, is that ten thousand hours is an *enormous* amount of time. It's all but impossible to reach that number all by yourself by the time you're a young adult. You have to have parents who encourage and support you. You can't be poor, because if you have to hold down a part-time job on the side to help make ends meet, there won't be time left in the day to practice enough. In fact, most people can reach that number only if they get into some kind of special program—like a hockey all-star squad—or if they get some kind of extraordinary opportunity that gives them a chance to put in those hours.

3.

So, back to Bill Joy. It's 1971. He's tall and gawky and sixteen years old. He's the math whiz, the kind of student that schools like MIT and Caltech and the University of Waterloo attract by the hundreds. "When Bill was a little kid, he wanted to know everything about everything way before he should've even known he wanted to know," his father, William, says. "We answered him when we could. And when we couldn't, we would just give him a book." When it came time to apply to college, Joy got a perfect score on the math portion of the Scholastic Aptitude Test. "It wasn't particularly hard," he says matter-of-factly. "There was plenty of time to check it twice."

He has talent by the truckload. But that's not the only consideration. It never is. The key to his development is that he stumbled across that nondescript building on Beal Avenue.

In the early 1970s, when Joy was learning about programming, computers were the size of rooms. A single machine (which might have less power and memory than your microwave now has) could cost upwards of a million dollars—and that's in 1970s dollars. Computers were rare. If you found one, it was hard to get access to it; if you managed to get access, renting time on it cost a fortune.

What's more, programming itself was extraordinarily tedious. This was the era when computer programs were created using cardboard punch cards. Each line of code was imprinted on the card using a keypunch machine. A complex program might include hundreds, if not thousands, of these cards in tall stacks. Once a program was ready, you walked over to whatever mainframe computer you had access to and gave the stack of cards to an operator. Since computers could handle only one task at a time, the operator made an appointment for your program, and depending on how many people were ahead of you in line, you might not get your cards back for a few hours or even a day. And if you made even a single error—even a typographical error—in your program, you had to take the cards back, track down the error, and begin the whole process again.

Under those circumstances, it was exceedingly difficult for anyone to become a programming expert. Certainly becoming an expert by your early twenties was all but impossible. When you can "program" for only a few minutes out of every hour you spend in the computer room, how can you ever get in ten thousand hours of practice? "Programming with cards," one computer scientist from that era remembers, "did not teach you programming. It taught you patience and proofreading."

It wasn't until the mid-1960s that a solution to the programming problem emerged. Computers were finally powerful enough that they could handle more than one "appointment" at once. If the computer's operating system was rewritten, computer scientists realized, the machine's time could be shared; the computer could be trained to handle hundreds of tasks at the same time. That, in turn, meant that programmers didn't have to physically hand their stacks of computer cards to the operator anymore. Dozens of terminals could be built, all linked to the mainframe by a telephone line, and everyone could be working—online—all at once.

Here is how one history of the period describes the advent of time-sharing:

> This was not just a revolution. It was a revelation. Forget the operator, the card decks, the wait. With time-sharing, you could sit at your Teletype, bang

> in a couple of commands, and get an answer then and there. Time-sharing was interactive: A program could ask for a response, wait for you to type it in, act on it while you waited, and show you the result, all in "real time."

This is where Michigan came in, because Michigan was one of the first universities in the world to switch over to time-sharing. By 1967, a prototype of the system was up and running. By the early 1970s, Michigan had enough computing power that a hundred people could be programming simultaneously in the Computer Center. "In the late sixties, early seventies, I don't think there was anyplace else that was exactly like Michigan," Mike Alexander, one of the pioneers of Michigan's computing system, said. "Maybe MIT. Maybe Carnegie Mellon. Maybe Dartmouth. I don't think there were any others."

This was the opportunity that greeted Bill Joy when he arrived on the Ann Arbor campus in the fall of 1971. He hadn't chosen Michigan because of its computers. He had never done anything with computers in high school. He was interested in math and engineering. But when the programming bug hit him in his freshman year, he found himself—by the happiest of accidents—in one of the few places in the world where a seventeen-year-old could program all he wanted.

"Do you know what the difference is between the computing cards and time-sharing?" Joy says. "It's the difference between playing chess by mail and speed chess." Programming wasn't an exercise in frustration anymore. It was *fun*.

"I lived in the north campus, and the Computer Center was in the north campus," Joy went on. "How much time did I spend there? Oh, a phenomenal amount of time. It was open twenty-four hours. I would stay there all night, and just walk home in the morning. In an average week in those years, I was spending more time in the Computer Center than on my classes. All of us down there had this recurring nightmare of forgetting to show up for class at all, of not even realizing we were enrolled.

"The challenge was that they gave all the students an account with a fixed amount of money, so your time would run out. When you signed on, you would put in how long you wanted to spend on the computer. They gave you, like, an hour of time. That's all you'd get. But someone figured out that if you put in 'time equals' and then a letter, like *t* equals *k,* they wouldn't charge you," he said, laughing at the memory. "It was a bug in the software. You could put in *t* equals *k* and sit there forever."

Just look at the stream of opportunities that came Bill Joy's way. Because he happened to go to a farsighted school like the University of Michigan, he was able to practice on a time-sharing system instead of with punch cards; because the Michigan system happened to have a bug in it, he could program all he wanted; because the university was willing to spend the money to keep the Computer Center open twenty-four hours, he could stay up all night; and because he was able to put in so many hours, by the time he happened to be presented with the opportunity to rewrite UNIX, he was up to the task. Bill Joy was brilliant. He wanted to learn. That was a big part of it. But before he could become an expert, someone had to give him the opportunity to learn *how* to be an expert.

"At Michigan, I was probably programming eight or ten hours a day," he went on. "By the time I was at Berkeley I was doing it day and night. I had a terminal at home. I'd stay up until two or three o'clock in the morning, watching old movies and programming. Sometimes I'd fall asleep at the keyboard"—he mimed his head falling on the keyboard—"and you know how the key repeats until the end, and it starts to go beep, beep, beep? After that happens three times, you have to go to bed. I was still relatively incompetent even when I got to Berkeley. I was proficient by my second year there. That's when I wrote programs that are still in use today, thirty years later." He paused for a moment to do the math in his head—which for someone like Bill Joy doesn't take very long. Michigan in 1971. Programming in earnest by sophomore year. Add in the summers, then the days and nights in his first year at Berkeley. "So, so maybe...ten thousand hours?" he said, finally. "That's about right."

4.

Is the ten-thousand-hour rule a general rule of success? If we scratch below the surface of every great achiever, do we always find the equivalent of the Michigan Computer Center or the hockey all-star team—some sort of special opportunity for practice?

Let's test the idea with two examples, and for the sake of simplicity, let's make them as familiar as possible: the Beatles, one of the most famous rock bands ever; and Bill Gates, one of the world's richest men.

The Beatles—John Lennon, Paul McCartney, George Harrison, and Ringo Starr—came to the United States in February of 1964, starting the so-called British Invasion of the American music scene and putting out a string of hit records that transformed the face of popular music.

The first interesting thing about the Beatles for our purposes is how long they had already been together by the time they reached the United States. Lennon and McCartney first started playing together in 1957, seven years prior to landing in America. (Incidentally, the time that elapsed between their founding and their arguably greatest artistic achievements—*Sgt. Pepper's Lonely Hearts Club Band* and *The Beatles* [White Album]—is ten years.) And if you look even more closely at those long years of preparation, you'll find an experience that, in the context of hockey players and Bill Joy and world-class violinists, sounds awfully familiar. In 1960, while they were still just a struggling high school rock band, they were invited to play in Hamburg, Germany.

"Hamburg in those days did not have rock-and-roll music clubs. It had strip clubs," says Philip Norman, who wrote the Beatles biography *Shout!* "There was one particular club owner called Bruno, who was originally a fairground showman. He had the idea of bringing in rock groups to play in various clubs. They had this formula. It was a huge nonstop show, hour after hour, with a lot of people lurching in and the other lot lurching out. And the bands would play all the time to catch the passing traffic. In an American red-light district, they would call it nonstop striptease.

"Many of the bands that played in Hamburg were from Liverpool," Norman went on. "It was an accident. Bruno went to London to look for bands. But he happened to meet an entrepreneur from Liverpool in Soho who was down in London by pure chance. And he arranged to send some bands over. That's how the connection was established. And eventually the Beatles made a connection not just with Bruno but with other club owners as well. They kept going back because they got a lot of alcohol and a lot of sex."

And what was so special about Hamburg? It wasn't that it paid well. It didn't. Or that the acoustics were fantastic. They weren't. Or that the audiences were savvy and appreciative. They were anything but. It was the sheer amount of time the band was forced to play.

Here is John Lennon, in an interview after the Beatles disbanded, talking about the band's performances at a Hamburg strip club called the Indra:

> We got better and got more confidence. We couldn't help it with all the experience playing all night long. It was handy them being foreign. We had to try even harder, put our heart and soul into it, to get ourselves over.
>
> In Liverpool, we'd only ever done one-hour sessions, and we just used to do our best numbers, the same ones, at every one. In Hamburg, we had to play for eight hours, so we really had to find a new way of playing.

Eight hours?

Here is Pete Best, the Beatles' drummer at the time: "Once the news got out about that we were making a show, the club started packing them in. We played seven nights a week. At first we played almost nonstop till twelve-thirty, when it closed, but as we got better the crowds stayed till two most mornings."

Seven days a week?

The Beatles ended up traveling to Hamburg five times between 1960 and the end of 1962. On the first trip, they played 106 nights, five or more hours a night. On their second trip, they played 92 times. On their third trip, they played 48 times, for a total of 172 hours on stage. The last two Hamburg gigs, in November and December of 1962, involved another 90 hours of performing. All told, they performed for 270 nights in just over a year and a half. By the time they had their first burst of success in 1964, in fact, they had performed live an estimated twelve hundred times. Do you know how extraordinary that is? Most bands today don't perform twelve hundred times in their entire careers. The Hamburg crucible is one of the things that set the Beatles apart.

"They were no good onstage when they went there and they were very good when they came back," Norman went on. "They learned not only stamina. They had to learn an enormous amount of numbers—cover versions of everything you can think of, not just rock and roll, a bit of jazz too. They weren't disciplined onstage at all before that. But when they came back, they sounded like no one else. It was the making of them."

5.

Let's now turn to the history of Bill Gates. His story is almost as well known as the Beatles'. Brilliant, young math whiz discovers computer programming. Drops out of Harvard. Starts a little computer company called Microsoft with his friends. Through sheer brilliance and ambition and guts builds it into the giant of the software world. That's the broad outline. Let's dig a little bit deeper.

Gates's father was a wealthy lawyer in Seattle, and his mother was the daughter of a well-to-do banker. As a child Bill was precocious and easily bored by his studies. So his parents took him out of public school and, at the beginning of seventh grade, sent him to Lakeside, a private school that catered to Seattle's elite families. Midway through Gates's second year at Lakeside, the school started a computer club.

"The Mothers' Club at school did a rummage sale every year, and there was always the question of what the money would go to," Gates remembers. "Some went to the summer program, where inner-city kids would come up to the campus. Some of it would go for teachers. That year, they put three thousand dollars into a computer terminal down in this funny little room that we subsequently took control of. It was kind of an amazing thing."

It was an "amazing thing," of course, because this was 1968. Most *colleges* didn't have computer clubs in the 1960s. Even more remarkable was the kind of computer Lakeside bought. The school didn't have its students learn programming by the laborious computer-card system, like virtually everyone else was doing in the 1960s. Instead, Lakeside installed what was called an ASR-33 Teletype, which was a time-sharing terminal with a direct link to a mainframe computer in downtown Seattle.

"The whole idea of time-sharing only got invented in nineteen sixty-five," Gates continued. "Someone was pretty forward-looking." Bill Joy got an extraordinary, early opportunity to learn programming on a time-share system as a freshman in college, in 1971. Bill Gates got to do real-time programming *as an eighth grader in 1968.*

From that moment forward, Gates lived in the computer room. He and a number of others began to teach themselves how to use this strange new device. Buying time on the mainframe computer the ASR was hooked up to was, of course, expensive—even for a wealthy institution like Lakeside—and it wasn't long before the $3,000 put up by the Mothers' Club ran out. The parents raised more money. The students spent it. Then a group of programmers at the University of Washington formed an outfit called Computer Center Corporation (or C-Cubed), which leased computer time to local companies. As luck would have it, one of the founders of the firm—Monique Rona—had a son at Lakeside, a year ahead of Gates. Would the Lakeside computer club, Rona wondered, like to test out the company's software programs on the weekends in exchange for free programming time? Absolutely! After school, Gates took the bus to the C-Cubed offices and programmed long into the evening.

C-Cubed eventually went bankrupt, so Gates and his friends began hanging around the computer center at the University of Washington. Before long, they latched onto an outfit called ISI (Information Sciences Inc.), which agreed to let them have free computer time in exchange for working on a piece of software that could be used to automate company payrolls. In one seven-month period in 1971, Gates and his cohorts ran up 1,575 hours of computer time on the ISI mainframe, which averages out to eight hours a day, seven days a week.

"It was my obsession," Gates says of his early high school years. "I skipped athletics. I went up there at night. We were programming on weekends. It would be a rare week that we wouldn't get twenty or thirty hours in. There was a period where Paul Allen and I got in trouble for stealing a bunch of passwords and crashing the system. We got kicked out. I didn't get to use the computer the whole summer. This is when I was fifteen and sixteen. Then I found out Paul had found a computer that was free at the University of Washington. They had these machines in the medical center and the physics department. They were on a twenty-four-hour schedule, but with this big slack period, so that between three and six in the morning they never scheduled anything." Gates laughed. "I'd leave at night, after my bedtime. I could walk up to the University of Washington from my house. Or I'd take the bus. That's why I'm always so generous to the University of Washington, because they let me steal so much computer time." (Years later, Gates's mother said, "We always wondered why it was so hard for him to get up in the morning.")

One of the founders of ISI, Bud Pembroke, then got a call from the technology company TRW, which had just signed a contract to set up a computer system at the huge Bonneville Power station in southern Washington State.

TRW desperately needed programmers familiar with the particular software the power station used. In these early days of the computer revolution, programmers with that kind of specialized experience were hard to find. But Pembroke knew exactly whom to call: those high school kids from Lakeside who had been running up thousands of hours of computer time on the ISI mainframe. Gates was now in his senior year, and somehow he managed to convince his teachers to let him decamp for Bonneville under the guise of an independent study project. There he spent the spring writing code, supervised by a man named John Norton, who Gates says taught him as much about programming as almost anyone he'd ever met.

Those five years, from eighth grade through the end of high school, were Bill Gates's Hamburg, and by any measure, he was presented with an even more extraordinary series of opportunities than Bill Joy.

Opportunity number one was that Gates

got sent to Lakeside. How many high schools in the world had access to a time-sharing terminal in 1968? Opportunity number two was that the mothers of Lakeside had enough money to pay for the school's computer fees. Number three was that, when that money ran out, one of the parents happened to work at C-Cubed, which happened to need someone to check its code on the weekends, and which also happened not to care if weekends turned into weeknights. Number four was that Gates just happened to find out about ISI, and ISI just happened to need someone to work on its payroll software. Number five was that Gates happened to live within walking distance of the University of Washington. Number six was that the university happened to have free computer time between three and six in the morning. Number seven was that TRW happened to call Bud Pembroke. Number eight was that the best programmers Pembroke knew for that particular problem happened to be two high school kids. And number nine was that Lakeside was willing to let those kids spend their spring term miles away, writing code.

And what did virtually all of those opportunities have in common? They gave Bill Gates extra time to practice. By the time Gates dropped out of Harvard after his sophomore year to try his hand at his own software company, he'd been programming practically nonstop for seven consecutive years. He was *way* past ten thousand hours. How many teenagers in the world had the kind of experience Gates had? "If there were fifty in the world, I'd be stunned," he says. "There was C-Cubed and the payroll stuff we did, then TRW—all those things came together. I had a better exposure to software development at a young age than I think anyone did in that period of time, and all because of an incredibly lucky series of events."

6.

If we put the stories of hockey players and the Beatles and Bill Joy and Bill Gates together,

I think we get a more complete picture of the path to success. Joy and Gates and the Beatles are all undeniably talented. Lennon and McCartney had a musical gift of the sort that comes along once in a generation, and Bill Joy, let us not forget, had a mind so quick that he was able to make up a complicated algorithm on the fly that left his professors in awe. That much is obvious.

But what truly distinguishes their histories is not their extraordinary talent but their extraordinary opportunities. The Beatles, for the most random of reasons, got invited to go to Hamburg. Without Hamburg, the Beatles might well have taken a different path. "I was very lucky," Bill Gates said at the beginning of our interview. That doesn't mean he isn't brilliant or an extraordinary entrepreneur. It just means that he understands what incredible good fortune it was to be at Lakeside in 1968.

All the outliers we've looked at so far were the beneficiaries of some kind of unusual opportunity. Lucky breaks don't seem like the exception with software billionaires and rock bands and star athletes. They seem like the rule.

Let me give you one final example of the hidden opportunities that outliers benefit from. Suppose we do another version of the calendar analysis we did in the previous chapter with hockey players, only this time looking at birth years, not birth months. To start with, take a close look at the following list of the seventy-five richest people in human history. The net worth of each person is calculated in current US dollars. As you can see, it includes queens and kings and pharaohs from centuries past, as well as contemporary billionaires, such as Warren Buffett and Carlos Slim.

No.	Name	Wealth in Billions (USD)	Origin	Company or Source of Wealth
1	John D. Rockefeller	318.3	United States	Standard Oil
2	Andrew Carnegie	298.3	Scotland	Carnegie Steel Company

No.	Name	Wealth in Billions (USD)	Origin	Company or Source of Wealth
3	Nicholas II of Russia	253.5	Russia	House of Romanov
4	William Henry Vanderbilt	231.6	United States	Chicago, Burlington and Quincy Railroad
5	Osman Ali Khan, Asaf Jah VII	210.8	Hyderabad	Monarchy
6	Andrew W. Mellon	188.8	United States	Gulf Oil
7	Henry Ford	188.1	United States	Ford Motor Company
8	Marcus Licinius Crassus	169.8	Roman Republic	Roman Senate
9	Basil II	169.4	Byzantine Empire	Monarchy
10	Cornelius Vanderbilt	167.4	United States	New York and Harlem Railroad
11	Alanus Rufus	166.9	England	Investments
12	Amenophis III	155.2	Ancient Egypt	Pharaoh
13	William de Warenne, 1st Earl of Surrey	153.6	England	Earl of Surrey
14	William II of England	151.7	England	Monarchy
15	Elizabeth I	142.9	England	House of Tudor

No.	Name	Wealth in Billions (USD)	Origin	Company or Source of Wealth
16	John D. Rockefeller Jr.	141.4	United States	Standard Oil
17	Sam Walton	128.0	United States	Wal-Mart
18	John Jacob Astor	115.0	Germany	American Fur Company
19	Odo of Bayeux	110.2	England	Monarchy
20	Stephen Girard	99.5	France	First Bank of the United States
21	Cleopatra	95.8	Ancient Egypt	Ptolemaic Inheritance
22	Stephen Van Rensselaer III	88.8	United States	Rensselaerswyck Estate
23	Richard B. Mellon	86.3	United States	Gulf Oil
24	Alexander Turney Stewart	84.7	Ireland	Long Island Rail Road
25	William Backhouse Astor Jr.	84.7	United States	Inheritance
26	Don Simon Iturbi Patiño	81.2	Bolivia	Huanuni tin mine
27	Sultan Hassanal Bolkiah	80.7	Brunei	Kral

No.	Name	Wealth in Billions (USD)	Origin	Company or Source of Wealth
28	Frederick Weyerhaeuser	80.4	Germany	Weyerhaeuser Corporation
29	Moses Taylor	79.3	United States	Citibank
30	Vincent Astor	73.9	United States	Inheritance
31	Carlos Slim Helú	72.4	Mexico	Telmex
32	T. V. Soong	67.8	China	Central Bank of China
33	Jay Gould	67.1	United States	Union Pacific
34	Marshall Field	66.3	United States	Marshall Field and Company
35	George F. Baker	63.6	United States	Central Railroad of New Jersey
36	Hetty Green	58.8	United States	Seaboard National Bank
37	Bill Gates	58.0	United States	Microsoft
38	Lawrence Joseph Ellison	58.0	United States	Oracle Corporation
39	Richard Arkwright	56.2	England	Derwent Valley Mills
40	Mukesh Ambani	55.8	India	Reliance Industries
41	Warren Buffett	52.4	United States	Berkshire Hathaway
42	Lakshmi Mittal	51.0	India	Mittal Steel Company
43	J. Paul Getty	50.1	United States	Getty Oil Company

No.	Name	Wealth in Billions (USD)	Origin	Company or Source of Wealth
44	James G. Fair	47.2	United States	Consolidated Virginia Mining Company
45	William Weightman	46.1	United States	Merck & Company
46	Russell Sage	45.1	United States	Western Union
47	John Blair	45.1	United States	Union Pacific
48	Anil Ambani	45.0	India	Reliance Communications
49	Leland Stanford	44.9	United States	Central Pacific Railroad
50	Howard Hughes Jr.	43.4	United States	Hughes Tool Company, Hughes Aircraft Company, Summa Corporation, TWA
51	Cyrus Curtis	43.2	United States	Curtis Publishing Company
52	John Insley Blair	42.4	United States	Delaware, Lackawanna and Western Railroad
53	Edward Henry Harriman	40.9	United States	Union Pacific Railroad
54	Henry H. Rogers	40.9	United States	Standard Oil Company
55	Paul Allen	40.0	United States	Microsoft, Vulcan Inc.

No.	Name	Wealth in Billions (USD)	Origin	Company or Source of Wealth
56	John Kluge	40.0	Germany	Metropolitan Broadcasting Company
57	J. P. Morgan	39.8	United States	General Electric, US Steel
58	Oliver H. Payne	38.8	United States	Standard Oil Company
59	Yoshiaki Tsutsumi	38.1	Japan	Seibu Corporation
60	Henry Clay Frick	37.7	United States	Carnegie Steel Company
61	John Jacob Astor IV	37.0	United States	Inheritance
62	George Pullman	35.6	United States	Pullman Company
63	Collis Potter Huntington	34.6	United States	Central Pacific Railroad
64	Peter Arrell Brown Widener	33.4	United States	American Tobacco Company
65	Philip Danforth Armour	33.4	United States	Armour Refrigerator Line
66	William S. O'Brien	33.3	United States	Consolidated Virginia Mining Company
67	Ingvar Kamprad	33.0	Sweden	IKEA

No.	Name	Wealth in Billions (USD)	Origin	Company or Source of Wealth
68	K. P. Singh	32.9	India	DLF Universal Limited
69	James C. Flood	32.5	United States	Consolidated Virginia Mining Company
70	Li Ka-shing	32.0	China	Hutchison Whampoa Limited
71	Anthony N. Brady	31.7	United States	Brooklyn Rapid Transit
72	Elias Hasket Derby	31.4	United States	Shipping
73	Mark Hopkins	30.9	United States	Central Pacific Railroad
74	Edward Clark	30.2	United States	Singer Sewing Machine
75	Prince Al-Waleed bin Talal	29.5	Saudi Arabia	Kingdom Holding Company

Do you know what's interesting about that list? Of the seventy-five names, an astonishing fourteen are Americans born within nine years of one another in the mid-nineteenth century. Think about that for a moment. Historians start with Cleopatra and the pharaohs and comb through every year in human history every since, looking in every corner of the world for evidence of extraordinary wealth, and almost 20 percent of the names they end up with come from a single generation in a single country.

Here's the list of those Americans and their birth years:

1. John D. Rockefeller, 1839
2. Andrew Carnegie, 1835
28. Frederick Weyerhaeuser, 1834
33. Jay Gould, 1836
34. Marshall Field, 1834
35. George F. Baker, 1840
36. Hetty Green, 1834
44. James G. Fair, 1831
54. Henry H. Rogers, 1840
57. J. P. Morgan, 1837
58. Oliver H. Payne, 1839
62. George Pullman, 1831
64. Peter Arrell Brown Widener, 1834
65. Philip Danforth Armour, 1832

What's going on here? The answer becomes obvious if you think about it. In the 1860s and 1870s, the American economy went through perhaps the greatest transformation in its history. This was when the railroads were being built and when Wall Street emerged. It was when industrial manufacturing started in earnest. It was when all the rules by which the traditional economy had functioned were broken and remade. What this list says is that it really matters how old you were when that transformation happened.

If you were born in the late 1840s you missed it. You were too young to take advantage of that moment. If you were born in the 1820s you were too old: your mind-set was shaped by the pre–Civil War paradigm. But there was a particular, narrow nine-year window that was just perfect for seeing the potential that the future held. All of the fourteen men and women on the list above had vision and talent. But they also were given an extraordinary opportunity, in the same way that hockey and soccer players born in January, February, and March are given an extraordinary opportunity.*

Now let's do the same kind of analysis for people like Bill Joy and Bill Gates.

If you talk to veterans of Silicon Valley, they'll tell you that the most important date in the history of the personal computer revolution was January 1975. That was when the magazine *Popular Electronics* ran a cover story on an extraordinary machine called the Altair 8800.

* The sociologist C. Wright Mills made an additional observation about that special cohort from the 1830s. He looked at the backgrounds of the American business elite from the Colonial Era to the twentieth century. In most cases, not surprisingly, he found that business leaders tended to come from privileged backgrounds. The one exception? The 1830s group. That shows how big the advantage was of being born in that decade. It was the only time in American history when those born in modest circumstances had a realistic shot at real riches. He writes: "The best time during the history of the United States for the poor boy ambitious for high business success to have been born was around the year 1835."

The Altair cost $397. It was a do-it-yourself contraption that you could assemble at home. The headline on the story read: "PROJECT BREAKTHROUGH! World's First Minicomputer Kit to Rival Commercial Models."

To the readers of *Popular Electronics,* in those days the bible of the fledgling software and computer world, that headline was a revelation. Computers up to that point had been the massive, expensive mainframes of the sort sitting in the white expanse of the Michigan Computer Center. For years, every hacker and electronics whiz had dreamt of the day when a computer would come along that was small and inexpensive enough for an ordinary person to use and own. That day had finally arrived.

If January 1975 was the dawn of the personal computer age, then who would be in the best position to take advantage of it? The same principles apply here that applied to the era of John Rockefeller and Andrew Carnegie.

"If you're too old in nineteen seventy-five, then you'd already have a job at IBM out of college, and once people started at IBM, they had a real hard time making the transition to the new world," says Nathan Myhrvold, who was a top executive at Microsoft for many years. "You had this multibillion-dollar company making mainframes, and if you were part of that, you'd think, Why screw around with these little pathetic computers? That was the computer industry to those people, and it had nothing to do with this new revolution. They were blinded by that being the only vision of computing. They made a nice living. It's just that there was no opportunity to become a zillionaire and make an impact on the world."

If you were more than a few years out of college in 1975, then you belonged to the old paradigm. You had just bought a house. You're married. A baby is on the way. You're in no position to give up a good job and pension for some pie-in-the-sky $397 computer kit. So let's rule out all those born before, say, 1952.

At the same time, though, you don't want to be too young. You really want to get in on the ground floor, right in 1975, and you can't do that if you're still in high school. So let's also rule out anyone born after, say, 1958. The perfect age to be in 1975, in other words, is old enough to be a part of the coming revolution but not so old that you missed it. Ideally, you want to be twenty or twenty-one, which is to say, born in 1954 or 1955.

There is an easy way to test this theory. When was Bill Gates born?

Bill Gates: October 28, 1955

That's the perfect birth date! Gates is the hockey player born on January 1. Gates's best friend at Lakeside was Paul Allen. He also hung out in the computer room with Gates and shared those long evenings at ISI and C-Cubed. Allen went on to found Microsoft with Bill Gates. When was Paul Allen born?

Paul Allen: January 21, 1953

The third-richest man at Microsoft is the one who has been running the company on a day-today basis since 2000, one of the most respected executives in the software world, Steve Ballmer. Ballmer's birth date?

Steve Ballmer: March 24, 1956

Let's not forget a man every bit as famous as Gates: Steve Jobs, the cofounder of Apple Computer. Unlike Gates, Jobs wasn't from a rich family and he didn't go to Michigan, like Joy. But it doesn't take much investigation of his upbringing to realize that he had his Hamburg too. He grew up in Mountain View, California, just south of San Francisco, which is the absolute epicenter of Silicon Valley. His neighborhood was filled with engineers from Hewlett-Packard, then as now one of the most important electronics firms in the world. As a teenager he prowled the flea markets of Mountain View, where electronics hobbyists and tinkerers sold spare parts. Jobs came of age breathing the air of the very business he would later dominate.

This paragraph from *Accidental Millionaire,* one of the many Jobs biographies, gives us a sense of how extraordinary his childhood experiences were. Jobs

> attended evening talks by Hewlett-Packard scientists. The talks were about the latest advances in electronics and Jobs, exercising a style that was a trademark of his personality, collared Hewlett-Packard engineers and drew additional information from them. Once he even called Bill Hewlett, one of the company's founders, to request parts. Jobs not only received the parts he asked for, he managed to wrangle a summer job. Jobs worked on an assembly line to build computers and was so fascinated that he tried to design his own...

Wait. *Bill Hewlett gave him spare parts?* That's on a par with Bill Gates getting unlimited access to a time-share terminal at age thirteen. It's as if you were interested in fashion and your neighbor when you were growing up happened to be Giorgio Armani. And when was Jobs born?

Steve Jobs: February 24, 1955

Another of the pioneers of the software revolution was Eric Schmidt. He ran Novell, one of Silicon Valley's most important software firms, and in 2001, he became the chief executive officer of Google. Birth date?

Eric Schmidt: April 27, 1955

I don't mean to suggest, of course, that every software tycoon in Silicon Valley was born in 1955. Some weren't, just as not every business titan in the United States was born in the mid-1830s. But there are very clearly patterns here, and what's striking is how little we seem to want to acknowledge them. We pretend that success is exclusively a matter of individual merit. But there's nothing in any of the histories we've looked at so far to suggest things are that simple. These are stories, instead, about people who were given a special opportunity to work really hard and seized it, and who happened to come of age at a time when that extraordinary effort was rewarded by the rest of society. Their success was not just of their own making. It was a product of the world in which they grew up.

By the way, let's not forget Bill Joy. Had he been just a little bit older and had he had to face the drudgery of programming with computer cards, he says, he would have studied science. Bill Joy the computer legend would have been Bill Joy the biologist. And had he come along a few years later, the little window that gave him the chance to write the supporting code for the Internet would have closed. Again, Bill Joy the computer legend might well have been Bill Joy the biologist. When was Bill Joy born?

Bill Joy: November 8, 1954

Joy would go on, after his stint at Berkeley, to become one of the four founders of Sun Microsystems, one of the oldest and most important of Silicon Valley's software companies. And if you still think that accidents of time and place and birth don't matter all that much, here are the birthdays of the three other founders of Sun Microsystems:

Scott McNealy: November 13, 1954
Vinod Khosla: January 28, 1955
Andy Bechtolsheim: September 30, 1955

CHAPTER THREE

The Trouble with Geniuses, Part 1

"KNOWLEDGE OF A BOY'S IQ IS OF LITTLE HELP IF YOU ARE FACED WITH A FORMFUL OF CLEVER BOYS."

1.

In the fifth episode of the 2008 season, the American television quiz show *1 vs. 100* had as its special guest a man named Christopher Langan.

The television show *1 vs. 100* is one of many that sprang up in the wake of the phenomenal success of *Who Wants to Be a Millionaire*. It features a permanent gallery of one hundred ordinary people who serve as what is called the "mob." Each week they match wits with a special invited guest. At stake is a million dollars. The guest has to be smart enough to answer more questions correctly than his or her one hundred adversaries—and by that standard, few have ever seemed as superbly qualified as Christopher Langan.

"Tonight the mob takes on their fiercest competition yet," the voice-over began. "Meet Chris Langan, who many call the smartest man in America." The camera did a slow pan of a stocky, muscular man in his fifties. "The average person has an IQ of one hundred," the voice-over continued. "Einstein one fifty. Chris has an IQ of one ninety-five. He's currently wrapping his big brain around a theory of the universe. But will his king-size cranium be enough to take down the mob for one million dollars? Find out right now on *One versus One Hundred*."

Out strode Langan onto the stage amid wild applause.

"You don't think you need to have a high

intellect to do well on *One versus One Hundred,* do you?" the show's host, Bob Saget, asked him. Saget looked at Langan oddly, as if he were some kind of laboratory specimen.

"Actually, I think it could be a hindrance," Langan replied. He had a deep, certain voice. "To have a high IQ, you tend to specialize, think deep thoughts. You avoid trivia. But now that I see these people"—he glanced at the mob, the amusement in his eyes betraying just how ridiculous he found the proceedings—"I think I'll do okay."

Over the past decade, Chris Langan has achieved a strange kind of fame. He has become the public face of genius in American life, a celebrity outlier. He gets invited on news shows and profiled in magazines, and he has been the subject of a documentary by the filmmaker Errol Morris, all because of a brain that appears to defy description.

The television news show *20/20* once hired a neuropsychologist to give Langan an IQ test, and Langan's score was literally off the charts—too high to be accurately measured. Another time, Langan took an IQ test specially designed for people too smart for ordinary IQ tests. He got all the questions right except one.* He was speaking at six months of age. When he was three, he would listen to the radio on Sundays as the announcer read the comics aloud, and he would follow along on his own until he had taught himself to read. At five, he began questioning his grandfather about the existence of God—and remembers being disappointed in the answers he got.

In school, Langan could walk into a test in a foreign-language class, not having studied at all, and if there were two or three minutes before the instructor arrived, he could skim through the textbook and ace the test. In his

* The super IQ test was created by Ronald K. Hoeflin, who is himself someone with an unusually high IQ. Here's a sample question, from the verbal analogies section. "Teeth is to Hen as Nest is to ?" If you want to know the answer, I'm afraid I have no idea.

early teenage years, while working as a farmhand, he started to read widely in the area of theoretical physics. At sixteen, he made his way through Bertrand Russell and Alfred North Whitehead's famously abstruse masterpiece *Principia Mathematica*. He got a perfect score on his SAT, even though he fell asleep at one point during the test.

"He did math for an hour," his brother Mark says of Langan's summer routine in high school. "Then he did French for an hour. Then he studied Russian. Then he would read philosophy. He did that religiously, every day."

Another of his brothers, Jeff, says, "You know, when Christopher was fourteen or fifteen, he would draw things just as a joke, and it would be like a photograph. When he was fifteen, he could match Jimi Hendrix lick for lick on a guitar. Boom. Boom. Boom. Half the time, Christopher didn't attend school at all. He would just show up for tests and there was nothing they could do about it. To us, it was hilarious. He could brief a semester's worth of textbooks in two days, and take care of whatever he had to take care of, and then get back to whatever he was doing in the first place."*

On the set of *1 vs. 100,* Langan was poised and confident. His voice was deep. His eyes

* To get a sense of what Chris Langan must have been like growing up, consider the following description of a child named "L," who had an IQ in the same 200 range as Langan's. It's from a study by Leta Stetter Hollingworth, who was one of the first psychologists to study exceptionally gifted children. As the description makes obvious, an IQ of 200 is really, really high: "Young L's erudition was astonishing. His passion for scholarly accuracy and thoroughness set a high standard for accomplishment. He was relatively large, robust and impressive, and was fondly dubbed 'Professor.' His attitudes and abilities were appreciated by both pupils and teachers. He was often allowed to lecture (for as long as an hour) on some special topic, such as the history of timepieces, ancient theories of engine construction, mathematics, and history. He constructed out of odds and ends (typewriter ribbon spools, for example) a homemade clock of the pendular type to illustrate some of the principles of chronometry, and this clock was set up before the class during the enrichment unit on 'Time and Time Keeping' to demonstrate some of

were small and fiercely bright. He did not circle about topics, searching for the right phrase, or double back to restate a previous sentence. For that matter, he did not say um, or ah, or use any form of conversational mitigation: his sentences came marching out, one after another, polished and crisp, like soldiers on a parade ground. Every question Saget threw at him, he tossed aside, as if it were a triviality. When his winnings reached $250,000, he appeared to make a mental calculation that the risks of losing everything were at that point greater than the potential benefits of staying in. Abruptly, he stopped. "I'll take the cash," he said. He shook Saget's hand firmly

---

the principles of chronometry. His notebooks were marvels of scholarly exposition.

"Being discontented with what he considered the inadequate treatment of land travel in a class unit on 'Transportation,' he agreed that time was too limited to do justice to everything. But he insisted that 'at least they should have covered ancient theory.' As an extra and voluntary project, 'he brought in elaborate drawings and accounts of the ancient theories of engines, locomotives etc.' . . . He was at that time 10 years of age."

and was finished—exiting on top as, we like to think, geniuses invariably do.

2.

Just after the First World War, Lewis Terman, a young professor of psychology at Stanford University, met a remarkable boy named Henry Cowell. Cowell had been raised in poverty and chaos. Because he did not get along with other children, he had been unschooled since the age of seven. He worked as a janitor at a one-room schoolhouse not far from the Stanford campus, and throughout the day, Cowell would sneak away from his job and play the school piano. And the music he made was beautiful.

Terman's specialty was intelligence testing; the standard IQ test that millions of people around the world would take during the following fifty years, the Stanford-Binet, was his creation. So he decided to test Cowell's IQ. The boy *must* be intelligent, he reasoned, and sure enough, he was. He had an IQ of above 140, which is near genius level. Terman was fascinated. How many other diamonds in the rough were there? he wondered.

He began to look for others. He found a girl who knew the alphabet at nineteen months, and another who was reading Dickens and Shakespeare by the time she was four. He found a young man who had been kicked out of law school because his professors did not believe that it was possible for a human being to precisely reproduce long passages of legal opinions from memory.

In 1921, Terman decided to make the study of the gifted his life work. Armed with a large grant from the Commonwealth Foundation, he put together a team of fieldworkers and sent them out into California's elementary schools. Teachers were asked to nominate the brightest students in their classes. Those children were given an intelligence test. The students who scored in the top 10 percent were then given a second IQ test, and those who scored above 130 on that test were given a third IQ test, and from that set of results Terman selected the best and the brightest. By the time Terman was finished, he had sorted through the records of some

250,000 elementary and high school students, and identified 1,470 children whose IQs averaged over 140 and ranged as high as 200. That group of young geniuses came to be known as the "Termites," and they were the subjects of what would become one of the most famous psychological studies in history.

For the rest of his life, Terman watched over his charges like a mother hen. They were tracked and tested, measured and analyzed. Their educational attainments were noted, marriages followed, illnesses tabulated, psychological health charted, and every promotion and job change dutifully recorded. Terman wrote his recruits letters of recommendation for jobs and graduate school applications. He doled out a constant stream of advice and counsel, all the time recording his findings in thick red volumes entitled *Genetic Studies of Genius.*

"There is nothing about an individual as important as his IQ, except possibly his morals," Terman once said. And it was to those with a very high IQ, he believed, that "we must look for production of leaders who advance science, art, government, education and social welfare generally." As his subjects grew older, Terman issued updates on their progress, chronicling their extraordinary achievements. "It is almost impossible," Terman wrote giddily, when his charges were in high school, "to read a newspaper account of any sort of competition or activity in which California boys and girls participate without finding among the winners the names of one or more . . . members of our gifted group." He took writing samples from some of his most artistically minded subjects and had literary critics compare them to the early writings of famous authors. They could find no difference. All the signs pointed, he said, to a group with the potential for "heroic stature." Terman believed that his Termites were destined to be the future elite of the United States.

Today, many of Terman's ideas remain central to the way we think about success. Schools have programs for the "gifted." Elite universities often require that students take an intelligence test (such as the American Scholastic Aptitude Test) for admission. High-tech companies like

Google or Microsoft carefully measure the cognitive abilities of prospective employees out of the same belief: they are convinced that those at the very top of the IQ scale have the greatest potential. (At Microsoft, famously, job applicants are asked a battery of questions designed to test their smarts, including the classic "Why are manhole covers round?" If you don't know the answer to that question, you're not smart enough to work at Microsoft.*)

If I had magical powers and offered to raise your IQ by 30 points, you'd say yes—right? You'd assume that would help you get further ahead in the world. And when we hear about someone like Chris Langan, our instinctive response is the same as Terman's instinctive response when he met Henry Cowell almost a century ago. We feel awe. Geniuses are the ultimate outliers. Surely there is nothing that can hold someone like that back.

---

* The answer is that a round manhole cover can't fall into the manhole, no matter how much you twist and turn it. A rectangular cover can: All you have to do is tilt it sideways. There: now you can get a job at Microsoft.

But is that true?

So far in *Outliers,* we've seen that extraordinary achievement is less about talent than it is about opportunity. In this chapter, I want to try to dig deeper into why that's the case by looking at the outlier in its purest and most distilled form—the genius. For years, we've taken our cues from people like Terman when it comes to understanding the significance of high intelligence. But, as we shall see, Terman made an error. He was wrong about his Termites, and had he happened on the young Chris Langan working his way through *Principia Mathematica* at the age of sixteen, he would have been wrong about him for the same reason. Terman didn't understand what a real outlier was, and that's a mistake we continue to make to this day.

3.

One of the most widely used intelligence tests is something called Raven's Progressive Matrices. It requires no language skills or specific body of acquired knowledge. It's a measure of abstract reasoning skills. A typical Raven's test consists of forty-eight items, each one harder than the one before it, and IQ is calculated based on how many items are answered correctly.

Here's a question, typical of the sort that is asked on the Raven's.

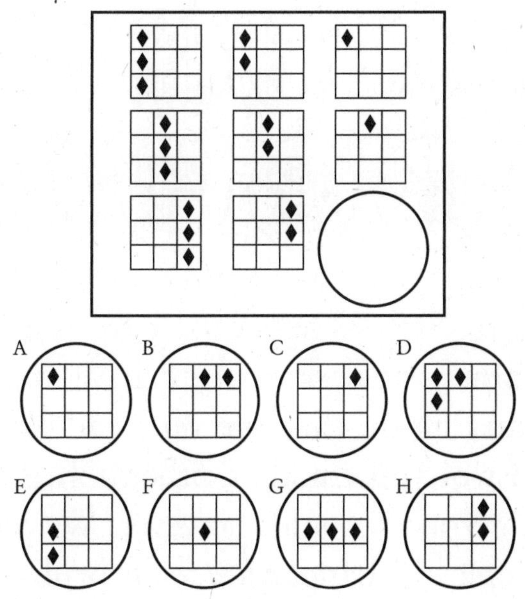

Did you get that? I'm guessing most of you did. The correct answer is C. But now try this one. It's the kind of really hard question that comes at the end of the Raven's.

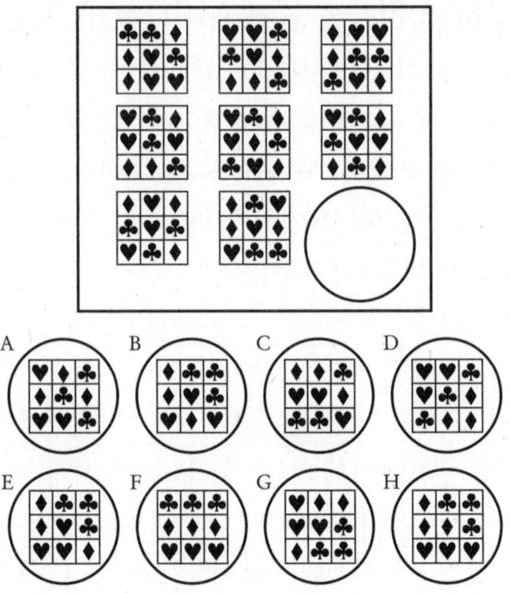

The correct answer is A. I have to confess I couldn't figure this one out, and I'm guessing most of you couldn't either. Chris Langan almost certainly could, however. When we say that people like Langan are really brilliant, what we mean is that they have the kind of mind that can figure out puzzles like that last question.

Over the years, an enormous amount of research has been done in an attempt to determine how a person's performance on an IQ test like the Raven's translates to real-life success. People at the bottom of the scale—with an IQ below 70—are considered mentally disabled. A score of 100 is average; you probably need to be just above that mark to be able to handle college. To get into and succeed in a reasonably competitive graduate program, meanwhile, you probably need an IQ of at least 115. In general, the higher your score, the more education you'll get, the more money you're likely to make, and—believe it or not—the longer you'll live.

But there's a catch. The relationship between success and IQ works only up to a point. Once someone has reached an IQ of somewhere around 120, having additional IQ points doesn't seem to translate into any measurable real-world advantage.*

* The "IQ fundamentalist" Arthur Jensen put it thusly in his 1980 book *Bias in Mental Testing* (p. 113): "The four socially and personally most important threshold regions on the IQ scale are those that differentiate with high probability between persons who, because of their level of general mental ability, can or cannot attend a regular school (about IQ 50), can or cannot

"It is amply proved that someone with an IQ of 170 is more likely to think well than someone whose IQ is 70," the British psychologist Liam Hudson has written, "and this holds true where the comparison is much closer—between IQs of, say, 100 and 130. But the relation seems to break down when one is making comparisons between two people both of whom have IQs

---

master the traditional subject matter of elementary school (about IQ 75), can or cannot succeed in the academic or college preparatory curriculum through high school (about IQ 105), can or cannot graduate from an accredited four-year college with grades that would qualify for admission to a professional or graduate school (about IQ 115). Beyond this, the IQ level becomes relatively unimportant in terms of ordinary occupational aspirations and criteria of success. That is not to say that there are not real differences between the intellectual capabilities represented by IQs of 115 and 150 or even between IQs of 150 and 180. But IQ differences in this upper part of the scale have far less personal implications than the thresholds just described and are generally of lesser importance for success in the popular sense than are certain traits of personality and character."

which are relatively high....A mature scientist with an adult IQ of 130 is as likely to win a Nobel Prize as is one whose IQ is 180."

What Hudson is saying is that IQ is a lot like height in basketball. Does someone who is five foot six have a realistic chance of playing professional basketball? Not really. You need to be at least six foot or six one to play at that level, and, all things being equal, it's probably better to be six two than six one, and better to be six three than six two. But past a certain point, height stops mattering so much. A player who is six foot eight is not automatically better than someone two inches shorter. (Michael Jordan, the greatest player ever, was six six after all.) A basketball player only has to be tall *enough*—and the same is true of intelligence. Intelligence has a threshold.

The introduction to the *1 vs. 100* episode pointed out that Einstein had an IQ of 150 and Langan has an IQ of 195. Langan's IQ is 30 percent higher than Einstein's. But that doesn't mean Langan is 30 percent *smarter* than Einstein. That's ridiculous. All we can say is that when it comes to thinking about really hard things like physics, they are both clearly smart *enough*.

The idea that IQ has a threshold, I realize, goes against our intuition. We think that, say, Nobel Prize winners in science must have the highest IQ scores imaginable; that they must be the kinds of people who got perfect scores on their entrance examinations to college, won every scholarship available, and had such stellar academic records in high school that they were scooped up by the top universities in the country.

But take a look at the following list of where the last twenty-five Americans to win the Nobel Prize in Medicine got their undergraduate degrees, starting in 2007.

Antioch College
Brown University
UC Berkeley
University of Washington
Columbia University
Case Institute of Technology
MIT
Caltech

Harvard University
Hamilton College
Columbia University
University of North Carolina
DePauw University
University of Pennsylvania
University of Minnesota
University of Notre Dame
Johns Hopkins University
Yale University
Union College, Kentucky
University of Illinois
University of Texas
Holy Cross
Amherst College
Gettysburg College
Hunter College

No one would say that this list represents the college choices of the absolute best high school students in America. Yale and Columbia and MIT are on the list, but so are DePauw, Holy Cross, and Gettysburg College. It's a list of *good* schools.

Along the same lines, here are the colleges of the last twenty-five American Nobel laureates in Chemistry:

City College of New York
City College of New York
Stanford University
University of Dayton, Ohio
Rollins College, Florida
MIT
Grinnell College
MIT
McGill University
Georgia Institute of Technology
Ohio Wesleyan University
Rice University
Hope College
Brigham Young University
University of Toronto
University of Nebraska
Dartmouth College
Harvard University
Berea College
Augsburg College

University of Massachusetts
Washington State University
University of Florida
University of California, Riverside
Harvard University

To be a Nobel Prize winner, apparently, you have to be smart enough to get into a college at least as good as Notre Dame or the University of Illinois. That's all.*

This is a radical idea, isn't it? Suppose that your teenage daughter found out that she had been accepted at two universities—Harvard University and Georgetown University, in Washington, DC. Where would you want her

* Just to be clear: it is still the case that Harvard produces more Nobel Prize winners than any other school. Just look at those lists. Harvard appears on both of them, a total of three times. A school like Holy Cross appears just once. But wouldn't you expect schools like Harvard to win more Nobels than they do? Harvard is, after all, the richest, most prestigious school in history and has its pick of the most brilliant undergraduates the world over.

to go? I'm guessing Harvard, because Harvard is a "better" school. Its students score a good 10 to 15 percent higher on their entrance exams.

But given what we are learning about intelligence, the idea that schools can be ranked, like runners in a race, makes no sense. Georgetown's students may not be as smart on an absolute scale as the students of Harvard. But they are all, clearly, smart enough, and future Nobel Prize winners come from schools like Georgetown as well as from schools like Harvard.

The psychologist Barry Schwartz recently proposed that elite schools give up their complex admissions process and simply hold a lottery for everyone above the threshold. "Put people into two categories," Schwartz says. "Good enough and not good enough. The ones who are good enough get put into a hat. And those who are not good enough get rejected." Schwartz concedes that his idea has virtually no chance of being accepted. But he's absolutely right. As Hudson writes (and keep in mind that he did his research at elite all-male English boarding schools in the 1950s and 1960s), "Knowledge of a boy's IQ is of little help *if you are faced with a formful of clever boys.*"*

Let me give you an example of the threshold effect in action. The University of Michigan law school, like many elite US educational institutions, uses a policy of affirmative action when it comes to applicants from disadvantaged backgrounds. Around 10 percent of the students Michigan enrolls each fall are members of racial minorities, and if the law school did

* To get a sense of how absurd the selection process at elite Ivy League schools has become, consider the following statistics. In 2008, 27,462 of the most highly qualified high school seniors in the world applied to Harvard University. Of these students, 2,500 of them scored a perfect 800 on the SAT critical reading test and 3,300 had a perfect score on the SAT math exam. More than 3,300 were ranked first in their high school class. How many did Harvard accept? About 1,600, which is to say they rejected 93 out of every 100 applicants. Is it really possible to say that one student is Harvard material and another isn't, when both have identical—and perfect—academic records? Of course not. Harvard is being dishonest. Schwartz is right. They should just have a lottery.

not significantly relax its entry requirements for those students—admitting them with lower undergraduate grades and lower standardized-test scores than everyone else—it estimates that percentage would be less than 3 percent. Furthermore, if we compare the grades that the minority and nonminority students get in law school, we see that the white students do better. That's not surprising: if one group has higher undergraduate grades and test scores than the other, it's almost certainly going to have higher grades in law school as well. This is one reason that affirmative action programs are so controversial. In fact, an attack on the University of Michigan's affirmative action program recently went all the way to the US Supreme Court. For many people it is troubling that an elite educational institution lets in students who are less qualified than their peers.

A few years ago, however, the University of Michigan decided to look closely at how the law school's minority students had fared after they graduated. How much money did they make? How far up in the profession did they go? How satisfied were they with their careers? What kind of social and community contributions did they make? What kind of honors had they won? They looked at everything that could conceivably be an indication of real-world success. And what they found surprised them.

"We knew that our minority students, a lot of them, were doing well," says Richard Lempert, one of the authors of the Michigan study. "I think our expectation was that we would find a half- or two-thirds-full glass, that they had not done as well as the white students but nonetheless a lot were quite successful. But we were completely surprised. We found that they were doing every bit as well. There was no place we saw any serious discrepancy."

What Lempert is saying is that by the only measure that a law school really ought to care about—how well its graduates do in the real world—minority students aren't less qualified. They're just as successful as white students. And why? Because even though the academic credentials of minority students at Michigan aren't as good as those of white students, the quality of students at the law school is high enough that *they're still above the threshold.* They are smart enough. Knowledge of a law student's test scores is of little help if you are faced with a classroom of clever law students.

4.

Let's take the threshold idea one step further. If intelligence matters only up to a point, then past that point, other things—things that have nothing to do with intelligence—must start to matter more. It's like basketball again: once someone is tall enough, then we start to care about speed and court sense and agility and ballhandling skills and shooting touch.

So, what might some of those other things be? Well, suppose that instead of measuring your IQ, I gave you a totally different kind of test.

Write down as many different uses that you can think of for the following objects:

1. a brick
2. a blanket

This is an example of what's called a "divergence test" (as opposed to a test like the Raven's, which asks you to sort through a list of possibilities and *converge* on the right answer). It requires you to use your imagination and take your mind in as many different directions as possible. With a divergence test, obviously there isn't a single right answer. What the test giver is looking for are the number and the uniqueness of your responses. And what the test is measuring isn't analytical intelligence but something profoundly different—something much closer to creativity. Divergence tests are every bit as challenging as convergence tests, and if you don't believe that, I encourage you to pause and try the brick-and-blanket test right now.

Here, for example, are answers to the "uses of objects" test collected by Liam Hudson from a student named Poole at a top British high school:

> (Brick). To use in smash-and-grab raids. To help hold a house together. To use in a game of Russian roulette if you want to keep fit at the same time (bricks at ten paces, turn and throw—no evasive

action allowed). To hold the eiderdown on a bed tie a brick at each corner. As a breaker of empty Coca-Cola bottles.

(Blanket). To use on a bed. As a cover for illicit sex in the woods. As a tent. To make smoke signals with. As a sail for a boat, cart or sled. As a substitute for a towel. As a target for shooting practice for short-sighted people. As a thing to catch people jumping out of burning skyscrapers.

It's not hard to read Poole's answers and get some sense of how his mind works. He's funny. He's a little subversive and libidinous. He has the flair for the dramatic. His mind leaps from violent imagery to sex to people jumping out of burning skyscrapers to very practical issues, such as how to get a duvet to stay on a bed. He gives us the impression that if we gave him another ten minutes, he'd come up with another twenty uses.*

* Here's another student's answers. These might be even better than Poole's: "(Brick). To break windows

Now, for the sake of comparison, consider the answers of another student from Hudson's sample. His name is Florence. Hudson tells us that Florence is a prodigy, with one of the highest IQs in his school.

> (Brick). Building things, throwing.
>
> (Blanket). Keeping warm, smothering fire, tying to trees and sleeping in (as a hammock), improvised stretcher.

Where is Florence's imagination? He identified the most common and most functional uses for bricks and blankets and simply stopped. Florence's IQ is higher than Poole's. But that

---

for robbery, to determine depth of wells, to use as ammunition, as pendulum, to practice carving, wall building, to demonstrate Archimedes' Principle, as part of abstract sculpture, costh, ballast, weight for dropping things in river, etc., as a hammer, keep door open, footwiper, use as rubble for path filling, chock, weight on scale, to prop up wobbly table, paperweight, as firehearth, to block up rabbit hole."

means little, since both students are above the threshold. What is more interesting is that Poole's mind can leap from violent imagery to sex to people jumping out of buildings without missing a beat, and Florence's mind can't. Now which of these two students do you think is better suited to do the kind of brilliant, imaginative work that wins Nobel Prizes?

That's the second reason Nobel Prize winners come from Holy Cross as well as Harvard, because Harvard isn't selecting its students on the basis of how well they do on the "uses of a brick" test—and maybe "uses of a brick" is a better predictor of Nobel Prize ability. It's also the second reason Michigan Law School couldn't find a difference between its affirmative action graduates and the rest of its alumni. Being a successful lawyer is about a lot more than IQ. It involves having the kind of fertile mind that Poole had. And just because Michigan's minority students have lower scores on convergence tests doesn't mean they don't have that other critical trait in abundance.

5.

This was Terman's error. He fell in love with the fact that his Termites were at the absolute pinnacle of the intellectual scale—at the ninety-ninth percentile of the ninety-ninth percentile—without realizing how little that seemingly extraordinary fact meant.

By the time the Termites reached adulthood, Terman's error was plain to see. Some of his child geniuses had grown up to publish books and scholarly articles and thrive in business. Several ran for public office, and there were two superior court justices, one municipal court judge, two members of the California state legislature, and one prominent state official. But few of his geniuses were nationally known figures. They tended to earn good incomes—but not *that* good. The majority had careers that could only be considered ordinary, and a surprising number ended up with careers that even Terman considered failures. Nor were there any Nobel Prize winners in his exhaustively selected group of geniuses. His fieldworkers actually tested two elementary students who went on to be Nobel laureates—William Shockley and Luis Alvarez—and rejected them both. Their IQs weren't high enough.

In a devastating critique, the sociologist Pitirim Sorokin once showed that if Terman had simply put together a randomly selected group of children from the same kinds of family backgrounds as the Termites—and dispensed with IQs altogether—he would have ended up with a group doing almost as many impressive things as his painstakingly selected group of geniuses. "By no stretch of the imagination or of standards of genius," Sorokin concluded, "is the 'gifted group' as a whole 'gifted.'" By the time Terman came out with his fourth volume of *Genetic Studies of Genius,* the word "genius" had all but vanished. "We have seen," Terman concluded, with more than a touch of disappointment, "that intellect and achievement are far from perfectly correlated."

What I told you at the beginning of this chapter about the extraordinary intelligence of Chris Langan, in other words, is of little use if we want to understand his chances of being a success in the world. Yes, he is a man with a one-in-a-million mind and the ability to get through *Principia Mathematica* at sixteen. And yes, his sentences come marching out one after another, polished and crisp like soldiers on a parade ground. But so what? If we want to understand the likelihood of his becoming a true outlier, we have to know a lot more about him than that.

CHAPTER FOUR

The Trouble with Geniuses, Part 2

"AFTER PROTRACTED NEGOTIATIONS, IT WAS AGREED THAT ROBERT WOULD BE PUT ON PROBATION."

1.

Chris Langan's mother was from San Francisco and was estranged from her family. She had four sons, each with a different father. Chris was the eldest. His father disappeared before Chris was born; he was said to have died in Mexico. His mother's second husband was murdered. Her third committed suicide. Her fourth was a failed journalist named Jack Langan.

"To this day I haven't met anybody who was as poor when they were kids as our family was," Chris Langan says. "We didn't have a pair of matched socks. Our shoes had holes in them. Our pants had holes in them. We only had one set of clothes. I remember my brothers and I going into the bathroom and using the bathtub to wash our only set of clothes and we were bare-assed naked when we were doing that because we didn't have anything to wear."

Jack Langan would go on drinking sprees and disappear. He would lock the kitchen cabinets so the boys couldn't get to the food. He used a bullwhip to keep the boys in line. He would get jobs and then lose them, moving the family on to the next town. One summer the family lived on an Indian reservation in a teepee, subsisting on government-surplus peanut butter and cornmeal. For a time, they lived in Virginia City, Nevada. "There was only one law officer in town, and when the Hell's Angels came to town, he would crouch down in the back of his office," Mark Langan remembers.

"There was a bar there, I'll always remember. It was called the Bucket of Blood Saloon."

When the boys were in grade school, the family moved to Bozeman, Montana. One of Chris's brothers spent time in a foster home. Another was sent to reform school.

"I don't think the school ever understood just how gifted Christopher was," his brother Jeff says. "He sure as hell didn't play it up. This was Bozeman. It wasn't like it is today. It was a small hick town when we were growing up. We weren't treated well there. They'd just decided that my family was a bunch of deadbeats." To stick up for himself and his brothers, Chris started to lift weights. One day, when Chris was fourteen, Jack Langan got rough with the boys, as he sometimes did, and Chris knocked him out cold. Jack left, never to return. Upon graduation from high school, Chris was offered two full scholarships, one to Reed College in Oregon and the other to the University of Chicago. He chose Reed.

"It was a huge mistake," Chris recalls. "I had a real case of culture shock. I was a crew-cut kid who had been working as a ranch hand in the summers in Montana, and there I was, with a whole bunch of long-haired city kids, most of them from New York. And these kids had a whole different style than I was used to. I couldn't get a word in edgewise at class. They were very inquisitive. Asking questions all the time. I was crammed into a dorm room. There were four of us, and the other three guys had a whole different other lifestyle. They were smoking pot. They would bring their girlfriends into the room. I had never smoked pot before. So basically I took to hiding in the library."

He continued: "Then I lost that scholarship. . . . My mother was supposed to fill out a parents' financial statement for the renewal of that scholarship. She neglected to do so. She was confused by the requirements or whatever. At some point, it came to my attention that my scholarship had not been renewed. So I went to the office to ask why, and they told me, Well, no one sent us the financial statement, and we allocated all the scholarship money and it's all gone, so I'm afraid that you don't have a scholarship here anymore. That was the style of the place. They simply didn't care. They didn't give a shit about their students. There was no counseling, no mentoring, nothing."

Chris left Reed before the final set of exams, leaving him with a row of Fs on his transcript. In the first semester, he had earned As. He went back to Bozeman and worked in construction and as a forest services firefighter for a year and a half. Then he enrolled at Montana State University.

"I was taking math and philosophy classes," he recalled. "And then in the winter quarter, I was living thirteen miles out of town, out on Beach Hill Road, and the transmission fell out of my car. My brothers had used it when I was gone that summer. They were working for the railroad and had driven it on the railroad tracks. I didn't have the money to repair it. So I went to my adviser and the dean in sequence and said, I have a problem. The transmission fell out of my car, and you have me in a seven-thirty a.m. and eight-thirty a.m. class. If you could please just transfer me to the afternoon sections of these classes, I would appreciate it because of this car problem. There was a neighbor who was a rancher who was going to take me in at eleven o'clock. My adviser was this cowboy-looking guy with a handlebar mustache, dressed in a tweed jacket. He said, 'Well, son, after looking at your transcript at Reed College, I see that you have yet to learn that everyone has to make sacrifices to get an education. Request denied.' So then I went to the dean. Same treatment."

His voice grew tight. He was describing things that had happened more than thirty years ago, but the memory still made him angry. "At that point I realized, here I was, knocking myself out to make the money to make my way back to school, and it's the middle of the Montana winter. I am willing to hitchhike into town every day, do whatever I had to do, just to get into school and back, and they are unwilling to do anything for me. So bananas. And that was the point I decided I could do without the higher-education system. Even if I couldn't do without it, it was sufficiently repugnant to me that I wouldn't do it anymore. So I dropped out of college, simple as that."

Chris Langan's experiences at Reed and Montana State represented a turning point in his life. As a child, he had dreamt of becoming an academic. He *should* have gotten a PhD; universities are institutions structured, in large part, for people with his kind of deep intellectual interests and curiosity. "Once he got into the university environment, I thought he would prosper, I really did," his brother Mark says. "I thought he would somehow find a niche. It made absolutely no sense to me when he left that."

Without a degree, Langan floundered. He worked in construction. One frigid winter he worked on a clam boat on Long Island. He took factory jobs and minor civil service positions and eventually became a bouncer in a bar on Long Island, which was his principal occupation for much of his adult years. Through it all, he continued to read deeply in philosophy, mathematics, and physics as he worked on a sprawling treatise he calls the "CTMU"—the "Cognitive Theoretic Model of the Universe." But without academic credentials, he despairs of ever getting published in a scholarly journal.

"I am a guy who has a year and a half of college," he says, with a shrug. "And at some point this will come to the attention of the editor, as he is going to take the paper and send it off to the referees, and these referees are going to try and look me up, and they are not going to find me. And they are going to say, This guy has a year and a half of college. How can he know what he's talking about?"

It is a heartbreaking story. At one point I asked Langan—hypothetically—whether he would take a job at Harvard University were it offered to him. "Well, that's a difficult question," he replied. "Obviously, as a full professor at Harvard I would count. My ideas would have weight and I could use my position, my affiliation at Harvard, to promote my ideas. An institution like that is a great source of intellectual energy, and if I were at a place like that, I could absorb the vibration in the air." It was suddenly clear how lonely his life has been. Here he was, a man with an insatiable appetite for learning, forced for most of his adult life to live in intellectual isolation. "I even noticed that kind of intellectual energy in the year and a half I was in college," he said, almost wistfully. "Ideas are in the air constantly. It's such a stimulating place to be.

"On the other hand," he went on, "Harvard is basically a glorified corporation, operating with a profit incentive. That's what makes it tick. It has an endowment in the billions of dollars. The people running it are not necessarily searching for truth and knowledge. They want to be big shots, and when you accept a paycheck from these people, it is going to come down to what you want to do and what you feel is right versus what the man says you can do to receive another paycheck. When you're there, they got a thumb right on you. They are out to make sure you don't step out of line."

2.

What does the story of Chris Langan tell us? His explanations, as heartbreaking as they are, are also a little strange. His mother forgets to sign his financial aid form and—just like that—no scholarship. He tries to move from a morning to an afternoon class, something students do every day, and gets stopped cold. And why were Langan's teachers at Reed and Montana State so indifferent to his plight? Teachers typically delight in minds as brilliant as his. Langan talks about dealing with Reed and Montana State as if they were some kind of vast and unyielding government bureaucracy. But colleges, particularly small liberal arts colleges like Reed, tend not to be rigid bureaucracies. Making allowances in the name of helping someone stay in school is what professors do all the time.

Even in his discussion of Harvard, it's as if Langan has no conception of the culture and particulars of the institution he's talking about. *When you accept a paycheck from these people, it is going to come down to what you want to do and what you feel is right versus what the man says you can do to receive another paycheck.* What? One of the main reasons college professors accept a lower paycheck than they could get in private industry is that university life gives them the freedom to do what they want to do and what they feel is right. Langan has Harvard backwards.

When Langan told me his life story, I couldn't help thinking of the life of Robert Oppenheimer, the physicist who famously headed the American effort to develop the nuclear bomb during World War II. Oppenheimer, by all accounts, was a child with a mind very much like Chris Langan's. His parents considered him a genius. One of his teachers recalled that "he received every new idea as perfectly beautiful." He was doing lab experiments by the third grade and studying physics and chemistry by the fifth grade. When he was nine, he once told one of his cousins, "Ask me a question in Latin and I will answer you in Greek."

Oppenheimer went to Harvard and then

on to Cambridge University to pursue a doctorate in physics. There, Oppenheimer, who struggled with depression his entire life, grew despondent. His gift was for theoretical physics, and his tutor, a man named Patrick Blackett (who would win a Nobel Prize in 1948), was forcing him to attend to the minutiae of experimental physics, which he hated. He grew more and more emotionally unstable, and then, in an act so strange that to this day no one has properly made sense of it, Oppenheimer took some chemicals from the laboratory and tried to poison his tutor.

Blackett, luckily, found out that something was amiss. The university was informed. Oppenheimer was called on the carpet. And what happened next is every bit as unbelievable as the crime itself. Here is how the incident is described in *American Prometheus,* Kai Bird and Martin Sherwin's biography of Oppenheimer: "After protracted negotiations, it was agreed that Robert would be put on probation and have regular sessions with a prominent Harley Street psychiatrist in London."

On probation?

Here we have two very brilliant young students, each of whom runs into a problem that imperils his college career. Langan's mother has missed a deadline for his financial aid. Oppenheimer has tried to poison his tutor. To continue on, they are required to plead their cases to authority. And what happens? Langan gets his scholarship taken away, and Oppenheimer gets sent to a psychiatrist. Oppenheimer and Langan might both be geniuses, but in other ways, they could not be more different.

The story of Oppenheimer's appointment to be scientific director of the Manhattan Project twenty years later is perhaps an even better example of this difference. The general in charge of the Manhattan Project was Leslie Groves, and he scoured the country, trying to find the right person to lead the atomic-bomb effort. Oppenheimer, by rights, was a long shot. He was just thirty-eight, and junior to many of the people whom he would have to manage. He was a theorist, and this was a job that called for experimenters and engineers. His political affiliations were dodgy: he had all kinds of friends who were Communists. Perhaps more striking, he had never had any administrative experience. "He was a very impractical fellow," one of Oppenheimer's friends later said. "He walked about with scuffed shoes and a funny hat, and, more important, he didn't know anything about equipment." As one Berkeley scientist put it, more succinctly: "He couldn't run a hamburger stand."

Oh, and by the way, in graduate school *he tried to kill his tutor*. This was the résumé of the man who was trying out for what might be said to be—without exaggeration—one of the most important jobs of the twentieth century. And what happened? The same thing that happened twenty years earlier at Cambridge: he got the rest of the world to see things his way.

Here are Bird and Sherwin again: "Oppenheimer understood that Groves guarded the entrance to the Manhattan Project, and he therefore turned on all his charm and brilliance. It was an irresistible performance." Groves was smitten. " 'He's a genius,' Groves later told a reporter.

'A real genius.'" Groves was an engineer by training with a graduate degree from MIT, and Oppenheimer's great insight was to appeal to that side of Groves. Bird and Sherwin go on: "Oppenheimer was the first scientist Groves had met on his tour [of potential candidates] who grasped that building an atomic bomb required finding practical solutions to a variety of cross-disciplinary problems.... [Groves] found himself nodding in agreement when Oppenheimer pitched the notion of a central laboratory devoted to this purpose, where, as he later testified, 'we could begin to come to grips with chemical, metallurgical, engineering and ordnance problems that had so far received no consideration.'"

Would Oppenheimer have lost his scholarship at Reed? Would he have been unable to convince his professors to move his classes to the afternoon? Of course not. And that's not because he was smarter than Chris Langan. It's because he possessed the kind of savvy that allowed him to get what he wanted from the world.

"They required that everyone take introductory calculus," Langan said of his brief stay at Montana State. "And I happened to get a guy who taught it in a very dry, very trivial way. I didn't understand why he was teaching it this way. So I asked him questions. I actually had to chase him down to his office. I asked him, 'Why are you teaching this way? Why do you consider this practice to be relevant to calculus?' And this guy, this tall, lanky guy, always had sweat stains under his arms, he turned and looked at me and said, 'You know, there is something you should probably get straight. Some people just don't have the intellectual firepower to be mathematicians.' "

There they are, the professor and the prodigy, and what the prodigy clearly wants is to be engaged, at long last, with a mind that loves mathematics as much as he does. But he fails. In fact—and this is the most heartbreaking part of all—he manages to have an entire conversation with his calculus professor without ever communicating the one fact most likely to appeal to a calculus professor. The professor never realizes that Chris Langan is good at calculus.

3.

The particular skill that allows you to talk your way out of a murder rap, or convince your professor to move you from the morning to the afternoon section, is what the psychologist Robert Sternberg calls "practical intelligence." To Sternberg, practical intelligence includes things like "knowing what to say to whom, knowing when to say it, and knowing how to say it for maximum effect." It is procedural: it is about knowing *how* to do something without necessarily knowing why you know it or being able to explain it. It's practical in nature: that is, it's not knowledge for its own sake. It's knowledge that helps you read situations correctly and get what you want. And, critically, it is a kind of intelligence separate from the sort of analytical ability measured by IQ. To use the technical term, general intelligence and practical intelligence are "orthogonal": the presence of one doesn't imply the presence of the other. You can have lots of analytical intelligence and very little practical intelligence, or lots of practical intelligence and not much analytical intelligence, or—as in the lucky case of someone like Robert Oppenheimer—you can have lots of both.

So where does something like practical intelligence come from? We know where analytical intelligence comes from. It's something, at least in part, that's in your genes. Chris Langan started talking at six months. He taught himself to read at three years of age. He was *born* smart. IQ is a measure, to some degree, of innate ability.* But social savvy is *knowledge*. It's a set of skills that have to be learned. It has to come from somewhere, and the place where we seem to get these kinds of attitudes and skills is from our families.

Perhaps the best explanation we have of this process comes from the sociologist Annette

* Most estimates put the heritability of IQ at roughly 50 percent.

Lareau, who a few years ago conducted a fascinating study of a group of third graders. She picked both blacks and whites and children from both wealthy homes and poor homes, zeroing in, ultimately, on twelve families. Lareau and her team visited each family at least twenty times, for hours at a stretch. She and her assistants told their subjects to treat them like "the family dog," and they followed them to church and to soccer games and to doctor's appointments, with a tape recorder in one hand and a notebook in the other.

You might expect that if you spent such an extended period in twelve different households, what you would gather is twelve different ideas about how to raise children: there would be the strict parents and the lax parents and the hyperinvolved parents and the mellow parents and on and on. What Lareau found, however, is something much different. There were only two parenting "philosophies," and they divided almost perfectly along class lines. The wealthier parents raised their kids one way, and the poorer parents raised their kids another way.

The wealthier parents were heavily involved in their children's free time, shuttling them from one activity to the next, quizzing them about their teachers and coaches and teammates. One of the well-off children Lareau followed played on a baseball team, two soccer teams, a swim team, and a basketball team in the summer, as well as playing in an orchestra and taking piano lessons.

That kind of intensive scheduling was almost entirely absent from the lives of the poor children. Play for them wasn't soccer practice twice a week. It was making up games outside with their siblings and other kids in the neighborhood. What a child did was considered by his or her parents as something separate from the adult world and not particularly consequential. One girl from a working-class family—Katie Brindle—sang in a choir after school. But she signed up for it herself and walked to choir practice on her own. Lareau writes:

> What Mrs. Brindle doesn't do that is routine for middle-class mothers is view her daughter's interest

> in singing as a signal to look for other ways to help her develop that interest into a formal talent. Similarly Mrs. Brindle does not discuss Katie's interest in drama or express regret that she cannot afford to cultivate her daughter's talent. Instead she frames Katie's skills and interests as character traits—singing and acting are part of what makes Katie "Katie." She sees the shows her daughter puts on as "cute" and as a way for Katie to "get attention."

The middle-class parents talked things through with their children, reasoning with them. They didn't just issue commands. They expected their children to talk back to them, to negotiate, to question adults in positions of authority. If their children were doing poorly at school, the wealthier parents challenged their teachers. They intervened on behalf of their kids. One child Lareau follows just misses qualifying for a gifted program. Her mother arranges for her to be retested privately, petitions the school, and gets her daughter admitted. The poor parents, by contrast, are intimidated by authority. They react passively and stay in the background. Lareau writes of one low-income parent:

> At a parent-teacher conference, for example, Ms. McAllister (who is a high school graduate) seems subdued. The gregarious and outgoing nature she displays at home is hidden in this setting. She sits hunched over in the chair and she keeps her jacket zipped up. She is very quiet. When the teacher reports that Harold has not been turning in his homework, Ms. McAllister clearly is flabbergasted, but all she says is, "He did it at home." She does not follow up with the teacher or attempt to intervene on Harold's behalf. In her view, it is up to the teachers to manage her son's education. That is their job, not hers.

Lareau calls the middle-class parenting style "concerted cultivation." It's an attempt to actively "foster and assess a child's talents, opinions and skills." Poor parents tend to follow, by contrast, a strategy of "accomplishment of natural growth."

They see as their responsibility to care for their children but to let them grow and develop on their own.

Lareau stresses that one style isn't morally better than the other. The poorer children were, to her mind, often better behaved, less whiny, more creative in making use of their own time, and had a well-developed sense of independence. But in practical terms, concerted cultivation has enormous advantages. The heavily scheduled middle-class child is exposed to a constantly shifting set of experiences. She learns teamwork and how to cope in highly structured settings. She is taught how to interact comfortably with adults, and to speak up when she needs to. In Lareau's words, the middle-class children learn a sense of "entitlement."

That word, of course, has negative connotations these days. But Lareau means it in the best sense of the term: "They acted as though they had a right to pursue their own individual preferences and to actively manage interactions in institutional settings. They appeared comfortable in those settings; they were open to sharing information and asking for attention. . . . It was common practice among middle-class children to shift interactions to suit their preferences." They knew the rules. "Even in fourth grade, middle-class children appeared to be acting on their own behalf to gain advantages. They made special requests of teachers and doctors to adjust procedures to accommodate their desires."

By contrast, the working-class and poor children were characterized by "an emerging sense of distance, distrust, and constraint." They didn't know how to get their way, or how to "customize"—using Lareau's wonderful term—whatever environment they were in, for their best purposes.

In one telling scene, Lareau describes a visit to the doctor by Alex Williams, a nine-year-old boy, and his mother, Christina. The Williamses are wealthy professionals.

"Alex, you should be thinking of questions you might want to ask the doctor," Christina says in the car on the way to the doctor's office. "You can ask him anything you want. Don't be shy. You can ask anything."

Alex thinks for a minute, then says, "I have some bumps under my arms from my deodorant." Christina: "Really? You mean from your new deodorant?" Alex: "Yes." Christina: "Well, you should ask the doctor."

Alex's mother, Lareau writes, "is teaching that he has the right to speak up"—that even though he's going to be in a room with an older person and authority figure, it's perfectly all right for him to assert himself. They meet the doctor, a genial man in his early forties. He tells Alex that he is in the ninety-fifth percentile in height. Alex then interrupts:

> ALEX: I'm in the what?
>
> DOCTOR: It means that you're taller than more than ninety-five out of a hundred young men when they're, uh, ten years old.
>
> ALEX: I'm not ten.
>
> DOCTOR: Well, they graphed you at ten. You're—nine years and ten months. They—they usually take the closest year to that graph.

Look at how easily Alex interrupts the doctor—"I'm not ten." That's entitlement: his mother permits that casual incivility because she wants him to learn to assert himself with people in positions of authority.

> THE DOCTOR TURNS TO ALEX: Well, now the most important question. Do you have any questions you want to ask me before I do your physical?
>
> ALEX: Um . . . only one. I've been getting some bumps on my arms, right around here (indicates underarm).
>
> DOCTOR: Underneath?
>
> ALEX: Yeah.
>
> DOCTOR: Okay. I'll have to take a look at those when I come in closer to do the checkup. And I'll see what they are and what I can do. Do they hurt or itch?
>
> ALEX: No, they're just there.
>
> DOCTOR: Okay, I'll take a look at those bumps for you.

This kind of interaction simply doesn't happen with lower-class children, Lareau says.

They would be quiet and submissive, with eyes turned away. Alex takes charge of the moment. "In remembering to raise the question he prepared in advance, he gains the doctor's full attention and focuses it on an issue of his choosing," Lareau writes.

> In so doing, he successfully shifts the balance of power away from the adults and toward himself. The transition goes smoothly. Alex is used to being treated with respect. He is seen as special and as a person worthy of adult attention and interest. These are key characteristics of the strategy of concerted cultivation. Alex is not showing off during his checkup. He is behaving much as he does with his parents—he reasons, negotiates, and jokes with equal ease.

It is important to understand where the particular mastery of that moment comes from. It's not genetic. Alex Williams didn't inherit the skills to interact with authority figures from his parents and grandparents the way he inherited the color of his eyes. Nor is it racial: it's not a practice specific to either black or white people.

As it turns out, Alex Williams is black and Katie Brindle is white. It's a *cultural* advantage. Alex has those skills because over the course of his young life, his mother and father—in the manner of educated families—have painstakingly taught them to him, nudging and prodding and encouraging and showing him the rules of the game, right down to that little rehearsal in the car on the way to the doctor's office.

When we talk about the advantages of class, Lareau argues, this is in large part what we mean. Alex Williams is better off than Katie Brindle because he's wealthier and because he goes to a better school, but also because—and perhaps this is even more critical—the sense of entitlement that he has been taught is an attitude perfectly suited to succeeding in the modern world.

4.

This is the advantage that Oppenheimer had and that Chris Langan lacked. Oppenheimer was raised in one of the wealthiest neighborhoods in

Manhattan, the son of an artist and a successful garment manufacturer. His childhood was the embodiment of concerted cultivation. On weekends, the Oppenheimers would go driving in the countryside in a chauffeur-driven Packard. Summers he would be taken to Europe to see his grandfather. He attended the Ethical Culture School on Central Park West, perhaps the most progressive school in the nation, where, his biographers write, students were "infused with the notion that they were being groomed to reform the world." When his math teacher realized he was bored, she sent him off to do independent work.

As a child, Oppenheimer was passionate about rock collecting. At the age of twelve, he began corresponding with local geologists about rock formations he had seen in Central Park, and he so impressed them that they invited him to give a lecture before the New York Mineralogical Club. As Sherwin and Bird write, Oppenheimer's parents responded to their son's hobby in an almost textbook example of concerted cultivation:

> Dreading the thought of having to talk to an audience of adults, Robert begged his father to explain that they had invited a twelve-year-old. Greatly amused, Julius encouraged his son to accept this honor. On the designated evening, Robert showed up at the club with his parents, who proudly introduced their son as J. Robert Oppenheimer. The startled audience of geologists and amateur rock collectors burst out laughing when he stepped up to the podium: a wooden box had to be found for him to stand on so that the audience could see more than the shock of his wiry black hair sticking up above the lectern. Shy and awkward, Robert nevertheless read his prepared remarks and was given a hearty round of applause.

Is it any wonder Oppenheimer handled the challenges of his life so brilliantly? If you are someone whose father has made his way up in the business world, then you've seen, firsthand, what it means to negotiate your way out of a tight spot. If you're someone who was sent to the Ethical Culture School, then you aren't going to be intimidated by a row of Cambridge dons arrayed in judgment against you. If you studied physics at Harvard, then you know how to talk to an army general who did engineering just down the road at MIT.

Chris Langan, by contrast, had only the bleakness of Bozeman, and a home dominated by an angry, drunken stepfather. "[Jack] Langan did this to all of us," said Mark. "We all have a true resentment of authority." That was the lesson Langan learned from his childhood: distrust authority and be independent. He never had a parent teach him on the way to the doctor how to speak up for himself, or how to reason and negotiate with those in positions of authority. He didn't learn entitlement. He learned constraint. It may seem like a small thing, but it was a crippling handicap in navigating the world beyond Bozeman.

"I couldn't get any financial aid either," Mark went on. "We just had zero knowledge, less than zero knowledge, of the process. How to apply. The forms. Checkbooks. It was not our environment."

"If Christopher had been born into a wealthy

family, if he was the son of a doctor who was well connected in some major market, I guarantee you he would have been one of those guys you read about, knocking back PhDs at seventeen," his brother Jeff says. "It's the culture you find yourself in that determines that. The issue with Chris is that he was always too bored to actually sit there and listen to his teachers. If someone had recognized his intelligence and if he was from a family where there was some kind of value on education, they would have made sure he wasn't bored."

5.

When the Termites were into their adulthood, Terman looked at the records of 730 of the men and divided them into three groups. One hundred and fifty—the top 20 percent—fell into what Terman called the A group. They were the true success stories, the stars—the lawyers and physicians and engineers and academics. Ninety percent of the As graduated from college and among them had earned 98 graduate degrees.

The middle 60 percent were the B group, those who were doing "satisfactorily." The bottom 150 were the Cs, the ones who Terman judged to have done the least with their superior mental ability. They were the postal workers and the struggling bookkeepers and the men lying on their couches at home without any job at all.

One third of the Cs were college dropouts. A quarter only had a high school diploma, and all 150 of the Cs — each one of whom, at one point in his life, had been dubbed a genius — had together earned a grand total of eight graduate degrees.

What was the difference between the As and the Cs? Terman ran through every conceivable explanation. He looked at their physical and mental health, their "masculinity-femininity scores," and their hobbies and vocational interests. He compared the ages when they started walking and talking and what their precise IQ scores were in elementary and high school. In the end, only one thing mattered: family background.

The As overwhelmingly came from the middle and the upper class. Their homes were filled with books. Half the fathers of the A group had a college degree or beyond, and this at a time when a university education was a rarity. The Cs, on the other hand, were from the other side of the tracks. Almost a third of them had a parent who had dropped out of school before the eighth grade.

At one point, Terman had his fieldworkers go and visit everyone from the A and C groups and rate their personalities and manner. What they found is everything you would expect to find if you were comparing children raised in an atmosphere of concerted cultivation with children raised in an atmosphere of natural growth. The As were judged to be much more alert, poised, attractive, and well dressed. In fact, the scores on those four dimensions are so different as to make you think you are looking at two different species of humans. You aren't, of course. You're simply seeing the difference between those schooled by their families to present their best face to the world, and those denied that experience.

The Terman results are deeply distressing. Let's not forget how highly gifted the C group was. If you had met them at five or six years of age, you would have been overwhelmed by their curiosity and mental agility and sparkle. They were true outliers. The plain truth of the Terman study, however, is that in the end almost *none* of the genius children from the lowest social and economic class ended up making a name for themselves.

What did the Cs lack, though? Not something expensive or impossible to find; not something encoded in DNA or hardwired into the circuits of their brains. They lacked something that could have been given to them if we'd only known they needed it: a community around them that prepared them properly for the world. The Cs were squandered talent. But they didn't need to be.

6.

Today, Chris Langan lives in rural Missouri on a horse farm. He moved there a few years ago, after he got married. He is in his fifties but looks many years younger. He has the build of a linebacker, thick through the chest, with enormous biceps. His hair is combed straight back from his forehead. He has a neat, graying moustache and aviator-style glasses. If you look into his eyes, you can see the intelligence burning behind them.

"A typical day is, I get up and make coffee. I go in and sit in front of the computer and begin working on whatever I was working on the night before," he told me not long ago. "I found if I go to bed with a question on my mind, all I have to do is concentrate on the question before I go to sleep and I virtually always have the answer in the morning. Sometimes I realize what the answer is because I dreamt the answer and I can remember it. Other times I just feel the answer, and I start typing and the answer emerges onto the page."

He had just been reading the work of the linguist Noam Chomsky. There were piles of books in his study. He ordered books from the library all the time. "I always feel that the closer you get to the original sources, the better off you are," he said.

Langan seemed content. He had farm animals to take care of, and books to read, and a wife he loved. It was a much better life than being a bouncer.

"I don't think there is anyone smarter than me out there," he went on. "I have never met anybody like me or never seen even an indication that there is somebody who actually has better powers of comprehension. Never seen it and I don't think I am going to. I could—my mind is open to the possibility. If anyone should challenge me—'Oh, I think that I am smarter than you are'—I think I could have them."

What he said sounded boastful, but it wasn't really. It was the opposite—a touch defensive. He'd been working for decades now on a project of enormous sophistication—but almost none of what he had done had ever been published much less read by the physicists and philosophers and mathematicians who might be able to judge its value. Here he was, a man with a one-in-a-million mind, and he had yet to have any impact on the world. He wasn't holding forth at academic conferences. He wasn't leading a graduate seminar at some prestigious university. He was living on a slightly tumbledown horse farm in northern Missouri, sitting on the back porch in jeans and a cutoff T-shirt. He knew how it looked: it was the great paradox of Chris Langan's genius.

"I have not pursued mainstream publishers as hard as I should have," he conceded. "Going around, querying publishers, trying to find an agent. I haven't done it, and I am not interested in doing it."

It was an admission of defeat. Every experience he had had outside of his own mind had ended in frustration. He knew he needed to do a better job of navigating the world, but he didn't know how. He couldn't even talk to his calculus teacher, for goodness' sake. These were things that others, with lesser minds, could master easily. But that's because those others had had help along the way, and

Chris Langan never had. It wasn't an excuse. It was a fact. He'd had to make his way alone, and no one—not rock stars, not professional athletes, not software billionaires, and not even geniuses—ever makes it alone.

CHAPTER FIVE

The Three Lessons of Joe Flom

"MARY GOT A QUARTER."

1.

Joe Flom is the last living "named" partner of the law firm Skadden, Arps, Slate, Meagher and Flom. He has a corner office high atop the Condé Nast tower in Manhattan. He is short and slightly hunched. His head is large, framed by long prominent ears, and his narrow blue eyes are hidden by oversize aviator-style glasses. He is slender now, but during his heyday, Flom was extremely overweight. He waddles when he walks. He doodles when he thinks. He mumbles when he talks, and when he makes his way down the halls of Skadden, Arps, conversations drop to a hush.

Flom grew up in the Depression in Brooklyn's Borough Park neighborhood. His parents were Jewish immigrants from Eastern Europe. His father, Isadore, was a union organizer in the garment industry who later went to work sewing shoulder pads for ladies' dresses. His mother worked at what was called piecework—doing appliqué at home. They were desperately poor. His family moved nearly every year when he was growing up because the custom in those days was for landlords to give new tenants a month's free rent, and without that, his family could not get by.

In junior high school, Flom took the entrance exam for the elite Townsend Harris public high school on Lexington Avenue in Manhattan, a school that in just forty years of existence produced three Nobel Prize winners, six Pulitzer Prize winners, and one Supreme Court Justice, not to mention George Gershwin and Jonas Salk, the inventor of the polio vaccine. He got in. His mother would give him a dime in the morning for breakfast—three donuts, orange juice, and coffee at Nedick's. After school, he pushed a hand truck in the garment district. He did two years of night school at City College in upper Manhattan—working during the days to make ends meet—signed up for the army, served his time, and applied to Harvard Law School.

"I wanted to get into the law since I was six years old," Flom says. He didn't have a degree from college. Harvard took him anyway. "Why? I wrote them a letter on why I was the answer to sliced bread," is how Flom explains it, with characteristic brevity. At Harvard, in the late 1940s, he never took notes. "All of us were going through this first year idiocy of writing notes carefully in the classroom and doing an outline of that, then a condensation of that, and then doing it again on onionskin paper, on top of other paper," remembers Charles Haar, who was a classmate of Flom's. "It was a routinized way of trying to learn the cases. Not Joe. He wouldn't have any of that. But he had that quality which we always vaguely subsumed under 'thinking like a lawyer.' He had the great capacity for judgment."

Flom was named to the *Law Review*—an honor reserved for the very top students in the class. During "hiring season," the Christmas break of his second year, he went down to New York to interview with the big corporate law firms of the day. "I was ungainly, awkward, a fat kid. I didn't feel comfortable," Flom remembers. "I was one of two kids in my class at the end of hiring season who didn't have a job. Then one day, one of my professors said that there are these guys starting a firm. I had a visit with them, and the entire time I met with them, they were telling me what the risks were of going with a firm that didn't have a client. The more they talked, the more I liked them. So I said, What the hell, I'll take a chance. They had to scrape together the thirty-six hundred a year, which was the starting salary." In the beginning, it was just Marshall Skadden,

Leslie Arps—both of whom had just been turned down for partner at a major Wall Street law firm—and John Slate, who had worked for Pan Am airlines. Flom was their associate. They had a tiny suite of offices on the top floor of the Lehman Brothers Building on Wall Street. "What kind of law did we do?" Flom says, laughing. "Whatever came in the door!"

In 1954, Flom took over as Skadden's managing partner, and the firm began to grow by leaps and bounds. Soon it had one hundred lawyers. Then two hundred. When it hit three hundred, one of Flom's partners—Morris Kramer—came to him and said that he felt guilty about bringing in young law school graduates. Skadden was so big, Kramer said, that it was hard to imagine the firm growing beyond that and being able to promote any of those hires. Flom told him, "Ahhh, we'll go to one thousand." Flom never lacked for ambition.

Today Skadden, Arps has nearly two thousand attorneys in twenty-three offices around the world and earns well over $1 billion a year, making it one of the largest and most powerful law firms in the world. In his office, Flom has pictures of himself with George Bush Sr. and Bill Clinton. He lives in a sprawling apartment in a luxurious building on Manhattan's Upper East Side. For a period of almost thirty years, if you were a Fortune 500 company about to be taken over or trying to take over someone else, or merely a big shot in some kind of fix, Joseph Flom has been your attorney and Skadden, Arps has been your law firm—and if they weren't, you probably wished they were.

2.

I hope by now that you are skeptical of this kind of story. Brilliant immigrant kid overcomes poverty and the Depression, can't get a job at the stuffy downtown law firms, makes it on his own through sheer hustle and ability. It's a rags-to-riches story, and everything we've learned so far from hockey players and software billionaires and the Termites suggests that success doesn't happen that way. Successful people don't do it alone. Where they come from matters. They're products of particular places and environments.

Just as we did, then, with Bill Joy and Chris Langan, let's start over with Joseph Flom, this time putting to use everything we've learned from the first four chapters of this book. No more talk of Joe Flom's intelligence, or personality, or ambition, though he obviously has these three things in abundance. No glowing quotations from his clients, testifying to his genius. No more colorful tales from the meteoric rise of Skadden, Arps, Slate, Meagher and Flom.

Instead, I'm going to tell a series of stories from the New York immigrant world that Joe Flom grew up in—of a fellow law student, a father and son named Maurice and Mort Janklow, and an extraordinary couple by the name of Louis and Regina Borgenicht—in the hopes of answering a critical question. What were Joe Flom's opportunities? Since we know that outliers always have help along the way, can we sort through the ecology of Joe Flom and identify the conditions that helped create him?

We tell rags-to-riches stories because we

find something captivating in the idea of a lone hero battling overwhelming odds. But the true story of Joe Flom's life turns out to be much more intriguing than the mythological version because all the things in his life that seem to have been disadvantages—that he was a poor child of garment workers; that he was Jewish at a time when Jews were heavily discriminated against; that he grew up in the Depression—turn out, unexpectedly, to have been advantages. Joe Flom is an outlier. But he's not an outlier for the reasons you might think, and the story of his rise provides a blueprint for understanding success in his profession. By the end of the chapter, in fact, we'll see that it is possible to take the lessons of Joe Flom, apply them to the legal world of New York City, and predict the family background, age, and origin of the city's most powerful attorneys, *without knowing a single additional fact about them.* But we're getting ahead of ourselves.

Lesson Number One: The Importance of Being Jewish

3.

One of Joe Flom's classmates at Harvard Law School was a man named Alexander Bickel. Like Flom, Bickel was the son of Eastern European Jewish immigrants who lived in Brooklyn. Like Flom, Bickel had gone to public school in New York and then to City College. Like Flom, Bickel was a star in his law school class. In fact, before his career was cut short by cancer, Bickel would become perhaps the finest constitutional scholar of his generation. And like Flom and the rest of their law school classmates, Bickel went to Manhattan during "hiring season" over Christmas of 1947 to find himself a job.

His first stop was at Mudge Rose, down on Wall Street, as traditional and stuffy as any firm of that era. Mudge Rose was founded in 1869. It was where Richard Nixon practiced in the years before he won the presidency in 1968. "We're like the lady who only wants her name in the newspaper twice—when she's born and when she dies," one of the senior partners famously said. Bickel was taken around the firm and interviewed by one partner after another, until he was led into the library to meet with the firm's senior partner. You can imagine the scene: a dark-paneled room, an artfully frayed Persian carpet, row upon row of leather-bound legal volumes, oil paintings of Mr. Mudge and Mr. Rose on the wall.

"After they put me through the whole interview and everything," Bickel said many years later, "I was brought to [the senior partner], who took it upon himself to tell me that for a boy of my *antecedents*"—and you can imagine how Bickel must have paused before repeating that euphemism for his immigrant background—"I certainly had come far. But I ought to understand how limited the possibilities of a firm like his were to hire a boy of my *antecedents*. And while he congratulated me on my progress, I should understand he certainly couldn't offer me a job. But they all enjoyed seeing me and all that."

It is clear from the transcript of Bickel's reminiscences that his interviewer does not quite know what to do with that information. Bickel was by the time of the interview at the height of his reputation. He had argued cases before the Supreme Court. He had written brilliant books. Mudge Rose saying no to Bickel because of his "antecedents" was like the Chicago Bulls turning down Michael Jordan because they were uncomfortable with black kids from North Carolina. It didn't make any sense.

"But for stars?" the interviewer asked, meaning, Wouldn't they have made an exception for *you?*

BICKEL: "Stars, schmars..."

In the 1940s and 1950s, the old-line law firms of New York operated like a private club. They were all headquartered in downtown Manhattan, in and around Wall Street, in somber, granite-faced buildings. The partners at the top firms graduated from the same Ivy League schools, attended the same churches, and summered in the same oceanside towns on Long Island. They wore conservative gray suits.

Their partnerships were known as "white-shoe" firms — in apparent reference to the white bucks favored at the country club or a cocktail party, and they were very particular in whom they hired. As Erwin Smigel wrote in *The Wall Street Lawyer,* his study of the New York legal establishment of that era, they were looking for:

> lawyers who are Nordic, have pleasing personalities and "clean-cut" appearances, are graduates of the "right schools," have the "right" social background and experience in the affairs of the world, and are endowed with tremendous stamina. A former law school dean, in discussing the qualities students need to obtain a job, offers a somewhat more realistic picture: "To get a job [students] should be long enough on family connections, long enough on ability or long enough on personality, or a combination of these. Something called acceptability is made up of the sum of its parts. If a man has any of these things, he could get a job. If he has two of them, he can have a choice of jobs; if he has three, he could go anywhere."

Bickel's hair was not fair. His eyes were not blue. He spoke with an accent, and his family connections consisted, principally, of being the son of Solomon and Yetta Bickel of Bucharest, Romania, by way, most recently, of Brooklyn. Flom's credentials were no better. He says he felt "uncomfortable" when he went for his interviews downtown, and of course he did: he was short and ungainly and Jewish and talked with the flat, nasal tones of his native Brooklyn, and you can imagine how he would have been perceived by some silver-haired patrician in the library. If you were not of the right background and religion and social class and you came out of law school in that era, you joined some smaller, second-rate, upstart law firm on a rung below the big names downtown, or you simply went into business for yourself and took "whatever came in the door"—that is, whatever legal work the big downtown firms did not want for themselves. That seems horribly unfair, and it was. But as is so often the case with outliers, buried in that setback was a golden opportunity.

4.

The old-line Wall Street law firms had a very specific idea about what it was that they did. They were corporate lawyers. They represented the country's largest and most prestigious companies, and "represented" meant they handled the taxes and the legal work behind the issuing of stocks and bonds and made sure their clients did not run afoul of federal regulators. They did not do litigation; that is, very few of them had a division dedicated to defending and filing lawsuits. As Paul Cravath, one of the founders of Cravath, Swaine and Moore, the very whitest of the white-shoe firms, once put it, the lawyer's job was to settle disputes in the conference room, not in the courtroom. "Among my classmates at Harvard, the thing that bright young guys did was securities work or tax," another white-shoe partner remembers. "Those were the distinguished fields. Litigation was for hams, not for serious people. Corporations just didn't sue each other in those days."

What the old-line firms also did not do was

involve themselves in hostile corporate takeovers. It's hard to imagine today, when corporate raiders and private-equity firms are constantly swallowing up one company after another, but until the 1970s, it was considered scandalous for one company to buy another company without the target agreeing to be bought. Places like Mudge Rose and the other establishment firms on Wall Street would not touch those kinds of deals.

"The problem with hostile takeovers is that they were hostile," says Steven Brill, who founded the trade magazine *American Lawyer*. "It wasn't gentlemanly. If your best buddy from Princeton is the CEO of Company X, and he's been coasting for a long time, and some corporate raider shows up and says this company sucks, it makes you uncomfortable. You think, If he goes, then maybe I go too. It's this whole notion of not upsetting the basic calm and stable order of things."*

* The lawyer and novelist Louis Auchincloss, who very much belongs to the old WASP-y white-shoe legal establishment in New York, has a scene in his book *The Scarlet Letters* that perfectly captures the

The work that "came in the door" to the generation of Jewish lawyers from the Bronx and Brooklyn in the 1950s and 1960s, then, was the work the white-shoe firms disdained: litigation and, more important, "proxy fights," which were the legal maneuvers at the center of any hostile-takeover bid. An investor would take an interest in a company; he would denounce the management as incompetent and send letters to share-

---

antipathy the downtown firms felt toward takeover law. "Face it, my dear, your husband and I are running a firm of shysters," a takeover attorney explains to the wife of his law partner.

He continues: "Nowadays when one wishes to acquire a company that doesn't wish to be acquired, one's counsel bring all kinds of nuisance suits to induce it to change its mind. We sue for mismanagement by the directors, for unpaid dividends, for violation of the bylaws, for improper issuance of stock. We allege criminal misconduct; we shout about antitrust; we sue for ancient and dubious liabilities. And our opponent's counsel will answer with inordinate demands for all our files and seek endless interrogatories in order to enmesh our client in a hopeless tangle of red tape.... It is simply war, and you know the quality that applies to that and love."

holders, trying to get them to give him their "proxy" so he could vote out the firm's executives. And to run the proxy fight, the only lawyer the investor could get was someone like Joe Flom.

In *Skadden,* the legal historian Lincoln Caplan describes that early world of takeovers:

> The winner of a proxy contest was determined in the snake pit. (Officially, it was called the counting room.) Lawyers for each side met with inspectors of elections, whose job it was to approve or eliminate questionable proxies. The event was often informal, contentious and unruly. Adversaries were sometimes in T-shirts, eating watermelon or sharing a bottle of scotch. In rare cases, the results of the snake pit could swing the outcome of a contest and turn on a single ballot.
>
> Lawyers occasionally tried to fix an election by engineering the appointment of inspectors who were beholden to them; inspectors commonly smoked cigars provided by each side. Management's lawyer would contest the proxies of the insurgents ("I challenge this!") and vice versa.... Lawyers who prevailed in the snake pit excelled at winging

> it. There were lawyers who knew more about the rules of proxy contests, but no one was better in a fight than Joe Flom...
>
> Flom was fat (a hundred pounds overweight then, one lawyer said...), physically unattractive (to a partner, he resembled a frog), and indifferent to social niceties (he would fart in public or jab a cigar close to the face of someone he was talking to, without apology). But in the judgment of colleagues and of some adversaries, his will to win was unsurpassed and he was often masterful.

The white-shoe law firms would call in Flom as well whenever some corporate raider made a run at one of their establishment clients. They wouldn't touch the case. But they were happy to outsource it to Skadden, Arps. "Flom's early specialty was proxy fights, and that was not what we did, just like we don't do matrimonial work," said Robert Rifkind, a longtime partner at Cravath, Swaine and Moore. "And therefore we purported not to know about it. I remember once we had an issue involving a proxy fight, and one of my senior corporate partners said, Well, let's get Joe in. And he came to a conference room, and we all sat around and described the problem and he told us what to do and he left. And I said, 'We can do that too, you know.' And the partner said, 'No, no, no, you can't. We're not going to do that.' It was just that we didn't do it."

Then came the 1970s. The old aversion to lawsuits fell by the wayside. It became easier to borrow money. Federal regulations were relaxed. Markets became internationalized. Investors became more aggressive, and the result was a boom in the number and size of corporate takeovers. "In nineteen eighty, if you went to the Business Roundtable [the association of major American corporate executives] and took surveys about whether hostile takeovers should be allowed, two-thirds would have said no," Flom said. "Now, the vote would be almost unanimously yes." Companies needed to be defended against lawsuits from rivals. Hostile suitors needed to be beaten back. Investors who wanted to devour unwilling targets needed help with their legal strategy, and shareholders needed formal representation. The dollar figures involved were enormous. From the mid-1970s to the end of the 1980s, the amount of money involved in mergers and acquisitions every year on Wall Street increased *2,000 percent,* peaking at almost a quarter of a trillion dollars.

All of a sudden the things that the old-line law firms didn't want to do—hostile takeovers and litigation—were the things that *every* law firm wanted to do. And who was the expert in these two suddenly critical areas of law? The once marginal, second-tier law firms started by the people who couldn't get jobs at the downtown firms ten and fifteen years earlier.

"[The white-shoe firms] thought hostile takeovers were beneath contempt until relatively late in the game, and until they decided that, hey, maybe we ought to be in that business, they left me alone," Flom said. "And once you get the reputation for doing that kind of work, the business comes to you first."

Think of how similar this is to the stories of Bill Joy and Bill Gates. Both of them toiled away in a relatively obscure field without any great hopes for worldly success. But then—boom!—the personal computer revolution happened, and they had their ten thousand hours in. They were ready. Flom had the same experience. For twenty years he perfected his craft at Skadden, Arps. Then the world changed and he was ready. He didn't triumph over adversity. Instead, what started out as adversity ended up being an opportunity.

"It's not that those guys were smarter lawyers than anyone else," Rifkind says. "It's that they had a skill that they had been working on for years that was suddenly very valuable."*

---

* The best analysis of how adversity turned into opportunity for Jewish lawyers has been done by the legal scholar Eli Wald. Wald is careful to make the point, however, that Flom and his ilk weren't merely lucky. Lucky is winning the lottery. They were given an opportunity, and they seized it. As Wald says: "Jewish lawyers were lucky *and* they helped themselves. That's the best way to put it. They took advantage of the circumstances that came their way. The lucky part was the unwillingness of the WASP firms to step into takeover law. But that word luck fails to capture the work and the efforts and the imagination and the acting on opportunities that might have been hidden and not so obvious."

Lesson Number Two: Demographic Luck

5.

Maurice Janklow enrolled in Brooklyn Law School in 1919. He was the eldest son of Jewish immigrants from Romania. He had seven brothers and sisters. One ended up running a small department store in Brooklyn. Two others were in the haberdashery business, one had a graphic design studio, another made feather hats, and another worked in the finance department at Tishman Realty.

Maurice, however, was the family intellectual, the only one to go to college. He got his law degree and set up a practice on Court Street in downtown Brooklyn. He was an elegant man who dressed in a homburg and Brooks Brothers suits. In the summer, he wore a straw boater. He married the very beautiful Lillian Levantin, who was the daughter of a prominent Talmudist. He drove a big car. He moved to Queens. He and a partner then took over a writing-paper business that gave every indication of making a fortune.

Here was a man who looked, for all the world, like the kind of person who should thrive as a lawyer in New York City. He was intelligent and educated. He came from a family well schooled in the rules of the system. He was living in the most economically vibrant city in the world. But here is the strange thing: it never happened. Maurice Janklow's career did not take off the way that he'd hoped. In his mind, he never really made it beyond Court Street in Brooklyn. He struggled and floundered.

Maurice Janklow had a son named Mort, however, who became a lawyer as well, and the son's story is very different from that of the father. Mort Janklow built a law firm from scratch in the 1960s, then put together one of the very earliest cable television franchises and sold it for a fortune to Cox Broadcasting. He started a literary agency in the 1970s, and it is today one of the most prestigious in the world.*

* Janklow and Nesbit, the agency he started, is, in fact, my literary agency. That is how I heard about Janklow's family history.

He has his own plane. Every dream that eluded the father was fulfilled by the son.

Why did Mort Janklow succeed where Maurice Janklow did not? There are, of course, a hundred potential answers to that question. But let's take a page from the analysis of the business tycoons born in the 1830s and the software programmers born in 1955 and look at the differences between the two Janklows in terms of their generation. Is there a perfect time for a New York Jewish lawyer to be born? It turns out there is, and this same fact that helps explain Mort Janklow's success is the second key to Joe Flom's success as well.

6.

Lewis Terman's genius study, as you will recall from the chapter about Chris Langan, was an investigation into how some children with really high IQs who were born between 1903 and 1917 turned out as adults. And the study found that there was a group of real successes and there was a group of real failures, and that the successes were far more likely to have come from wealthier families. In that sense, the Terman study underscores the argument Annette Lareau makes, that what your parents do for a living, and the assumptions that accompany the class your parents belong to, *matter.*

There's another way to break down the Terman results, though, and that's by *when* the Termites were born. If you divide the Termites into two groups, with those born between 1903 and 1911 on one side, and those between 1912 and 1917 on the other, it turns out that the Terman failures are far more likely to have been born in the earlier group.

The explanation has to do with two of the great cataclysmic events of the twentieth century: the Great Depression and World War II. If you were born after 1912—say, in 1915—you got out of college after the worst of the Depression was over, and you were drafted at a young enough age that going away to war for three or four years was as much an opportunity as it was a disruption (provided you weren't killed, of course).

The Termites born before 1911, though,

graduated from college at the height of the Depression, when job opportunities were scarce, and they were already in their late thirties when the Second World War hit, meaning that when they were drafted, they had to disrupt careers and families and adult lives that were already well under way. To have been born before 1911 is to have been demographically unlucky. The most devastating events of the twentieth century hit you at exactly the wrong time.

This same demographic logic applies to Jewish lawyers in New York like Maurice Janklow. The doors were closed to them at the big downtown law firms. So they were overwhelmingly solo practitioners, handling wills and divorces and contracts and minor disputes, and in the Depression the work of the solo practitioner all but disappeared. "Nearly half of the members of the metropolitan bar earned less than the minimum subsistence level for American families," Jerold Auerbach writes of the Depression years in New York. "One year later 1,500 lawyers were prepared to take the pauper's oath to qualify for work relief. Jewish lawyers (approximately one-half of the metropolitan bar) discovered that their practice had become a 'dignified road to starvation.'" Regardless of the number of years they had spent in practice, their income was "strikingly less" than that of their Christian colleagues. Maurice Janklow was born in 1902. When the Depression started, he was newly married and had just bought his big car, moved to Queens, and made his great gamble on the writing-paper business. His timing could not have been worse.

"He was going to make a fortune," Mort Janklow says of his father. "But the Depression killed him economically. He didn't have any reserves, and he had no family to fall back on. And from then on, he became very much a scrivener-type lawyer. He didn't have the courage to take risks after that. It was too much for him. My father used to close titles for twenty-five dollars. He had a friend who worked at the Jamaica Savings Bank who would throw him some business. He would kill himself for twenty-five bucks, doing the whole closing, title reports. For twenty-five bucks!

"I can remember my father and mother in

the morning," Janklow continued. "He would say to her, 'I got a dollar seventy-five. I need ten cents for the bus, ten cents for the subway, a quarter for a sandwich,' and he would give her the rest. They were that close to the edge."

7.

Now contrast that experience with the experience of someone who, like Mort Janklow, was born in the 1930s.

Take a look at the following chart, which shows the birthrates in the United States from 1910 to 1950. In 1915, there are almost three million babies. In 1935, that number drops by almost six hundred thousand, and then, within a decade and a half, the number is back over three million again. To put it in more precise terms, for every thousand Americans, there were 29.5 babies born in 1915; 18.7 babies born in 1935; and 24.1 babies born in 1950. The decade of the 1930s is what is called a "demographic trough." In response to the economic hardship of the Depression, families simply stopped having children, and as a result, the generation born during that decade was markedly smaller than both the generation that preceded it and the generation that immediately followed it.

Year	Total Births	Births per 1,000
1910	2,777,000	30.1
1915	2,965,000	29.5
1920	2,950,000	27.7
1925	2,909,000	25.1
1930	2,618,000	21.3
1935	2,377,000	18.7
1940	2,559,000	19.4
1945	2,858,000	20.4
1950	3,632,000	24.1

Here is what the economist H. Scott Gordon once wrote about the particular benefits of being one of those people born in a small generation:

> When he opens his eyes for the first time, it is in a spacious hospital, well-appointed to serve the wave that preceded him. The staff is generous with their time, since they have little to do while they ride

> out the brief period of calm until the next wave hits. When he comes to school age, the magnificent buildings are already there to receive him; the ample staff of teachers welcomes him with open arms. In high school, the basketball team is not as good as it was but there is no problem getting time on the gymnasium floor. The university is a delightful place; lots of room in the classes and residences, no crowding in the cafeteria, and the professors are solicitous. Then he hits the job market. The supply of new entrants is low, and the demand is high, because there is a large wave coming behind him providing a strong demand for the goods and services of his potential employers.

In New York City, the early 1930s cohort was so small that class sizes were at least half of what they had been twenty-five years earlier. The schools were new, built for the big generation that had come before, and the teachers had what in the Depression was considered a high-status job.

"The New York City public schools of the 1940s were considered the best schools in the country," says Diane Ravitch, a professor at New York University who has written widely on the city's educational history. "There was this generation of educators in the thirties and forties who would have been in another time and place college professors. They were brilliant, but they couldn't get the jobs they wanted, and public teaching was what they did because it was security and it had a pension and you didn't get laid off."

The same dynamic benefited the members of that generation when they went off to college. Here is Ted Friedman, one of the top litigators in New York in the 1970s and 1980s. Like Flom, he grew up poor, the child of struggling Jewish immigrants.

"My options were City College and the University of Michigan," Friedman said. City College was free, and Michigan—then, as now, one of the top universities in the United States—was $450 a year. "And the thing was, after the first year, you could get a scholarship if your grades were high," Friedman said. "So it was only the first year I had to pay that, if I did well." Friedman's first inclination was to stay in New York. "Well, I went to City College for one day, I didn't like it. I thought, This is going to be four more years of Bronx Science [the high school he had attended], and came home, packed my bags, and hitchhiked to Ann Arbor." He went on:

> I had a couple of hundred dollars in my pocket from the summer. I was working the Catskills to make enough money to pay the four-hundred-fifty-dollar tuition, and I had some left over. Then there was this fancy restaurant in Ann Arbor where I got a job waiting tables. I also worked the night shift at River Rouge, the big Ford plant. That was real money. It wasn't so hard to get that job. The factories were looking for people. I had another job too, which paid me the best pay I ever had before I became a lawyer, which was working in construction. During the summer, in Ann Arbor, we built the Chrysler proving grounds. I worked there a few summers during law school. Those jobs were really high paying, probably because you worked so much overtime.

Think about this story for a moment. The first lesson is that Friedman was willing to work hard, take responsibility for himself, and put himself through school. But the second, perhaps more important lesson is that he happened to come along at a time in America when if you were willing to work hard, you *could* take responsibility for yourself and put yourself through school. Friedman was, at the time, what we would today call "economically disadvantaged." He was an inner-city kid from the Bronx, neither of whose parents went to college. But look at how easy it was for him to get a good education. He graduated from his public high school in New York at a time when New York City public schools were the envy of the world. His first option, City College, was free, and his second option, the University of Michigan, cost just $450—and the admissions process was casual enough, apparently, that he could try one school one day and the other the next.

And how did he get there? He hitchhiked, with the money that he made in the summer in his pocket, and when he arrived, he immediately got a series of really good jobs to help pay his way, because the factories were "looking for people." And of course they were: they had to feed the needs of the big generation just ahead of those born in the demographic trough of the 1930s, and the big generation of baby boomers coming up behind them. The sense of possibility so necessary for success comes not just from inside us or from our parents. It comes from our time: from the particular opportunities that our particular place in history presents us with. For a young would-be lawyer, being born in the early 1930s was a magic time, just as being born in 1955 was for a software programmer, or being born in 1835 was for an entrepreneur.

Today, Mort Janklow has an office high above Park Avenue filled with gorgeous works of modern art—a Dubuffet, an Anselm Kiefer. He tells hilarious stories. ("My mother had two sisters. One lived to be ninety-nine and the other died at ninety. The ninety-nine-year-old was a smart woman. She married my Uncle Al, who was the chief of sales for Maidenform. Once I said to him, 'What's the rest of the country like, Uncle Al?' And he said, 'Kiddo. When you leave New York, every place is Bridgeport.'") He gives the sense that the world is his for the taking. "I've always been a big risk taker," he says. "When I built the cable company, in the early stages, I was making deals where I would have been bankrupt if I hadn't pulled it off. I had confidence that I could make it work."

Mort Janklow went to New York City public schools when they were at their best. Maurice Janklow went to New York City public schools when they were at their most overcrowded. Mort Janklow went to Columbia University Law School, because demographic trough babies have their pick of selective schools. Maurice Janklow went to Brooklyn Law School, which was as good as an immigrant child could do in 1919. Mort Janklow sold his cable business for tens of millions of dollars. Maurice Janklow closed titles for twenty-five dollars. The story of the Janklows tells us that the meteoric rise of Joe Flom could not have happened at just any time. Even the most gifted of lawyers, equipped with the best of family lessons, cannot escape the limitations of their generation.

"My mother was coherent until the last five or six months of her life," Mort Janklow said. "And in her delirium she talked about things that she'd never talked about before. She shed tears over her friends dying in the 1918 flu epidemic. That generation—my parents' generation—lived through a lot. They lived through that epidemic, which took, what? ten percent of the world's population. Panic in the streets. Friends dying. And then the First World War, then the Depression, then the Second World War. They didn't have much of a chance. That was a very tough period. My father would have been much more successful in a different kind of world."

Lesson Number Three: The Garment Industry and Meaningful Work

8.

In 1889, Louis and Regina Borgenicht boarded an ocean liner in Hamburg bound for America.

Louis was from Galacia, in what was then Poland. Regina was from a small town in Hungary. They had been married only a few years and had one small child and a second on the way. For the thirteen-day journey, they slept on straw mattresses on a deck above the engine room, hanging tight to their bunk beds as the ship pitched and rolled. They knew one person in New York: Borgenicht's sister, Sallie, who had immigrated ten years before. They had enough money to last a few weeks, at best. Like so many other immigrants to America in those years, theirs was a leap of faith.

Louis and Regina found a tiny apartment on Eldridge Street, on Manhattan's Lower East Side, for $8 a month. Louis then took to the streets, looking for work. He saw peddlers and fruit sellers and sidewalks crammed with pushcarts. The noise and activity and energy dwarfed what he had known in the Old World. He was first overwhelmed, then invigorated. He went to his sister's fish store on Ludlow Street and persuaded her to give him a consignment of herring on credit. He set up shop on the sidewalk with two barrels of fish, hopping back and forth between them and chanting in German:

For frying
For baking
For cooking
Good also for eating
Herring will do for every meal,
And for every class!

By the end of the week, he had cleared $8. By the second week, $13. Those were considerable sums. But Louis and Regina could not see how selling herring on the street would lead to a constructive business. Louis then decided to try being a pushcart peddler. He sold towels and tablecloths, without much luck. He switched to notebooks, then bananas, then socks and stockings. Was there really a future in pushcarts? Regina gave birth to a second child, a daughter, and Louis's urgency grew. He now had four mouths to feed.

The answer came to him after five long days of walking up and down the streets of the Lower

East Side, just as he was about to give up hope. He was sitting on an overturned box, eating a late lunch of the sandwiches Regina had made for him. *It was clothes.* Everywhere around him stores were opening—suits, dresses, overalls, shirts, skirts, blouses, trousers, all made and ready to be worn. Coming from a world where clothing was sewn at home by hand or made to order by tailors, this was a revelation.

"To me the greatest wonder in this was not the mere quantity of garments—although that was a miracle in itself—" Borgenicht would write years later, after he became a prosperous manufacturer of women's and children's clothing, "but the fact that in America even poor people could save all the dreary, time-consuming labor of making their own clothes simply by going into a store and walking out with what they needed. *There* was a field to go into, a field to thrill to."

Borgenicht took out a small notebook. Everywhere he went, he wrote down what people were wearing and what was for sale—menswear, women's wear, children's wear. He wanted to find a "novel" item, something that people would wear that was not being sold in the stores. For four more days he walked the streets. On the evening of the final day as he walked toward home, he saw a half dozen girls playing hopscotch. One of the girls was wearing a tiny embroidered apron over her dress, cut low in the front with a tie in the back, and it struck him, suddenly, that in his previous days of relentlessly inventorying the clothing shops of the Lower East Side, he had *never* seen one of those aprons for sale.

He came home and told Regina. She had an ancient sewing machine that they had bought upon their arrival in America. The next morning, he went to a dry-goods store on Hester Street and bought a hundred yards of gingham and fifty yards of white crossbar. He came back to their tiny apartment and laid the goods out on the dining room table. Regina began to cut the gingham—small sizes for toddlers, larger for small children—until she had forty aprons. She began to sew. At midnight, she went to bed and Louis took up where she had left off. At dawn, she rose and began cutting buttonholes and adding buttons. By ten in the morning, the aprons were finished. Louis gathered them up over his arm and ventured out onto Hester Street.

"Children's aprons! Little girls' aprons! Colored ones, ten cents. White ones, fifteen cents! Little girls' aprons!"

By one o'clock, all forty were gone.

"Ma, we've got our business," he shouted out to Regina, after running all the way home from Hester Street.

He grabbed her by the waist and began swinging her around and around.

"You've got to help me," he cried out. "We'll work together! Ma, *this is our business.*"

9.

Jewish immigrants like the Floms and the Borgenichts and the Janklows were not like the other immigrants who came to America in the nineteenth and early twentieth centuries. The Irish and the Italians were peasants, tenant farmers from the impoverished countryside of Europe. Not so the Jews. For centuries in Europe, they had been forbidden to own land, so they had clustered in cities and towns, taking up urban trades and professions. Seventy percent of the Eastern European Jews who came through Ellis Island in the thirty years or so before the First World War had some kind of occupational skill. They had owned small groceries or jewelry stores. They had been bookbinders or watchmakers. Overwhelmingly, though, their experience lay in the clothing trade. They were tailors and dressmakers, hat and cap makers, and furriers and tanners.

Louis Borgenicht, for example, left the impoverished home of his parents at age twelve to work as a salesclerk in a general store in the Polish town of Brzesko. When the opportunity came to work in *Schnittwaren Handlung* (literally, the handling of cloth and fabrics or "piece goods," as they were known), he jumped at it. "In those days, the piece-goods man was clothier to the world," he writes, "and of the three fundamentals required for life in that simple society, food and shelter were humble. Clothing was the aristocrat. Practitioners of the clothing art, dealers in wonderful cloths from every corner of Europe, traders who visited the centers of industry on their annual buying tours—these were the merchant princes of my youth. Their voices were heard, their weight felt."

Borgenicht worked in piece goods for a man named Epstein, then moved on to a store in neighboring Jaslow called Brandstatter's. It was there that the young Borgenicht learned the ins and outs of all the dozens of different varieties of cloth, to the point where he could run his hand over a fabric and tell you the thread count, the name of the manufacturer, and its place of origin. A few years later, Borgenicht moved to Hungary and met Regina. She had been running a dressmaking business since the age of sixteen. Together they opened a series of small piece-goods stores, painstakingly learning the details of small-business entrepreneurship.

Borgenicht's great brainstorm that day on the upturned box on Hester Street, then, did not come from nowhere. He was a veteran of *Schnittwaren Handlung,* and his wife was a seasoned dressmaker. This was their field. And at the same time as the Borgenichts set up shop inside their tiny apartment, thousands of other Jewish immigrants were doing the same thing, putting their sewing and dressmaking and tailoring skills to use, to the point where by 1900, control of the garment industry had passed almost entirely into the hands of the Eastern European newcomers. As Borgenicht puts it, the Jews "bit deep into the welcoming land and worked like madmen *at what they knew.*"

Today, at a time when New York is at the center of an enormous and diversified metropolitan area, it is easy to forget the significance of the set of skills that immigrants like the Borgenichts brought to the New World. From the late nineteenth century through the middle of the twentieth century, the garment trade was the largest and most economically vibrant industry in the city. More people worked making clothes in New York than at anything else, and more clothes were manufactured in New York than in any other city in the world. The distinctive buildings that still stand on the lower half of Broadway in Manhattan—from the big ten- and fifteen-story industrial warehouses in the twenty blocks below Times Square to the cast-iron lofts of SoHo and Tribeca—were almost all built to house coat makers and hatmakers and lingerie manufacturers and huge rooms of men and women hunched over sewing machines. To come to New York City in the 1890s with a background in dressmaking or sewing or *Schnittwaren Handlung* was a stroke of extraordinary good fortune. It was like showing up in Silicon Valley in 1986 with ten thousand hours of computer programming already under your belt.

"There is no doubt that those Jewish immigrants arrived at the perfect time, with the perfect skills," says the sociologist Stephen Steinberg. "To exploit that opportunity, you had to have certain virtues, and those immigrants worked hard. They sacrificed. They scrimped and saved and invested wisely. But still, you have to remember that the garment industry in those years was growing by leaps and bounds. The economy was desperate for the skills that they possessed."

Louis and Regina Borgenicht and the thousands of others who came over on the boats with them were given a golden opportunity. And so were their children and grandchildren, because the lessons those garment workers brought home with them in the evenings turned out to be critical for getting ahead in the world.

10.

The day after Louis and Regina Borgenicht sold out their first lot of forty aprons, Louis made his way to H. B. Claflin and Company. Claflin was a dry-goods "commission" house, the equivalent of Brandstatter's back in Poland. There, Borgenicht asked for a salesman who spoke German, since his English was almost nonexistent. He had in his hand his and Regina's life savings—$125—and with that money, he bought enough cloth to make ten dozen aprons. Day and night, he and Regina cut and sewed. He sold all ten dozen in two days. Back he went to Claflin for another round. They sold those too. Before long, he and Regina hired another immigrant just off the boat to help with the children so Regina could sew full-time, and then another to serve as an apprentice. Louis ventured uptown as far as Harlem, selling to the mothers in the tenements. He rented a storefront on Sheriff Street, with living quarters in the back. He hired three more girls, and bought sewing machines for all of them. He became known as "the apron man." He and Regina were selling aprons as fast as they could make them.

Before long, the Borgenichts decided to branch out. They started making adult aprons, then petticoats, then women's dresses. By January of 1892, the Borgenichts had twenty people working for them, mostly immigrant Jews like themselves. They had their own factory on the Lower East Side of Manhattan and a growing list of customers, including a store uptown owned by another Jewish immigrant family, the Bloomingdale brothers. Keep in mind the Borgenichts had been in the country for only three years at this point. They barely spoke English. And they weren't rich yet by any stretch of the imagination. Whatever profit they made got plowed back into their business, and Borgenicht says he had only $200 in the bank. But already he was in charge of his own destiny.

This was the second great advantage of the garment industry. It wasn't just that it was growing by leaps and bounds. It was also explicitly entrepreneurial. Clothes weren't made in a single big factory. Instead, a number of established firms designed patterns and prepared the fabric, and then the complicated stitching and pressing and button attaching were all sent out to small contractors. And if a contractor got big enough, or ambitious enough, he started designing his own patterns and preparing his own fabric. By 1913, there were approximately sixteen thousand separate companies in New York City's garment business, many just like the Borgenichts' shop on Sheriff Street.

"The threshold for getting involved in the business was very low. It's basically a business built on the sewing machine, and sewing machines don't cost that much," says Daniel Soyer, a historian who has written widely on the garment industry. "So you didn't need a lot of capital. At the turn of the twentieth century, it was probably fifty dollars to buy a machine or two. All you had to do to be a contractor was to have a couple sewing machines, some irons, and a couple of workers. The profit margins were very low but you could make some money."

Listen to how Borgenicht describes his decision to expand beyond aprons:

> From my study of the market I knew that only three men were making children's dresses in 1890. One was an East Side tailor near me, who made only to order, while the other two turned out an expensive product with which I had no desire at all to compete. I wanted to make "popular price" stuff—wash dresses, silks, and woolens. It was my goal to produce dresses that the great mass of the people could afford, dresses that would—from the business angle—sell equally well to both large and small, city and country stores. With Regina's help—she always had excellent taste, and judgment—I made up a line of samples. Displaying them to all my "old" customers and friends, I hammered

> home every point—my dresses would save mothers endless work, the materials and sewing were as good and probably better than anything that could be done at home, the price was right for quick disposal.

On one occasion, Borgenicht realized that his only chance to undercut bigger firms was to convince the wholesalers to sell cloth to him directly, eliminating the middleman. He went to see a Mr. Bingham at Lawrence and Company, a "tall, gaunt, white-bearded Yankee with steel-blue eyes." There the two of them were, the immigrant from rural Poland, his eyes ringed with fatigue, facing off in his halting English against the imperious Yankee. Borgenicht said he wanted to buy forty cases of cashmere. Bingham had never before sold to an individual company, let alone a shoestring operation on Sheriff Street.

"You have a hell of a cheek coming in here and asking me for favors!" Bingham thundered. But he ended up saying yes.

What Borgenicht was getting in his eighteen-hour days was a lesson in the modern economy. He was learning market research. He was learning manufacturing. He was learning how to negotiate with imperious Yankees. He was learning how to plug himself into popular culture in order to understand new fashion trends.

The Irish and Italian immigrants who came to New York in the same period didn't have that advantage. They didn't have a skill specific to the urban economy. They went to work as day laborers and domestics and construction workers—jobs where you could show up for work every day for thirty years and never learn market research and manufacturing and how to navigate the popular culture and how to negotiate with the Yankees, who ran the world.

Or consider the fate of the Mexicans who immigrated to California between 1900 and the end of the 1920s to work in the fields of the big fruit and vegetable growers. They simply exchanged the life of a feudal peasant in Mexico for the life of a feudal peasant in California. "The conditions in the garment industry were every bit as bad," Soyer goes on. "But as a garment worker, you were closer to the center of the industry. If you are working in a field in California, you have no clue what's happening to the produce when it gets on the truck. If you are working in a small garment shop, your wages are low, and your conditions are terrible, and your hours are long, but you can see exactly what the successful people are doing, and you can see how you can set up your own job."*

When Borgenicht came home at night to his children, he may have been tired and poor and overwhelmed, but he was alive. He was his

* I realize that it seems strange to refer to American Jewish immigrants as lucky when the families and relatives they left behind in Europe were on the verge of extermination at the hands of the Nazis. Borgenicht, in fact, unwittingly captures this poignancy in his memoir, which was published in 1942. He called it *The Happiest Man.* After numerous chapters brimming with optimism and cheer, the book ends with the sobering reality of Nazi-dominated Europe. Had *The Happiest Man* been published in 1945, when the full story of the Holocaust was known, one imagines it would have had a very different title.

own boss. He was responsible for his own decisions and direction. His work was complex: it engaged his mind and imagination. And in his work, there was a relationship between effort and reward: the longer he and Regina stayed up at night sewing aprons, the more money they made the next day on the streets.

Those three things—autonomy, complexity, and a connection between effort and reward—are, most people agree, the three qualities that work has to have if it is to be satisfying. It is not how much money we make that ultimately makes us happy between nine and five. It's whether our work fulfills us. If I offered you a choice between being an architect for $75,000 a year and working in a tollbooth every day for the rest of your life for $100,000 a year, which would you take? I'm guessing the former, because there is complexity, autonomy, and a relationship between effort and reward in doing creative work, and that's worth more to most of us than money.

Work that fulfills those three criteria is *meaningful*. Being a teacher is meaningful.

Being a physician is meaningful. So is being an entrepreneur, and the miracle of the garment industry—as cutthroat and grim as it was—was that it allowed people like the Borgenichts, just off the boat, to find something meaningful to do as well.* When Louis Borgenicht came home after first seeing that child's apron, he danced a jig. He hadn't sold anything yet. He was still penniless and desperate, and he knew that to make something of his idea was going to require years of backbreaking labor. But he was ecstatic, because the prospect of those endless years of hard labor did not seem like a burden to him. Bill Gates had that same feeling when he first sat down at the keyboard at Lakeside. And the Beatles didn't recoil in horror when they were told they had to play eight hours a night, seven days a week. They jumped at the chance. Hard work is a prison sentence only if it does not have meaning. Once

* Just to be clear: to say that garment work was meaningful is not to romanticize it. It was incredibly hard and often miserable labor. The conditions were

it does, it becomes the kind of thing that makes you grab your wife around the waist and dance a jig.

The most important consequence of the miracle of the garment industry, though, was what happened to the children growing up in those homes where meaningful work was practiced. Imagine what it must have been like to watch the meteoric rise of Regina and Louis Borgenicht through the eyes of one of their offspring. They learned the same lesson that little Alex Williams would learn nearly a century later—a lesson crucial to those who wanted to tackle the upper reaches of a profession like law or medicine: if

---

inhuman. One survey in the 1890s put the average workweek at eighty-four hours, which comes to twelve hours a day. At times, it was higher. "During the busy season," David Von Drehle writes in *Triangle: The Fire That Changed Amierca,* "it was not unusual to find workers on stools or broken chairs, bent over their sewing or hot irons, from 5 A.M. to 9 P.M., a hundred or more hours a week. Indeed, it was said that during the busy seasons the grinding hum of sewing machines never entirely ceased on the Lower East Side, day or night."

you work hard enough and assert yourself, and use your mind and imagination, you can shape the world to your desires.

11.

In 1982, a sociology graduate student named Louise Farkas went to visit a number of nursing homes and residential hotels in New York City and Miami Beach. She was looking for people like the Borgenichts, or, more precisely, the children of people like the Borgenichts, who had come to New York in the great wave of Jewish immigration at the turn of the last century. And for each of the people she interviewed, she constructed a family tree showing what a line of parents and children and grandchildren and, in some cases, great-grandchildren did for a living.

Here is her account of "subject #18":

> A Russian tailor artisan comes to America, takes to the needle trade, works in a sweat shop for a small salary. Later takes garments to finish at home with

the help of his wife and older children. In order to increase his salary he works through the night. Later he makes a garment and sells it on New York streets. He accumulates some capital and goes into a business venture with his sons. They open a shop to create men's garments. The Russian tailor and his sons become men's suit manufacturers supplying several men's stores.... The sons and the father become prosperous.... The sons' children become educated professionals.

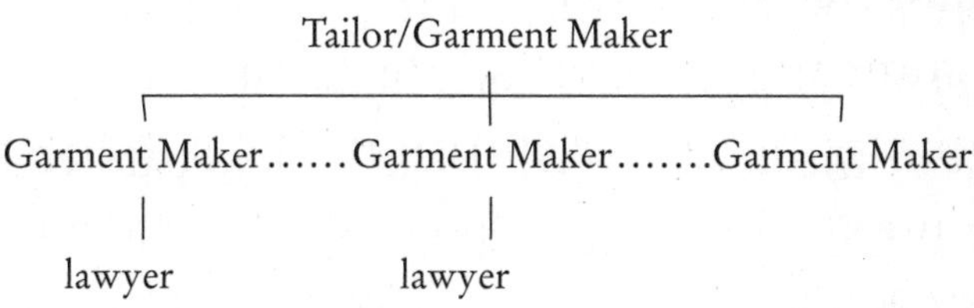

Here's another. It's a tanner who emigrated from Poland in the late nineteenth century.

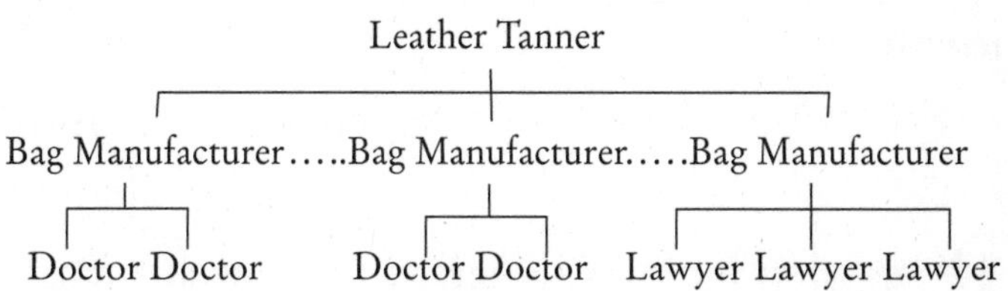

Farkas's Jewish family trees go on for pages, each virtually identical to the one before, until the conclusion becomes inescapable: Jewish doctors and lawyers did not become professionals in spite of their humble origins. They became professionals *because of* their humble origins.

Ted Friedman, the prominent litigator in the 1970s and 1980s, remembers as a child going to concerts with his mother at Carnegie Hall. They were poor and living in the farthest corners of the Bronx. How did they afford tickets? "Mary got a quarter," Friedman says. "There was a Mary who was a ticket taker, and if you gave Mary a quarter, she would let you stand in the second balcony, without a ticket. Carnegie Hall didn't know about it. It was just between you and Mary. It was a bit of a journey, but we would go back once or twice a month."*

Friedman's mother was a Russian immigrant.

* The conventional explanation for Jewish success, of course, is that Jews come from a literate, intellectual

She barely spoke English. But she had gone to work as a seamstress at the age of fifteen and had become a prominent garment union organizer, and what you learn in that world is that through your own powers of persuasion and initiative, you can take your kids to Carnegie Hall. There is no better lesson for a budding lawyer than that. The garment industry was boot camp for the professions.

What did Joe Flom's father do? He sewed shoulder pads for women's dresses. What did Robert Oppenheimer's father do? He was a garment manufacturer, like Louis Borgenicht. One flight up from Flom's corner office at Skadden, Arps is the office of Barry Garfinkel, who has

---

culture. They are famously "the people of the book." There is surely something to that. But it wasn't just the children of rabbis who went to law school. It was the children of garment workers. And their critical advantage in climbing the professional ladder wasn't the intellectual rigor you get from studying the Talmud. It was the practical intelligence and savvy you get from watching your father sell aprons on Hester Street.

been at Skadden, Arps nearly as long as Flom and who for many years headed the firm's litigation department. What did Garfinkel's mother do? She was a milliner. She made hats at home. What did two of Louis and Regina Borgenicht's sons do? They went to law school, and no less than nine of their grandchildren ended up as doctors and lawyers as well.

Here is the most remarkable of Farkas's family trees. It belongs to a Jewish family from Romania who had a small grocery store in the Old Country and then came to New York and opened another, on the Lower East Side of Manhattan. It is the most elegant answer to the question of where all the Joe Floms came from.

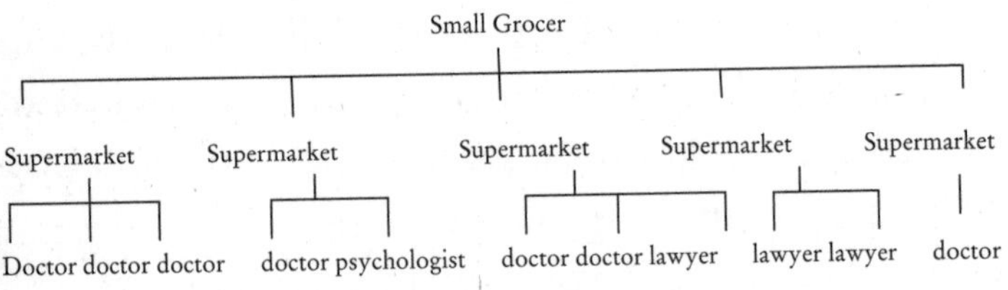

12.

Ten blocks north of the Skadden, Arps headquarters in midtown Manhattan are the offices of Joe Flom's great rival, the law firm generally regarded as the finest in the world.

It is headquartered in the prestigious office building known as Black Rock. To get hired there takes a small miracle. Unlike New York's other major law firms, all of which have hundreds of attorneys scattered around the major capitals of the world, it operates only out of that single Manhattan building. It turns down much more business than it accepts. Unlike every one of its competitors, it does not bill by the hour. It simply names a fee. Once, while defending Kmart against a takeover, the firm billed $20 million for two weeks' work. Kmart paid—happily. If its attorneys do not outsmart you, they will outwork you, and if they can't outwork you, they'll win through sheer intimidation. There is no firm in the world that has made more money, lawyer for lawyer, over the past two decades. On Joe Flom's wall, next to pictures of Flom with George Bush Sr. and Bill Clinton, there is a picture of him with the rival firm's managing partner.

No one rises to the top of the New York legal profession unless he or she is smart and ambitious and hardworking, and clearly the four men who founded the Black Rock firm fit that description. But we know far more than that, don't we? Success is not a random act. It arises out of a predictable and powerful set of circumstances and opportunities, and at this point, after examining the lives of Bill Joy and Bill Gates, pro hockey players and geniuses, and Joe Flom, the Janklows, and the Borgenichts, it shouldn't be hard to figure out where the perfect lawyer comes from.

This person will have been born in a demographic trough, so as to have had the best of New York's public schools and the easiest time in the job market. He will be Jewish, of course, and so, locked out of the old-line downtown law firms on account of his "antecedents." This person's parents will have done meaningful work in the garment business, passing on to their children autonomy and complexity and the connection between effort and reward. A good school—although it doesn't have to be a great school—will have been attended. He need not have been the smartest in the class, only smart enough.

In fact, we can be even more precise. Just as there is a perfect birth date for a nineteenth-century business tycoon, and a perfect birth date for a software tycoon, there is a perfect birth date for a New York Jewish lawyer as well. It's 1930, because that would give the lawyer the benefit of a blessedly small generation. It would also make him forty years of age in 1970, when the revolution in the legal world first began, which translates to a healthy fifteen-year Hamburg period in the takeover business while the white-shoe lawyers lingered, oblivious, over their two-martini lunches. If you want to be a great New York lawyer, it is an advantage to be an outsider, and it is an advantage to have parents who did meaningful work, and, better still, it is an advantage to have been born in the early 1930s. But if you have all three advantages—on top of a good dose of ingenuity and drive—then that's an unstoppable combination. That's like being a hockey player born on January 1.

The Black Rock law firm is Wachtell, Lipton, Rosen & Katz. The firm's first partner was Herbert Wachtell. He was born in 1931. He grew up in the Amalgamated Clothing Workers union housing across from Van Cortlandt Park, in the Bronx. His parents were Jewish immigrants from the Ukraine. His father was in the ladies' undergarment business with his brothers, on the sixth floor of what is now a fancy loft at Broadway and Spring Street in SoHo. He went to New York City public schools in the 1940s, then to City College in upper Manhattan, and then to New York University Law School.

The second partner was Martin Lipton. He was born in 1931. His father was a manager at a factory. He was a descendant of Jewish immigrants. He attended public schools in Jersey City, then the University of Pennsylvania, then New York University Law School.

The third partner was Leonard Rosen. He was born in 1930. He grew up poor in the Bronx, near Yankee Stadium. His parents were Jewish immigrants from the Ukraine. His father worked in the garment district in Manhattan as a presser. He went to New York City public schools in the 1940s, then to City College in upper Manhattan, and then to New York University Law School.

The fourth partner was George Katz. He was born in 1931. He grew up in a one-bedroom first-floor apartment in the Bronx. His parents were the children of Jewish immigrants from Eastern Europe. His father sold insurance. His grandfather, who lived a few blocks away, was a sewer in the garment trade, doing piecework out of his house. He went to New York City public schools in the 1940s, then to City College in upper Manhattan, and then to New York University Law School.

Imagine that we had met any one of these four fresh out of law school, sitting in the elegant waiting room at Mudge Rose next to a blue-eyed Nordic type from the "right" background. We'd all have bet on the Nordic type. And we would have been wrong, because the Katzes and the Rosens and the Liptons and the Wachtells and the Floms had something that the Nordic type did not. Their world—their culture and generation and family history—gave them the greatest of opportunities.

Part Two

LEGACY

CHAPTER SIX

Harlan, Kentucky

"DIE LIKE A MAN, LIKE YOUR BROTHER DID!"

1.

In the southeastern corner of Kentucky, in the stretch of the Appalachian Mountains known as the Cumberland Plateau, lies a small town called Harlan.

The Cumberland Plateau is a wild and mountainous region of flat-topped ridges, mountain walls five hundred to a thousand feet high, and narrow valleys, some wide enough only for a one-lane road and a creek. When the area was first settled, the plateau was covered with a dense primeval forest. Giant tulip poplars grew in the coves and at the foot of the hills, some with trunks as wide as seven or eight feet in diameter. Alongside them were white oaks, beeches, maples, walnuts, sycamores, birches, willows, cedars, pines, and hemlocks, all enmeshed in a lattice of wild grapevine, comprising one of the greatest assortment of forest trees in the Northern Hemisphere. On the ground were bears and mountain lions and rattlesnakes; in the treetops, an astonishing array of squirrels; and beneath the soil, one thick seam after another of coal.

Harlan County was founded in 1819 by eight immigrant families from the northern regions of the British Isles. They had come to Virginia in the eighteenth century and then moved west into the Appalachians in search of land. The county was never wealthy. For its first one hundred years, it was thinly populated, rarely numbering more than ten thousand people. The first settlers kept pigs and herded sheep on the hillsides, scratching out a living on small farms in the valleys. They made whiskey in backyard stills and felled trees, floating them down the Cumberland River in the spring, when the water was high. Until well into the twentieth century, getting to the nearest train station was a two-day wagon trip. The only way out of town was up Pine Mountain, which was nine steep miles on a road that turned on occasion into no more than a muddy, rocky trail. Harlan was a remote and strange place, unknown by the larger society around it, and it might well have remained so but for the fact that two of the town's founding families—the Howards and the Turners—did not get along.

The patriarch of the Howard clan was Samuel Howard. He built the town courthouse and the jail. His counterpart was William Turner, who owned a tavern and two general stores. Once a storm blew down the fence to the Turner property, and a neighbor's cow wandered onto their land. William Turner's grandson, "Devil Jim," shot the cow dead. The neighbor was too terrified to press charges and fled the county.

Another time, a man tried to open a competitor to the Turners' general store. The Turners had a word with him. He closed the store and moved to Indiana. These were not pleasant people.

One night Wix Howard and "Little Bob" Turner—the grandsons of Samuel and William, respectively—played against each other in a game of poker. Each accused the other of cheating. They fought. The following day they met in the street, and after a flurry of gunshots, Little Bob Turner lay dead with a shotgun blast to the chest. A group of Turners went to the Howards' general store and spoke roughly to Mrs. Howard. She was insulted and told her son Wilse Howard, and the following week he exchanged gunfire with another of Turner's grandsons, young Will Turner, on the road to Hagan, Virginia. That night one of the Turners and a friend attacked the Howard home. The two families then clashed outside the Harlan courthouse. In the gunfire, Will Turner was shot and killed. A contingent of Howards then went to see Mrs. Turner, the mother of Will Turner and Little Bob, to ask for a truce.

She declined: "You can't wipe out that blood," she said, pointing to the dirt where her son had died.

Things quickly went from bad to worse. Wilse Howard ran into "Little George" Turner near Sulphur Springs and shot him dead. The Howards ambushed three friends of the Turners—the Cawoods—killing all of them. A posse was sent out in search of the Howards. In the resulting gunfight, six more were killed or wounded. Wilse Howard heard the Turners were after him, and he and a friend rode into Harlan and attacked the Turner home. Riding back, the Howards were ambushed. In the fighting, another person died. Wilse Howard rode to Little George Turner's house and fired at him but missed and killed another man. A posse surrounded the Howard home. There was another gunfight. More dead. The county was in an uproar. I think you get the picture. There were places in nineteenth-century America where people lived in harmony. Harlan, Kentucky, was not one of them.

"Stop that!" Will Turner's mother snapped

at him when he staggered home, howling in pain after being shot in the courthouse gun battle with the Howards. "Die like a man, like your brother did!" She belonged to a world so well acquainted with fatal gunshots that she had certain expectations about how they ought to be endured. Will shut his mouth, and he died.

2.

Suppose you were sent to Harlan in the late nineteenth century to investigate the causes of the Howard-Turner feud. You lined up every surviving participant and interviewed them as carefully as you could. You subpoenaed documents and took depositions and pored over court records until you had put together a detailed and precise accounting of each stage in the deadly quarrel.

How much would you know? The answer is, not much. You'd learn that there were two families in Harlan who didn't much like each other, and you'd confirm that Wilse Howard, who was responsible for an awful lot of the violence, probably belonged behind bars. What happened in Harlan wouldn't become clear until you looked at the violence from a much broader perspective.

The first critical fact about Harlan is that at the same time that the Howards and the Turners were killing one another, there were almost identical clashes in other small towns up and down the Appalachians. In the famous Hatfield-McCoy feud on the West Virginia–Kentucky border not far from Harlan, several dozen people were killed in a cycle of violence that stretched over twenty years. In the French-Eversole feud in Perry County, Kentucky, twelve died, six of them killed by "Bad Tom" Smith (a man, John Ed Pearce writes in *Days of Darkness,* who was "just dumb enough to be fearless, just bright enough to be dangerous, and a dead shot"). The Martin-Tolliver feud, in Rowan County, Kentucky, in the mid-1880s featured three gunfights, three ambushes, and two house attacks, and ended in a two-hour gun battle involving one hundred armed men.

The Baker-Howard feud in Clay County, Kentucky, began in 1806, with an elk-hunting party gone bad, and didn't end until the 1930s, when a couple of Howards killed three Bakers in an ambush.

And these were just the well-known feuds. The Kentucky legislator Harry Caudill once looked in a circuit court clerk's office in one Cumberland Plateau town and found one thousand murder indictments stretching from the end of the Civil War, in the 1860s, to the beginning of the twentieth century—and this for a region that never numbered more than fifteen thousand people and where many violent acts never even made it to the indictment stage. Caudill writes of a murder trial in Breathitt County—or "Bloody Breathitt," as it came to be known—that ended abruptly when the defendant's father, "a man of about fifty with huge handlebar whiskers and two immense pistols," walked up to the judge and grabbed his gavel:

> The feudist rapped the bench and announced, "Court's over and ever'body can go. We ain't agoin'

> to have any court here this term, folks." The red-faced judge hastily acquiesced in this extraordinary order and promptly left town. When court convened at the next term the court and sheriff were bolstered by sixty militiamen, but by then the defendant was not available for trial. He had been slain from ambush.

When one family fights with another, it's a feud. When lots of families fight with one another in identical little towns up and down the same mountain range, it's a *pattern.*

What was the cause of the Appalachian pattern? Over the years, many potential explanations have been examined and debated, and the consensus appears to be that that region was plagued by a particularly virulent strain of what sociologists call a "culture of honor."

Cultures of honor tend to take root in highlands and other marginally fertile areas, such as Sicily or the mountainous Basque regions of Spain. If you live on some rocky mountainside, the explanation goes, you can't farm. You probably raise goats or sheep, and the kind of culture that grows up around being a herdsman is very different from the culture that grows up around growing crops. The survival of a farmer depends on the cooperation of others in the community. But a herdsman is off by himself. Farmers also don't have to worry that their livelihood will be stolen in the night, because crops can't easily be stolen unless, of course, a thief wants to go to the trouble of harvesting an entire field on his own. But a herdsman does have to worry. He's under constant threat of ruin through the loss of his animals. So he has to be aggressive: he has to make it clear, through his words and deeds, that he is not weak. He has to be willing to fight in response to even the slightest challenge to his reputation—and that's what a "culture of honor" means. It's a world where a man's reputation is at the center of his livelihood and self-worth.

"The critical moment in the development of the young shepherd's reputation is his first quarrel," the ethnographer J. K. Campbell writes of one herding culture in Greece. "Quarrels are necessarily public. They may occur in the coffee shop, the village square, or most frequently on a grazing boundary where a curse or a stone aimed at one of his straying sheep by another shepherd is an insult which inevitably requires a violent response."

So why was Appalachia the way it was? It was because of where the original inhabitants of the region came from. The so-called American backcountry states—from the Pennsylvania border south and west through Virginia and West Virginia, Kentucky and Tennessee, North Carolina and South Carolina, and the northern end of Alabama and Georgia—were settled overwhelmingly by immigrants from one of the world's most ferocious cultures of honor. They were "Scotch-Irish"—that is, from the lowlands of Scotland, the northern counties of England, and Ulster in Northern Ireland.

The borderlands—as this region was known—were remote and lawless territories that had been fought over for hundreds of years. The people of the region were steeped in violence. They were herdsmen, scraping out a living on rocky and infertile land. They were clannish, responding to the harshness and turmoil of their environment by forming tight family bonds and placing loyalty to blood above all else. And when they immigrated to North America, they moved into the American interior, to remote, lawless, rocky, and marginally fertile places like Harlan that allowed them to reproduce in the New World the culture of honor they had created in the Old World.

"To the first settlers, the American backcountry was a dangerous environment, just as the British borderlands had been," the historian David Hackett Fischer writes in *Albion's Seed.*

> Much of the southern highlands were "debatable lands" in the border sense of a contested territory without established government or the rule of law. The borderers were more at home than others in this anarchic environment, which was well suited to their family system, their warrior ethic, their farming and herding economy, their attitudes toward land and wealth and their ideas of work and power. So well adapted was the border culture to this environment that other ethnic groups tended to copy it. The ethos of the North British borders came to dominate this "dark and bloody ground," partly by force of num-

bers, but mainly because it was a means of survival in a raw and dangerous world.*

The triumph of a culture of honor helps to explain why the pattern of criminality in the American South has always been so distinctive. Murder rates are higher there than in the

* David Hackett Fischer's book *Albion's Seed: Four British Folkways in America* is the most definitive and convincing treatment of the idea that cultural legacies cast a long historical shadow. (If you read my first book, *The Tipping Point,* you'll remember that the discussion of Paul Revere was drawn from Fischer's *Paul Revere's Ride.*) In *Albion's Seed,* Fischer argues that there were four distinct British migrations to America in its first 150 years: first the Puritans, in the 1630s, who came from East Anglia to Massachusetts; then the Cavaliers and indentured servants, who came from southern England to Virginia in the mid-seventeenth century; then the Quakers, from the North Midlands to the Delaware Valley between the late seventeenth and early eighteenth centuries; and finally, the people of the borderlands to the Appalachian interior in the eighteenth century. Fischer argues brilliantly that those four cultures—each profoundly different—characterize those four regions of the United States even to this day.

rest of the country. But crimes of property and "stranger" crimes—like muggings—are lower. As the sociologist John Shelton Reed has written, "The homicides in which the South seems to specialize are those in which someone is being killed by someone he (or often she) knows, for reasons both killer and victim understand." Reed adds: "The statistics show that the Southerner who can avoid arguments and adultery is as safe as any other American, and probably safer." In the backcountry, violence wasn't for economic gain. It was *personal.* You fought over your honor.

Many years ago, the southern newspaperman Hodding Carter told the story of how as a young man he served on a jury. As Reed describes it:

> The case before the jury involved an irascible gentleman who lived next door to a filling station. For several months he had been the butt of various jokes played by the attendants and the miscellaneous loafers who hung around the station, despite his warnings and his notorious short temper. One morning, he emptied both barrels of his shotgun at his tormenters, killing one, maiming another permanently,

> and wounding a third. . . . When the jury was polled by the incredulous judge, Carter was the only juror who recorded his vote as guilty. As one of the others put it, "He wouldn't of been much of a man if he hadn't shot them fellows."

Only in a culture of honor would it have occurred to the irascible gentleman that shooting someone was an appropriate response to a personal insult. And only in a culture of honor would it have occurred to a jury that murder—under those circumstances—was not a crime.

I realize that we are often wary of making these kinds of broad generalizations about different cultural groups—and with good reason. This is the form that racial and ethnic stereotypes take. We want to believe that we are not prisoners of our ethnic histories.

But the simple truth is that if you want to understand what happened in those small towns in Kentucky in the nineteenth century, you *have* to go back into the past—and not just one or two generations. You have to go back two or three or four hundred years, to a country on the other side of the ocean, and look closely at what exactly the people in a very specific geographic area of that country did for a living. The "culture of honor" hypothesis says that it matters where you're from, not just in terms of where you grew up or where your parents grew up, but in terms of where your great-grandparents and great-great-grandparents grew up and even where your great-great-great-grandparents grew up. That is a strange and powerful fact. It's just the beginning, though, because upon closer examination, cultural legacies turn out to be even stranger and more powerful than that.

3.

In the early 1990s, two psychologists at the University of Michigan—Dov Cohen and Richard Nisbett—decided to conduct an experiment on the culture of honor. They knew that what happened in places like Harlan in the nineteenth century was, in all likelihood, a product of patterns laid down in the English borderlands centuries before. But their interest was in the present day.

Was it possible to find remnants of the culture of honor in the modern era? So they decided to gather together a group of young men and insult them. "We sat down and tried to figure out what is the insult that would go to the heart of an eighteen-to-twenty-year-old's brain," Cohen says. "It didn't take too long to come up with 'asshole.' "

The experiment went like this. The social sciences building at the University of Michigan has a long, narrow hallway in the basement lined with filing cabinets. The young men were called into a classroom, one by one, and asked to fill out a questionnaire. Then they were told to drop off the questionnaire at the end of the hallway and return to the classroom—a simple, seemingly innocent academic exercise.

For half the young men, that was it. They were the control group. For the other half, there was a catch. As they walked down the hallway with their questionnaire, a man—a confederate of the experimenters—walked past them and pulled out a drawer in one of the filing cabinets. The already narrow hallway now became even narrower. As the young men tried to squeeze by, the confederate looked up, annoyed. He slammed the filing cabinet drawer shut, jostled the young men with his shoulder, and, in a low but audible voice, said the trigger word: "Asshole."

Cohen and Nisbett wanted to measure, as precisely as possible, what being called that word meant. They looked at the faces of their subjects and rated how much anger they saw. They shook the young men's hands to see if their grip was firmer than usual. They took saliva samples from the students, both before and after the insult, to see if being called an asshole caused their levels of testosterone and cortisol—the hormones that drive arousal and aggression—to go up. Finally they asked the students to read the following story and supply a conclusion:

> It had only been about twenty minutes since they had arrived at the party when Jill pulled Steve aside, obviously bothered about something.
>
> "What's wrong?" asked Steve.
>
> "It's Larry. I mean, he knows that you and I are engaged, but he's already made two passes at me tonight."

> Jill walked back into the crowd, and Steve decided to keep his eye on Larry. Sure enough, within five minutes, Larry was reaching over and trying to kiss Jill.

If you've been insulted, are you more likely to imagine Steve doing something violent to Larry?

The results were unequivocal. There were clear differences in how the young men responded to being called a bad name. For some, the insult changed their behavior. For some it didn't. The deciding factor in how they reacted wasn't how emotionally secure they were, or whether they were intellectuals or jocks, or whether they were physically imposing or not. What mattered—and I think you can guess where this is headed—*was where they were from*. Most of the young men from the northern part of the United States treated the incident with amusement. They laughed it off. Their handshakes were unchanged. Their levels of cortisol actually went down, as if they were unconsciously trying to defuse their own anger. Only a few of them had Steve get violent with Larry.

But the southerners? Oh, my. They were *angry*. Their cortisol and testosterone jumped. Their handshakes got firm. Steve was all over Larry.

"We even played this game of chicken," Cohen said. "We sent the students back down the hallways, and around the corner comes another confederate. The hallway is blocked, so there's only room for one of them to pass. The guy we used was six three, two hundred fifty pounds. He used to play college football. He was now working as a bouncer in a college bar. He was walking down the hall in business mode—the way you walk through a bar when you are trying to break up a fight. The question was: how close do they get to the bouncer before they get out of the way? And believe me, they always get out of the way."

For the northerners, there was almost no effect. They got out of the way five or six feet beforehand, whether they had been insulted or not. The southerners, by contrast, were downright deferential in normal circumstances, stepping aside with more than nine feet to go. But if they had just been insulted? Less than *two* feet. Call a southerner an asshole, and he's itching for a fight. What Cohen and Nisbett were seeing in that long hall was the culture of honor in action: the southerners were reacting like Wix Howard did when Little Bob Turner accused him of cheating at poker.

4.

That study is strange, isn't it? It's one thing to conclude that groups of people living in circumstances pretty similar to their ancestors' act a lot like their ancestors. But those southerners in the hallway study weren't living in circumstances similar to their British ancestors. They didn't even necessarily have British ancestors. They just happened to have grown up in the South. None of them were herdsmen. Nor were their parents herdsmen. They were living in the late twentieth century, not the late nineteenth century. They were students at the University of Michigan, in one of the northernmost states in America, which meant they were sufficiently cosmopolitan to travel hundreds of miles from the south to go to college. And none of that mattered. *They still acted like they were living in nineteenth-century Harlan, Kentucky.*

"Your median student in those studies comes from a family making over a hundred thousand dollars, and that's in nineteen ninety dollars," Cohen says. "The southerners we see this effect with aren't kids who come from the hills of Appalachia. They are more likely to be the sons of upper-middle management Coca-Cola executives in Atlanta. And that's the big question. Why should we get this effect with them? Why should one get it hundreds of years later? Why are these suburban-Atlanta kids acting out the ethos of the frontier?"*

Cultural legacies are powerful forces. They have deep roots and long lives. They persist, gen-

* Cohen has done other experiments looking again for evidence of "southernness," and each time he finds the same thing. "Once, we bothered students with persistent annoyances," he said. "They come

eration after generation, virtually intact, even as the economic and social and demographic conditions that spawned them have vanished, and they play such a role in directing attitudes and behavior that we cannot make sense of our world without them.*

---

into the lab and they are supposed to draw pictures from their childhood. They are doing this with the confederate, and he's being a jerk. He does all these things to persistently annoy the subject. He'll wad up his drawing and throw it at the wastebasket and hit the subject. He'll steal the subject's crayons and not give them back. He keeps on calling the subject 'Slick,' and he says, 'I'm going to put your name on your drawing,' and writes 'Slick.' What you find is that northerners tend to give off displays of anger, up to a certain point, at which point they level off. Southerners are much less likely to be angry early on. But at some point they catch up to the northerners and shoot past them. They are more likely to explode, much more volatile, much more explosive."

* How are these kinds of attitudes passed down from generation to generation? Through social heritance. Think of the way accents persist over time. David Hackett Fischer points out that the original settlers

So far in *Outliers* we've seen that success arises out of the steady accumulation of advantages: when and where you are born, what your parents did for a living, and what the circumstances of your upbringing were all make a significant difference in how well you do in the world. The question for the second part of *Outliers* is whether the traditions and attitudes we inherit from our forebears can play the same role. Can we learn something about why people succeed and how to make people better at what they do by taking cultural legacies seriously? I think we can.

---

of Appalachia said: "whar for where, thar for there, hard for hired, critter for creature, sartin for certain, a-goin for going, hit for it, he-it for hit, far for fire, deef for deaf, pizen for poison, nekkid for naked, eetch for itch, boosh for bush, wrassle for wrestle, chaw for chew, poosh for push, shet for shut, ba-it for bat, be-it for be, narrer for narrow, winder for window, widder for widow, and young-uns for young one." Recognize that? It's the same way many rural people in the Appalachians speak today. Whatever mechanism passes on speech patterns probably passes on behavioral and emotional patterns as well.

CHAPTER SEVEN

The Ethnic Theory of Plane Crashes

"CAPTAIN, THE WEATHER RADAR HAS HELPED US A LOT."

1.

On the morning of August 5, 1997, the captain of Korean Air flight 801 woke at six. His family would later tell investigators that he went to the gym for an hour, then came home and studied the flight plan for that evening's journey to Guam. He napped and ate lunch. At three in the afternoon, he left for Seoul, departing early enough, his wife said, to continue his preparations at Kimpo International Airport. He had been a pilot with Korean Air for almost four years after coming over from the Korean Air Force. He had eighty-nine hundred hours of flight time, including thirty-two hundred hours of experience in jumbo jets. A few months earlier, he had been given a flight safety award by his airline for successfully handling a jumbo-jet engine failure at low altitude. He was forty-two years old and in excellent health, with the exception of a bout of bronchitis that had been diagnosed ten days before.

At seven p.m., the captain, his first officer, and the flight engineer met and collected the trip's paperwork. They would be flying a Boeing 747—the model known in the aviation world as the "classic." The aircraft was in perfect working order. It had once been the Korean presidential plane. Flight 801 departed the gate at ten-thirty in the evening and was airborne twenty minutes later. Takeoff was without incident. Just before one-thirty in the morning, the plane broke out of the clouds, and the flight crew glimpsed lights off in the distance.

"Is it Guam?" the flight engineer asked. Then, after a pause, he said, "It's Guam, Guam."

The captain chuckled. "Good!"

The first officer reported to Air Traffic Control (ATC) that the airplane was "clear of Charlie Bravo [cumulonimbus clouds]" and requested "radar vectors for runway six left."

The plane began its descent toward Guam airport. They would make a visual approach, the captain said. He had flown into Guam airport from Kimpo eight times previously, most recently a month ago, and he knew the airport and the surrounding terrain well. The landing gear went down. The flaps were extended ten degrees. At 01:41 and 48 seconds, the captain said, "Wiper on," and the flight engineer turned them on. It was raining. The first officer then said, "Not in sight?" He was looking for the runway. He couldn't see it. One second later, the Ground Proximity Warning System called out in its electronic voice: "Five hundred [feet]." The plane was five hundred feet off the ground. But how could that be if they couldn't see the runway? Two seconds passed. The flight engineer said, "Eh?" in an astonished tone of voice.

At 01:42 and 19 seconds, the first officer said, "Let's make a missed approach," meaning, Let's pull up and make a large circle and try the landing again.

One second later, the flight engineer said, "Not in sight." The first officer added, "Not in sight, missed approach."

At 01:42 and 22 seconds, the flight engineer said again, "Go around."

At 01:42 and 23 seconds, the captain repeated, "Go around," but he was slow to pull the plane out of its descent.

At 01:42 and 26 seconds, the plane hit the side of Nimitz Hill, a densely vegetated mountain three miles southwest of the airport—$60 million and 212,000 kilograms of steel slamming into rocky ground at one hundred miles per hour. The plane skidded for two thousand feet, severing an oil pipeline and snapping pine trees, before falling into a ravine and bursting into flames. By the time rescue workers reached the crash site, 228 of the 254 people on board were dead.

2.

Twenty years before the crash of KAL 801, a Korean Air Boeing 707 wandered into Russian airspace and was shot down by a Soviet military jet over the Barents Sea. It was an accident, meaning the kind of rare and catastrophic event that, but for the grace of God, could happen to any airline. It was investigated and analyzed. Lessons were learned. Reports were filed.

Then, two years later, a Korean Air Boeing 747 crashed in Seoul. Two accidents in two years is not a good sign. Three years after that, the airline lost another 747 near Sakhalin Island, in Russia, followed by a Boeing 707 that went down over the Andaman Sea in 1987, two more crashes in 1989 in Tripoli and Seoul, and then another in 1994 in Cheju, South Korea.*

To put that record in perspective, the "loss"

* Korean Air was called Korean Airlines before it changed its name after the Guam accident. And the Barents Sea incident was actually preceded by two other crashes, in 1971 and 1976.

rate for an airline like the American carrier United Airlines in the period 1988 to 1998 was .27 per million departures, which means that they lost a plane in an accident about once in every four million flights. The loss rate for Korean Air, in the same period, was 4.79 per million departures — more than *seventeen* times higher.

Korean Air's planes were crashing so often that when the National Transportation Safety Board (NTSB) — the US agency responsible for investigating plane crashes within American jurisdiction — did its report on the Guam crash, it was forced to include an addendum listing all the new Korean Air accidents that had happened just since its investigation began: the Korean Air 747 that crash-landed at Kimpo in Seoul, almost a year to the day after Guam; the jetliner that overran a runway at Korea's Ulsan Airport eight weeks after that; the Korean Air McDonnell Douglas 83 that rammed into an embankment at Pohang Airport the following March; and then, a month after that, the Korean Air passenger jet that crashed in a residential area of Shanghai. Had the NTSB waited just a few more months, it could have added another: the Korean Air cargo plane that crashed just after takeoff from London's Stansted airport, despite the fact that a warning bell went off in the cockpit no fewer than fourteen times.

In April 1999, Delta Air Lines and Air France suspended their flying partnership with Korean Air. In short order, the US Army, which maintains thousands of troops in South Korea, forbade its personnel from flying with the airline. South Korea's safety rating was downgraded by the US Federal Aviation Authority, and Canadian officials informed Korean Air's management that they were considering revoking the company's overflight and landing privileges in Canadian airspace.

In the midst of the controversy, an outside audit of Korean Air's operations was leaked to the public. The forty-page report was quickly denounced by Korean Air officials as sensationalized and unrepresentative, but by that point, it was too late to save the company's reputation. The audit detailed instances of flight crews smoking cigarettes on the tarmac during refueling and in the freight area; and when the plane was in the air. "Crew read newspapers throughout the flight," the audit stated, "often with newspapers held up in such a way that if a warning light came on, it would not be noticed." The report detailed bad morale, numerous procedural violations, and the alarming conclusion that training standards for the 747 "classic" were so poor that "there is some concern as to whether First Officers on the Classic fleet could land the aircraft if the Captain became totally incapacitated."

By the time of the Shanghai crash, the Korean president, Kim Dae-jung, felt compelled to speak up. "The issue of Korean Air is not a matter of an individual company but a matter of the whole country," he said. "Our country's credibility is at stake." Dae-jung then switched the presidential plane from Korean Air to its newer rival, Asiana.

But then a small miracle happened. Korean Air turned itself around. Today, the airline is a member in good standing of the prestigious

SkyTeam alliance. Its safety record since 1999 is spotless. In 2006, Korean Air was given the Phoenix Award by Air Transport World in recognition of its transformation. Aviation experts will tell you that Korean Air is now as safe as any airline in the world.

In this chapter, we're going to conduct a crash investigation: listen to the "black box" cockpit recorder; examine the flight records; look at the weather and the terrain and the airport conditions; and compare the Guam crash with other very similar plane crashes, all in an attempt to understand precisely how the company transformed itself from the worst kind of outlier into one of the world's best airlines. It is a complex and sometimes strange story. But it turns on a very simple fact, the same fact that runs through the tangled history of Harlan and the Michigan students. Korean Air did not succeed—it did not right itself—until it acknowledged the importance of its cultural legacy.

3.

Planes crashes rarely happen in real life the same way they happen in the movies. Some engine part does not explode in a fiery bang. The rudder doesn't suddenly snap under the force of takeoff. The captain doesn't gasp, "Dear God," as he's thrown back against his seat. The typical commercial jetliner—at this point in its stage of development—is about as dependable as a toaster. Plane crashes are much more likely to be the result of an accumulation of minor difficulties and seemingly trivial malfunctions.*

* This is true not just of plane crashes. It's true of virtually all industrial accidents. One of the most famous accidents in history, for example, was the near meltdown at Pennsylvania's Three Mile Island nuclear station in 1979. Three Mile Island so traumatized the American public that it sent the US nuclear power industry into a tailspin from which it has never fully recovered. But what actually happened at that nuclear reactor began as something far from dramatic. As the sociologist Charles Perrow shows in his classic *Normal Accidents,* there was a relatively routine blockage in

In a typical crash, for example, the weather is poor—not terrible, necessarily, but bad enough that the pilot feels a little bit more stressed than usual. In an overwhelming number of crashes, the plane is behind schedule, so the pilots are hurrying. In 52 percent of crashes, the pilot at the time of the accident has been awake for twelve hours or more, meaning that he is tired and not thinking sharply. And 44 percent of the time, the two pilots have never flown together before, so they're not comfortable with each other. Then the errors start—and it's not just one error. The typical accident involves seven

---

what is called the plant's "polisher"—a kind of giant water filter. The blockage caused moisture to leak into the plant's air system, inadvertently tripping two valves and shutting down the flow of cold water into the plant's steam generator. Like all nuclear reactors, Three Mile Island had a backup cooling system for precisely this situation. But on that particular day, for reasons that no one really understands, the valves for the backup system weren't open. Someone had closed them, and an indicator in the control room showing they were closed was blocked by a repair tag hanging

consecutive human errors. One of the pilots does something wrong that by itself is not a problem. Then one of them makes another error on top of that, which combined with the first error still does not amount to catastrophe. But then they make a third error on top of that, and then another and another and another *and another,* and it is the combination of all those errors that leads to disaster.

These seven errors, furthermore, are rarely

---

from a switch above it. That left the reactor dependent on another backup system, a special sort of relief valve. But, as luck would have it, the relief valve wasn't working properly that day either. It stuck open when it was supposed to close, and, to make matters even worse, a gauge in the control room that should have told the operators that the relief valve wasn't working was itself not working. By the time Three Mile Island's engineers realized what was happening, the reactor had come dangerously close to a meltdown.

No single big thing went wrong at Three Mile Island. Rather, five completely unrelated events occurred in sequence, each of which, had it happened in isolation, would have caused no more than a hiccup in the plant's ordinary operation.

problems of knowledge or flying skill. It's not that the pilot has to negotiate some critical technical maneuver and fails. The kinds of errors that cause plane crashes are invariably errors of teamwork and communication. One pilot knows something important and somehow doesn't tell the other pilot. One pilot does something wrong, and the other pilot doesn't catch the error. A tricky situation needs to be resolved through a complex series of steps—and somehow the pilots fail to coordinate and miss one of them.

"The whole flight-deck design is intended to be operated by two people, and that operation works best when you have one person checking the other, or both people willing to participate," says Earl Weener, who was for many years chief engineer for safety at Boeing. "Airplanes are very unforgiving if you don't do things right. And for a long time it's been clear that if you have two people operating the airplane cooperatively, you will have a safer operation than if you have a single pilot flying the plane and another person who is simply there to take over if the pilot is incapacitated."

Consider, for example, the famous (in aviation circles, anyway) crash of the Colombian airliner Avianca flight 052 in January of 1990. The Avianca accident so perfectly illustrates the characteristics of the "modern" plane crash that it is studied in flight schools. In fact, what happened to that flight is so similar to what would happen seven years later in Guam that it's a good place to start our investigation into the mystery of Korean Air's plane crash problem.

The captain of the plane was Laureano Caviedes. His first officer was Mauricio Klotz. They were en route from Medellin, Colombia, to New York City's Kennedy Airport. The weather that evening was poor. There was a nor'easter up and down the East Coast, bringing with it dense fog and high winds. Two hundred and three flights were delayed at Newark Airport. Two hundred flights were delayed at LaGuardia Airport, 161 at Philadelphia, 53 at Boston's Logan Airport, and 99 at Kennedy. Because of the weather, Avianca was held up by Air Traffic Control three times on its way to New York. The plane circled over Norfolk,

Virginia, for nineteen minutes, above Atlantic City for twenty-nine minutes, and forty miles south of Kennedy Airport for another twenty-nine minutes.

After an hour and a quarter of delay, Avianca was cleared for landing. As the plane came in on its final approach, the pilots encountered severe wind shear. One moment they were flying into a strong headwind, forcing them to add extra power to maintain their momentum on the glide down. The next moment, without warning, the headwind dropped dramatically, and they were traveling much too fast to make the runway. Typically, the plane would have been flying on autopilot in that situation, reacting immediately and appropriately to wind shear. But the autopilot on the plane was malfunctioning, and it had been switched off. At the last moment, the pilot pulled up, and executed a "go-around." The plane did a wide circle over Long Island, and reapproached Kennedy Airport. Suddenly, one of the plane's engines failed. Seconds later, a second engine failed. "Show me the runway!" the pilot cried out, hoping desperately that he was close enough to Kennedy to somehow glide his crippled plane to a safe landing. But Kennedy was sixteen miles away.

The 707 slammed into the estate owned by the father of the tennis champion John McEnroe, in the posh Long Island town of Oyster Bay. Seventy-three of the 158 passengers aboard died. It took less than a day for the cause of the crash to be determined: "fuel exhaustion." There was nothing wrong with the aircraft. There was nothing wrong with the airport. The pilots weren't drunk or high. The plane had run out of gas.

4.

"It's a classic case," said Suren Ratwatte, a veteran pilot who has been involved for years in "human factors" research, which is the analysis of how human beings interact with complex systems like nuclear power plants and airplanes. Ratwatte is Sri Lankan, a lively man in his forties who has been flying commercial jets his entire adult life. We were sitting in the lobby of the Sheraton Hotel in Manhattan. He'd just landed a jumbo jet at Kennedy Airport after a long flight from Dubai. Ratwatte knew the Avianca case well. He began to tick off the typical crash preconditions. The nor'easter. The delayed flight. The minor technical malfunction with the autopilot. The three long holding patterns—which meant not only eighty minutes of extra flying time but extra flying at low altitudes, where a plane burns far more fuel than it does in the thin air high above the clouds.

"They were flying a seven-oh-seven, which is an older airplane and is very challenging to fly," Ratwatte said. "That thing is a lot of work. The flight controls are not hydraulically powered. They are connected by a series of pulleys and pull rods to the physical metal surfaces of the airplane. You have to be quite strong to fly that airplane. You heave it around the sky. It's as much physical effort as rowing a boat. My current airplane I fly with my fingertips. I use a joystick. My instruments are huge. Theirs were the size of coffee cups. And his autopilot was gone. So the captain had to keep looking around these nine instruments, each the size of a coffee cup, while his right hand was controlling the speed, and his left hand was flying the airplane. He was maxed out. He had no resources left to do anything else. That's what happens when you're tired. Your decision-making skills erode. You start missing things—things that you would pick up on any other day."

In the black box recovered from the crash site, Captain Caviedes in the final hour of the flight is heard to repeatedly ask for the directions from ATC to be translated into Spanish, as if he no longer had the energy to make use of his English. On nine occasions, he also asked for directions to be repeated. "Tell me things louder," he said right near the end. "I'm not hearing them." When the plane was circling for forty minutes just southeast of Kennedy—when everyone on the flight deck clearly knew they were running out of fuel—the pilot could easily have asked to land at Philadelphia, which was just sixty-five miles away. But he didn't: it was as if he had locked in on New York. On the aborted landing, the plane's Ground Proximity Warning System went off no fewer than fifteen times, telling the captain that he was bringing in the plane too low. He seemed oblivious. When he aborted the landing, he should have circled back around immediately, and he didn't. He was exhausted.

Through it all, the cockpit was filled with a heavy silence. Sitting next to Caviedes was his first officer, Mauricio Klotz, and in the flight recorder, there are long stretches of nothing but rustling and engine noise. It was Klotz's responsibility to conduct all communication with ATC, which meant that his role that night was absolutely critical. But his behavior was oddly passive. It wasn't until the third holding pattern southwest of Kennedy Airport that Klotz told ATC that he didn't think the plane had enough fuel to reach an alternative airport. The next thing the crew heard from ATC was "Just stand by" and, following that, "Cleared to the Kennedy airport." Investigators later surmised that the Avianca pilots must have assumed that ATC was jumping them to the head of the queue, in front of the dozens of other planes circling Kennedy. In fact, they weren't. They were just being added to the end of the line. It was a crucial misunderstanding, upon which the fate of the plane would ultimately rest. But did the pilots raise the issue again, looking for clarification? No. Nor did they bring up the issue of fuel again for another thirty-eight minutes.

5.

To Ratwatte, the silence in the cockpit made no sense. And as a way of explaining why, Ratwatte began to talk about what had happened to him that morning on the way over from Dubai. "We had this lady in the back," he said. "We reckon she was having a stroke. Seizing. Vomiting. In bad shape. She was an Indian lady whose daughter lives in the States. Her husband spoke no English, no Hindi, only Punjabi. No one could communicate with him. He looked like he had just walked off a village in the Punjab, and they had absolutely no money. I was actually over Moscow when it happened, but I knew we couldn't go to Moscow. I didn't know what would happen to these people if we did. I said to the first officer, 'You fly the plane. We have to go to Helsinki.' "

The immediate problem Ratwatte faced was that they were less than halfway through a very long flight, which meant that they had far more fuel in their tanks than they usually do when it comes time to land. "We were sixty tons over maximum landing weight," he said. "So now I had to make a choice. I could dump the fuel. But countries hate it when you dump fuel. It's messy stuff and they would have routed me somewhere over the Baltic Sea, and it would have taken me forty minutes and the lady probably would have died. So I decided to land anyway. My choice."

That meant the plane was "landing heavy." They couldn't use the automated landing system because it wasn't set up to handle a plane with that much weight.

"At that stage, I took over the controls," he went on. "I had to ensure that the airplane touched down very softly; otherwise, there would have been the risk of structural damage. It could have been a real mess. There are also performance issues with being heavy. If you clear the runway and have to go around, you may not have enough thrust to climb back up.

"It was a lot of work. You're juggling a lot of balls. You've got to get it right. Because it was a long flight, there were two other pilots. So I got them up, and they got involved in doing everything as well. We had four people up there, which really helped in coordinating everything. I'd never been to Helsinki before. I had no idea how the airport was, no idea whether the runways were long enough. I had to find an approach, figure out if we could land there, figure out the performance parameters, and tell the company what we were doing. At one point I was talking to three different people—talking to Dubai, talking to MedLink, which is a service in Arizona where they put a doctor on call, and I was talking to the two doctors who were attending to the lady in the back. It was nonstop for forty minutes.

"We were lucky the weather was very good in Helsinki," he said. "Trying to do an approach in bad weather, plus a heavy plane, plus an unfamiliar airport, that's not good. Because it was Finland, a first-world country, they were well set up, very flexible. I said to them, 'I'm heavy. I would like to land into the wind.' You want to slow yourself down in that situation. They said, No problem. They landed us in the opposite direction than they normally use. We came in over the city, which they usually avoid for noise reasons."

Think about what was required of Ratwatte. He had to be a good pilot. That much goes without saying: he had to have the technical skill to land heavy. But almost everything else Ratwatte did that made that emergency landing a success fell outside the strict definition of piloting skills.

He had to weigh the risk of damaging his plane against the risk to the woman's life, and then, once that choice was made, he had to think through the implications of Helsinki versus Moscow for the sick passenger in the back. He had to educate himself, quickly, on the parameters of an airport he had never seen before: could it handle one of the biggest jets in the sky, at *sixty tons* over its normal landing weight? But most of all, he had to talk—to the passengers, to the doctors, to his copilot, to the second crew he woke up from their nap, to his superiors back home in Dubai, to ATC at Helsinki. It is safe to say that in the forty minutes that passed between the passenger's stroke and the landing in Helsinki, there were no more than a handful of seconds of silence in the cockpit. What was required of Ratwatte was that he *communicate,* and communicate not just in the sense of issuing commands but also in the sense of encouraging and cajoling and calming and negotiating and sharing information in the clearest and most transparent manner possible.

6.

Here, by contrast, is the transcript from Avianca 052, as the plane is going in for its abortive first landing. The issue is the weather. The fog is so thick that Klotz and Caviedes cannot figure out where they are. Pay close attention, though, not to the content of their conversation but to the *form.* In particular, note the length of the silences between utterances and to the tone of Klotz's remarks.

> CAVIEDES: The runway, where is it? I don't see it. I don't see it.

They take up the landing gear. The captain tells Klotz to ask for another traffic pattern. Ten seconds pass.

> CAVIEDES [SEEMINGLY TO HIMSELF]: We don't have fuel...

Seventeen seconds pass as the pilots give technical instructions to each other.

> CAVIEDES: I don't know what happened with the runway. I didn't see it.
>
> KLOTZ: I didn't see it.

Air Traffic Control comes in and tells them to make a left turn.

> CAVIEDES: Tell them we are in an emergency!
> KLOTZ [TO ATC]: That's right to one-eight-zero on the heading and, ah, we'll try once again. We're running out of fuel.

Imagine the scene in the cockpit. The plane is dangerously low on fuel. They have just blown their first shot at a landing. They have no idea how much longer the plane is capable of flying. The captain is desperate: "Tell them we are in an emergency!" And what does Klotz say? *That's right to one-eight-zero on the heading and, ah, we'll try once again. We're running out of fuel.*

To begin with, the phrase "running out of fuel" has no meaning in Air Traffic Control terminology. All planes, as they approach their destination, are by definition running out of fuel. Did Klotz mean that 052 no longer had enough fuel to make it to another, alternative airport? Did he mean that they were beginning to get worried about their fuel? Next, consider the structure of the critical sentence. Klotz begins with a routine acknowledgment of the instructions from ATC and doesn't mention his concern about fuel until the second half of the sentence. It's as if he were to say in a restaurant, "Yes, I'll have some more coffee and, ah, I'm choking on a chicken bone." How seriously would the waiter take him? The air traffic controller with whom Klotz was speaking testified later that he "just took it as a passing comment." On stormy nights, air traffic controllers hear pilots talking about running out of fuel all the time. Even the "ah" that Klotz inserts between the two halves of his sentence serves to undercut the importance of what he is saying. According to another of the controllers who handled 052 that night, Klotz spoke "in a very nonchalant manner.... There was no urgency in the voice."

7.

The term used by linguists to describe what Klotz was engaging in in that moment is "mitigated speech," which refers to any attempt to downplay or sugarcoat the meaning of what is being said. We mitigate when we're being polite, or when we're ashamed or embarrassed, or when we're being deferential to authority. If you want your boss to do you a favor, you don't say, "I'll need this by Monday." You mitigate. You say, "Don't bother, if it's too much trouble, but if you have a chance to look at this over the weekend, that would be wonderful." In a situation like that, mitigation is entirely appropriate. In other situations, however—like a cockpit on a stormy night—it's a problem.

The linguists Ute Fischer and Judith Orasanu once gave the following hypothetical scenario to a group of captains and first officers and asked them how they would respond:

> You notice on the weather radar an area of heavy precipitation 25 miles ahead. [The pilot] is maintaining his present course at Mach .73, even though embedded thunderstorms have been reported in your area and you encounter moderate turbulence. You want to ensure that your aircraft will not penetrate this area.
>
> Question: what do you say to the pilot?

In Fischer's and Orasanu's minds, there were at least six ways to try to persuade the pilot to change course and avoid the bad weather, each with a different level of mitigation.

1. *Command:* "Turn thirty degrees right." That's the most direct and explicit way of making a point imaginable. It's zero mitigation.
2. *Crew Obligation Statement:* "I think we need to deviate right about now." Notice the use of "we" and the fact that the request is now much less specific. That's a little softer.
3. *Crew Suggestion:* "Let's go around the weather." Implicit in that statement is "we're in this together."
4. *Query:* "Which direction would you like to deviate?" That's even softer than a crew suggestion, because the speaker is conceding that he's not in charge.
5. *Preference:* "I think it would be wise to turn left or right."
6. *Hint:* "That return at twenty-five miles looks mean." This is the most mitigated statement of all.

Fischer and Orasanu found that captains overwhelmingly said they would issue a command in that situation: "Turn thirty degrees right." They were talking to a subordinate. They had no fear of being blunt. The first officers, on the other hand, were talking to their boss, and so they overwhelmingly chose the most mitigated alternative. They hinted.

It's hard to read Fischer and Orasanu's study and not be just a little bit alarmed, because a hint is the hardest kind of request to decode and the easiest to refuse. In the 1982 Air Florida crash outside Washington, DC, the first officer tried three times to tell the captain that the plane had a dangerous amount of ice on its wings. But listen to how he says it. It's all hints:

> First Officer: Look how the ice is just hanging on his, ah, back, back there, see that?

Then:

> First Officer: See all those icicles on the back there and everything?

And then:

First Officer: Boy, this is a, this is a losing battle here on trying to de-ice those things, it [gives] you a false feeling of security, that's all that does.

Finally, as they get clearance for takeoff, the first officer upgrades two notches to a crew suggestion:

First Officer: Let's check those [wing] tops again, since we've been setting here awhile.

Captain: I think we get to go here in a minute.

The last thing the first officer says to the captain, just before the plane plunges into the Potomac River, is not a hint, a suggestion, or a command. It's a simple statement of fact—and this time the captain agrees with him.

First Officer: Larry, we're going down, Larry.

Captain: I know it.

Mitigation explains one of the great anomalies of plane crashes. In commercial airlines, captains and first officers split the flying duties equally. But historically, crashes have been far more likely to happen when the captain is in the "flying seat." At first that seems to make no sense, since the captain is almost always the pilot with the most experience. But think about the Air Florida crash. If the first officer had been the captain, would he have hinted three times? No, he would have commanded—and the plane wouldn't have crashed. Planes are safer when the least experienced pilot is flying, because it means the second pilot isn't going to be afraid to speak up.

Combating mitigation has become one of the great crusades in commercial aviation in the past fifteen years. Every major airline now has what is called "Crew Resource Management" training, which is designed to teach junior crew members how to communicate clearly and assertively. For example, many airlines teach a standardized procedure for copilots to challenge the pilot if he or she thinks something has gone terribly awry. ("Captain, I'm concerned about..." Then, "Captain, I'm uncomfortable with..." And if the captain still doesn't respond, "Captain, I believe the situation is unsafe." And if that fails, the first officer is required to take over the airplane.) Aviation experts will tell you that it is the success of this war on mitigation as much as anything else that accounts for the extraordinary decline in airline accidents in recent years.

"On a very simple level, one of the things we insist upon at my airline is that the first officer and the captain call each other by their first names," Ratwatte said. "We think that helps. It's just harder to say, 'Captain, you're doing something wrong,' than to use a name." Ratwatte took mitigation very seriously. You couldn't be a student of the Avianca crash and not feel that way. He went on: "One thing I personally try to do is, I try to put myself a little down. I say to my copilots, 'I don't fly very often. Three or four times a month. You fly a lot more. If you see me doing something stupid, it's because I don't fly very often. So tell me. Help me out.' Hopefully, that helps them speak up."

8.

Back to the cockpit of Avianca 052. The plane is now turning away from Kennedy, after the aborted first attempt at landing. Klotz has just been on the radio with ATC, trying to figure out when they can try to land again. Caviedes turns to him.

> CAVIEDES: What did he say?
>
> KLOTZ: I already advise him that we are going to attempt again because we now we can't..."

Four seconds of silence pass.

> CAVIEDES: Advise him we are in emergency.

Four more seconds of silence pass. The captain tries again.

> CAVIEDES: Did you tell him?
>
> KLOTZ: Yes, sir. I already advise him.

Klotz starts talking to ATC—going over routine details.

Klotz: One-five-zero maintaining two thousand Avianca zero-five-two heavy.

The captain is clearly at the edge of panic.

Caviedes: Advise him we don't have fuel.

Klotz gets back on the radio with ATC.

Klotz: Climb and maintain three thousand and, ah, we're running out of fuel, sir.

There it is again. No mention of the magic word "emergency," which is what air traffic controllers are trained to listen for. Just "running out of fuel, sir" at the end of a sentence, preceded by the mitigating "ah." If you're counting errors, the Avianca crew is now in double digits.

Caviedes: Did you already advise that we don't have fuel?
Klotz: Yes, sir. I already advise him...
Caviedes: Bueno.

If it were not the prelude to a tragedy, their back-and-forth would resemble an Abbott and Costello comedy routine.

A little over a minute passes.

> ATC: And Avianca zero-five-two heavy, ah, I'm gonna bring you about fifteen miles northeast and then turn you back onto the approach. Is that okay with you and your fuel?
>
> KLOTZ: I guess so. Thank you very much.

I guess so. Thank you very much. They are about to crash! One of the flight attendants enters the cockpit to find out how serious the situation is. The flight engineer points to the empty fuel gauge, and makes a throat-cutting gesture with his finger.* But he says nothing. Nor does anyone else for the next five minutes. There's radio chatter and routine business, and then the flight engineer cries out, "Flameout on engine number four!"

* We know this because the flight attendant survived the crash and testified at the inquest.

Caviedes says, "Show me the runway," but the runway is sixteen miles away.

Thirty-six seconds of silence pass. The plane's air traffic controller calls out one last time.

> ATC: You have, ah, you have enough fuel to make it to the airport?

The transcript ends.

9.

"The thing you have to understand about that crash," Ratwatte said, "is that New York air traffic controllers are famous for being rude, aggressive, and bullying. They are also very good. They handle a phenomenal amount of traffic in a very constrained environment. There is a famous story about a pilot who got lost trafficking around JFK. You have no idea how easy that is to do at JFK once you're on the ground. It's a maze. Anyway, a female controller got mad at him, and said, 'Stop. Don't do anything. Do not talk to me until I talk to you.' And she just left him there. Finally the pilot picks up the microphone and says, 'Madam. Was I married to you in a former life?'

"They are unbelievable. The way they look at it, it's 'I'm in control. Shut up and do what I say.' They will snap at you. And if you don't like what they tell you to do, you have to snap back. And then they'll say, 'All right, then.' But if you don't, they'll railroad you. I remember a British Airways flight was going into New York. They were being stuffed around by New York Air Traffic Control. The British pilots said, 'You people should go to Heathrow and learn how to control an airplane.' It's all in the spirit. If you are not used to that sort of give-and-take, New York ATC can be very, very intimidating. And those Avianca guys were just intimidated by the rapid fire."

It is impossible to imagine Ratwatte not making his case to Kennedy ATC — not because he is obnoxious or pushy or has an enormous ego, but because he sees the world differently. If he needed help in the cockpit, he would wake up the second crew. If he thought Moscow was wrong, well, he would just go to Helsinki, and if Helsinki was going to bring him in with the wind, well, he was going to talk them into bringing him in against the wind. That morning, when they were leaving Helsinki, he had lined up the plane on the wrong runway—and his first officer had quickly pointed out the error. The memory made Ratwatte laugh. "Masa is Swiss. He was very happy to correct me. He was giving me shit the whole way back."

Ratwatte continued: "All the guys had to do was tell the controller, 'We don't have the fuel to comply with what you are trying to do.' All they had to do was say, 'We can't do that. We have to land in the next ten minutes.' They weren't able to put that across to the controller."

It was at this point that Ratwatte began to speak carefully, because he was about to make the kind of cultural generalization that often leaves us uncomfortable. But what happened with Avianca was just so strange—so seemingly inexplicable—that it demanded a more complete explanation than simply that Klotz was incompetent and the captain was tired. There was something more profound—more structural—going on in that cockpit. What if there was something about the pilots' being Colombian that led to that crash? "Look, no American pilot would put up with that. That's the thing," Ratwatte said. "They would say, 'Listen, buddy. I have to land.' "

10.

In the 1960s and 1970s, the Dutch psychologist Geert Hofstede was working for the human resources department of IBM's European headquarters. Hofstede's job was to travel the globe and interview employees, asking about such things as how people solved problems and how they worked together and what their attitudes were to authority. The questionnaires were long and involved, and over time Hofstede was able to develop an enormous database for analyzing the ways in which cultures differ from one another. Today "Hofstede's Dimensions" are among the most widely used paradigms in crosscultural psychology.

Hofstede argued, for example, that cultures can be usefully distinguished according to how much they expect individuals to look after themselves. He called that measurement the "individualism-collectivism scale." The country that scores highest on the individualism end of that scale is the United States. Not surprisingly, the United States is also the only industrialized country in the world that does not provide its citizens with universal health care. At the opposite end of the scale is Guatemala.

Another of Hofstede's dimensions is "uncertainty avoidance." How well does a culture tolerate ambiguity? Here are the top five "uncertainty avoidance" countries, according to Hofstede's database—that is, the countries most reliant on rules and plans and most likely to stick to procedure regardless of circumstances:

1. Greece
2. Portugal
3. Guatemala
4. Uruguay
5. Belgium

The bottom five—that is, the cultures best able to tolerate ambiguity—are:

49. Hong Kong
50. Sweden
51. Denmark
52. Jamaica
53. Singapore

It is important to note that Hofstede wasn't suggesting that there was a right place or a wrong place to be on any one of these scales. Nor was he saying that a culture's position on one of his dimensions was an ironclad predictor of how someone from that country behaves: it's not impossible, for example, for someone from Guatemala to be highly individualistic.

What he was saying, instead, was something very similar to what Nisbett and Cohen argued after their hallway studies at the University of Michigan. Each of us has his or her own distinct personality. But overlaid on top of that are tendencies and assumptions and reflexes handed down to us by the history of the community we grew up in, and those differences are extraordinarily specific.

Belgium and Denmark are only an hour or so apart by airplane, for example. Danes look a lot like Belgians, and if you were dropped on a street corner in Copenhagen, you wouldn't find it all that different from a street corner in Brussels. But when it comes to uncertainty avoidance, the two nations could not be further apart. In fact, Danes have more in common with Jamaicans when it comes to tolerating ambiguity than they do with some of their European peers. Denmark and Belgium may share in a kind of broad European liberal-democratic tradition, but they have different histories, different political structures, different religious traditions, and different languages and food and architecture and literature—going back hundreds and hundreds of years. And the sum total of all those differences is that in certain kinds of situations that require dealing with risk and uncertainty, Danes tend to react in a very different way from Belgians.

Of all of Hofstede's Dimensions, though,

perhaps the most interesting is what he called the "Power Distance Index" (PDI). Power distance is concerned with attitudes toward hierarchy, specifically with how much a particular culture values and respects authority. To measure it, Hofstede asked questions like "How frequently, in your experience, does the following problem occur: employees being afraid to express disagreement with their managers?" To what extent do the "less powerful members of organizations and institutions accept and expect that power is distributed unequally?" How much are older people respected and feared? Are power holders entitled to special privileges?

"In low–power distance index countries," Hofstede wrote in his classic text *Culture's Consequences:*

> power is something of which power holders are almost ashamed and they will try to underplay. I once heard a Swedish (low PDI) university official state that in order to exercise power he tried not to look powerful. Leaders may enhance their informal status by renouncing formal symbols. In

> (low PDI) Austria, Prime Minister Bruno Kreisky was known to sometimes take the streetcar to work. In 1974, I actually saw the Dutch (low PDI) prime minister, Joop den Uyl, on vacation with his motor home at a camping site in Portugal. Such behavior of the powerful would be very unlikely in high-PDI Belgium or France.*

You can imagine the effect that Hofstede's findings had on people in the aviation industry. What was their great battle over mitigated

---

* Hofstede, similarly, references a study done a few years ago that compared German and French manufacturing plants that were in the same industry and were roughly the same size. The French plants had, on average, 26 percent of their employees in management and specialist positions; the Germans, 16 percent. The French, furthermore, paid their top management substantially more than the Germans did. What we are seeing in that comparison, Hofstede argued, is a difference in cultural attitudes toward hierarchy. The French have a power distance index twice that of the Germans. They require and support hierarchy in a way the Germans simply don't.

speech and teamwork all about, after all? It was an attempt to reduce power distance in the cockpit. Hofstede's question about power distance—"How frequently, in your experience, does the following problem occur: employees being afraid to express disagreement with their managers?"—was the very question aviation experts were asking first officers in their dealings with captains. And Hofstede's work suggested something that had not occurred to anyone in the aviation world: that the task of convincing first officers to assert themselves was going to depend an awful lot on their culture's power distance rating.

That's what Ratwatte meant when he said that no American would have been so fatally intimidated by the controllers at Kennedy Airport. America is a classic low–power distance culture. When push comes to shove, Americans fall back on their *American-ness,* and that American-ness means that the air traffic controller is thought of as an equal. But what country is at the other end of the power distance scale? Colombia.

In the wake of the Avianca crash, the psychologist Robert Helmreich, who has done more than anyone to argue for the role of culture in explaining pilot behavior, wrote a brilliant analysis of the accident in which he argued that you couldn't understand Klotz's behavior without taking into account his nationality, that his predicament that day was uniquely the predicament of someone who had a deep and abiding respect for authority. Helmreich wrote:

> The high–power distance of Colombians could have created frustration on the part of the first officer because the captain failed to show the kind of clear (if not autocratic) decision making expected in high–power distance cultures. The first and second officers may have been waiting for the captain to make decisions, but still may have been unwilling to pose alternatives.

Klotz sees himself as a subordinate. It's not his job to solve the crisis. It's the captain's—and the captain is exhausted and isn't saying anything. Then there's the domineering

Kennedy Airport air traffic controllers ordering the planes around. Klotz is trying to tell them he's in trouble. But he's using his own cultural language, speaking as a subordinate would to a superior. The controllers, though, aren't Colombian. They're low–power distance New Yorkers. They don't see any hierarchical gap between themselves and the pilots in the air, and to them, mitigated speech from a pilot doesn't mean the speaker is being appropriately deferential to a superior. *It means the pilot doesn't have a problem.*

There is a point in the transcript where the cultural miscommunication between the controllers and Klotz becomes so evident that it is almost painful to read. It's the last exchange between Avianca and the control tower, just minutes before the crash. Klotz has just said, "I guess so. Thank you very much" in response to the controller's question about their fuel state. Captain Caviedes then turns to Klotz.

CAVIEDES: What did he say?
KLOTZ: The guy is angry.

Angry! Klotz's feelings are hurt! His plane is moments from disaster. But he cannot escape the dynamic dictated to him by his culture in which subordinates must respect the dictates of their superiors. In his mind, he has tried and failed to communicate his plight, and his only conclusion is that he must have somehow offended his superiors in the control tower.

In the aftermath of the Kennedy crash, the management of Avianca airlines held a postmortem. Avianca had just had four accidents in quick succession—Barranquilla, Cucuta, Madrid, and New York—and all four cases, the airline concluded, "had to do with airplanes in perfect flight condition, aircrew without physical limitations and considered of average or above-average flight ability, and *still* the accidents happened." (italics mine)

In the company's Madrid crash, the report went on, the copilot tried to warn the captain about how dangerous the situation was:

> The copilot was right. But they died because... when the copilot asked questions, his implied

> suggestions were very weak. The captain's reply was to ignore him totally. Perhaps the copilot did not want to appear rebellious, questioning the judgment of the captain, or he did not want to play the fool because he knew that the pilot had a great deal of experience flying in that area. The copilot should have advocated for his own opinions in a stronger way...

Our ability to succeed at what we do is powerfully bound up with where we're from, and being a good pilot and coming from a high–power distance culture is a difficult mix. Colombia by no means has the highest PDI, by the way. Helmreich and a colleague, Ashleigh Merritt, once measured the PDI of pilots from around the world. Number one was Brazil. Number two was South Korea.*

---

* Here are the top five pilot PDIs by country. If you compare list to the ranking of plane crashes by country, they match up very nicely.

1. Brazil
2. South Korea

11.

The National Transportation Safety Board, the US agency responsible for investigating plane crashes, is headquartered in a squat, seventies-era office building on the banks of the Potomac River in Washington, DC. Off the agency's long hallways are laboratories filled with airplane wreckage: a mangled piece of an engine turbine, a problematic piece of a helicopter rotor. On a shelf in one of the laboratories is the cockpit voice and data recorder—the so-called black box—from the devastating ValuJet crash in Florida in 1996, in which 110 people

---

3. Morocco
4. Mexico
5. Philippines

The five lowest pilot PDIs by country are:

15. United States
16. Ireland
17. South Africa
18. Australia
19. New Zealand

were killed. The recorder is encased in a shoe box–size housing made out of thick hardened steel, and on one end of the box is a jagged hole, as if someone—or, rather, something—had driven a stake into it with tremendous force. Some of the NTSB investigators are engineers, who reconstruct crashes from the material evidence. Others are pilots. A surprising number of them, however, are psychologists, whose job it is to listen to the cockpit recorder and reconstruct what was said and done by the flight crew in the final minutes before a crash. One of the NTSB's leading black-box specialists is a gangly fiftyish PhD psychologist named Malcolm Brenner, and Brenner was one of the investigators into the Korean Air crash in Guam.

"Normally that approach into Guam is not difficult," Brenner began. Guam airport has what is called a glide scope, which is like a giant beam of light stretching up into the sky from the airport, and the pilot simply follows the beam all the way down to the runway. But on this particular night, the glide scope was down. "It was out of service," Brenner said. "It had been sent to another island to be repaired. So there was a notice to airmen that the glide scope was not operating."

In the grand scheme of things, this should not have been a big problem. In the month the glide scope had been under repair, there had been about fifteen hundred safe landings at Guam airport. It was just a small thing—an inconvenience, really—that made the task of landing a plane just a little bit more difficult.

"The second complication was the weather," Brenner continued. "Normally in the South Pacific, you've got these brief weather situations. But they go by quickly. You don't have storms. It's a tropical paradise. But that night, there were some little cells, and it just happens that that evening, they were going to be flying into one of those little cells, a few miles from the airport. So the captain has to decide, What exactly is my procedure for landing? Well, they were cleared for what's called a VOR/DME approach. It's complicated. It's a pain in the ass. It takes a lot of coordination to set it up. You have to come down in steps. But then, as it happens, from miles out, the captain sees the lights of Guam. So he relaxes. And he says, 'We're doing a visual approach.' "

The VOR is a beacon that sends out a signal that allows pilots to calculate their altitude as they approach an airport. It's what pilots relied on before the invention of the glide scope. The captain's strategy was to use the VOR to get the plane close and then, once he could see the lights of the runway, to land the plane visually. It seemed to make sense. Pilots do visual landings all the time. But every time a pilot chooses a plan, he is supposed to prepare a backup in case things go awry. And this captain didn't.

"They should have been coordinating. He should have been briefing for the [DME] step-downs," Brenner went on. "But he doesn't talk about that. The storm cells are all around them, and what the captain seems to be doing is assuming that at some point he's going to break out of the clouds and see the airport, and if he doesn't see it by five hundred sixty feet, he'll just go around. Now, that would work, except for one more thing. The VOR on which he's basing this strategy is not at the airport. It's two-point-five miles away on Nimitz Hill. There's a number of airports in the world where this is true. Sometimes you can follow the VOR down and it takes you straight to the airport. Here if you follow the VOR down, it takes you straight to Nimitz Hill."

The pilot knew about the VOR. It was clearly stated in the airport's navigational charts. He'd flown into Guam eight times before, and in fact, he had specifically mentioned it in the briefing he gave before takeoff. But then again, it was one in the morning, and he'd been up since six a.m. the previous day.

"We believe that fatigue was involved," Brenner went on. "It's a back-of-the-clock flight. You fly in and arrive at one in the morning, Korean time. Then you spend a few hours on the ground, and you fly back as the sun is coming up. The captain has flown it a month before. In that case, he slept on the first-class seat. Now he's flying in and says he's really tired."

So there they are, three classic preconditions of a plane crash, the same three that set the stage for Avianca 052: a minor technical malfunction;

bad weather; and a tired pilot. By itself, none of these would be sufficient for an accident. But all three in combination require the combined efforts of everyone in the cockpit. And that's where Korean Air 801 ran into trouble.

12.

Here is the flight recorder transcript of the final thirty minutes of KAL flight 801: It begins with the captain complaining of exhaustion.

> 0120:01. Captain: If this round-trip is more than a nine-hour trip, we might get a little something. With eight hours, we get nothing. Eight hours do not help us at all.... They make us work to maximum, up to maximum. Probably this way... hotel expenses will be saved for cabin crews, and maximize the flight hours. Anyway, they make us... work to maximum.

There is the sound of a man shifting in his seat. A minute passes.

0121:13. Captain: Eh . . . really . . . sleepy. [unintelligible words]
FIRST OFFICER: Of course.

Then comes one of the most critical moments in the flight. The first officer decides to speak up:

FIRST OFFICER: Don't you think it rains more? In this area, here?

The first officer must have thought long and hard before making that comment. He was not flying in the easy collegiality of Suren Ratwatte's cockpit. Among Korean Air flight crews, the expectation on layovers used to be that the junior officers would attend to the captain to the point of making him dinner or purchasing him gifts. As one former Korean Air pilot puts it, the sensibility in many of the airline's cockpits was that "the captain is in charge and does what he wants, when he likes, how he likes, and everyone else sits quietly and does nothing." In the Delta report on Korean Air that was posted anonymously on the Internet, one of the auditors tells a story of sitting in on a Korean Air flight where the first officer got confused while listening to Air Traffic Control and mistakenly put the plane on a course intended for another plane. "The Flight Engineer picked up something was wrong but said nothing. First Officer was also not happy but said nothing. . . . Despite [good] visual conditions, crew did not look out and see that current heading would not bring them to the airfield." Finally the plane's radar picks up the mistake, and then comes the key sentence: "Captain hit First Officer with the back of his hand for making the error."

Hit him with the back of his hand?

When the three pilots all met that evening at Kimpo for their preflight preparation, the first officer and the engineer would have bowed to the captain. They would all have then shaken hands. *"Cheo eom boeb seom ni da,"* the copilot might have said, respectfully. "It is first time to meet you." The Korean language has no fewer than six different levels of conversational address, depending on the relationship between the addressee and the addresser: formal deference, informal deference, blunt, familiar, intimate, and plain. The first officer would not have dared to use one of the more intimate or familiar forms when he addressed the captain. This is a culture in which enormous attention is paid to the relative standing of any two people in a conversation.

The Korean linguist Ho-min Sohn writes:

> At a dinner table, a lower-ranking person must wait until a higher-ranking person sits down and starts eating, while the reverse does not hold true; one does not smoke in the presence of a social superior; when drinking with a social superior, the subordinate hides his glass and turns away from the superior;...in greeting a social superior (though not an inferior) a Korean must bow; a Korean must rise when an obvious social superior appears on the scene, and he cannot pass in front of an obvious social superior. All social behavior and actions are conducted in the order of seniority or ranking; as the saying goes, *chanmul to wi alay ka issta,* there is order even to drinking cold water.

So, when the first officer says, "Don't you think it rains more? In this area, here?" we know what he means by that: *Captain. You have committed us to visual approach, with no backup plan, and the weather outside is terrible. You think that we will break out of the clouds in time to see the runway. But what if we don't? It's pitch-black outside and pouring rain and the glide scope is down.*

But he can't say that. He hints, and in his mind he's said as much as he can to a superior. The first officer will not mention the weather again.

It is just after that moment that the plane, briefly, breaks out of the clouds, and off in the distance the pilots see lights.

"Is it Guam?" the flight engineer asks. Then, after a pause, he says, "It's Guam, Guam."

The captain chuckles. "Good!"

But it isn't good. It's an illusion. They've come out of the clouds for a moment. But they are still twenty miles from the airport, and there is an enormous amount of bad weather still ahead of them. The flight engineer knows this, because it is his responsibility to track the weather, so now he decides to speak up.

"Captain, the weather radar has helped us a lot," he says.

The weather radar has helped us a lot? A second hint from the flight deck. What the engineer means is just what the first officer meant. *This isn't a night where you can rely on just your eyes to land the plane. Look at what the weather radar is telling us: there's trouble ahead.*

To Western ears, it seems strange that the flight engineer would bring up this subject just once. Western communication has what linguists call a "transmitter orientation"—that is, it is considered the responsibility of the speaker to communicate ideas clearly and unambiguously. Even in the tragic case of the Air Florida crash, where the first officer never does more than hint about the danger posed by the ice, he still hints *four* times, phrasing his comments four different ways, in an attempt to make his meaning clear. He may have been constrained by the power distance between himself and the captain, but he was still operating within a Western cultural context, which holds that if there is confusion, it is the fault of the speaker.

But Korea, like many Asian countries, is receiver oriented. It is up to the *listener* to make sense of what is being said. In the engineer's mind, he has said a lot.

Sohn gives the following conversation as an illustration, an exchange between an employee (Mr. Kim) and his boss, a division chief *(kwacang)*.

> KWACANG: It's cold and I'm kind of hungry.
> [MEANING: Why don't you buy a drink or something to eat?]
> MR. KIM: How about having a glass of liquor?
> [MEANING: I will buy liquor for you.]
> KWACANG: It's okay. Don't bother.
> [MEANING: I will accept your offer if you repeat it.]
> MR. KIM: You must be hungry. How about going out?
> [MEANING: I insist upon treating you.]
> KWACANG: Shall I do so?
> [MEANING: I accept.]

There is something beautiful in the subtlety of that exchange, in the attention that each party must pay to the motivations and desires of the other. It is civilized, in the truest sense of that word: it does not permit insensitivity or indifference.

But high–power distance communication works only when the listener is capable of paying close attention, and it works only if the two parties in a conversation have the luxury of time, in order to unwind each other's meanings. It doesn't work in an airplane cockpit on a stormy night with an exhausted pilot trying to land at an airport with a broken glide scope.

13.

In 2000, Korean Air finally acted, bringing in an outsider from Delta Air Lines, David Greenberg, to run their flight operations.

Greenberg's first step was something that would make no sense if you did not understand the true roots of Korean Air's problems. He evaluated the English language skills of all of the airline's flight crews. "Some of them were fine and some of them weren't," he remembers. "So we set up a program to assist and improve the proficiency of aviation English." His second step was to bring in a Western firm — a subsidiary of Boeing called Alteon — to take over the company's training and instruction programs. "Alteon conducted their training in English," Greenberg says. "They didn't speak Korean." Greenberg's rule was simple. The new language of Korean Air was English, and if you wanted to remain a pilot at the company, you had to be fluent in that language. "This was not a purge," he says. "Everyone had the same opportunity, and those who found the language issue challenging were allowed to go out and study on their own nickel. But language was the filter. I can't recall that anyone was fired for flying proficiency shortcomings."

Greenberg's rationale was that English was the language of the aviation world. When the pilots sat in the cockpit and worked their way through the written checklists that flight crews follow on every significant point of procedure, those checklists were in English. When they talked to Air Traffic Control anywhere in the world, those conversations would be in English.

"If you are trying to land at JFK at rush hour, there is no nonverbal communication," Greenberg says. "It's people talking to people, so you need to be darn sure you understand what's going on. You can say that two Koreans side by side don't need to speak English. But if they are arguing about what the guys outside said in English, then language is important."

Greenberg wanted to give his pilots an alternate identity. Their problem was that they were trapped in roles dictated by the heavy weight of their country's cultural legacy. They needed an opportunity to step outside those roles when they sat in the cockpit, and language was the key to that transformation. In English, they would be free of the sharply defined gradients of Korean hierarchy: formal deference, informal deference, blunt, familiar, intimate, and plain. Instead, the pilots could participate in a culture and language with a very different legacy.

The crucial part of Greenberg's reform, however, is what he didn't do. He didn't throw up his hands in despair. He didn't fire all of his Korean pilots and start again with pilots from a low–power distance culture. He knew that cultural legacies matter—that they are powerful and pervasive and that they persist, long after their original usefulness has passed. But he didn't assume that legacies are an indelible part of who we are. He believed that if the Koreans were honest about where they came from and were willing to confront those aspects of their heritage that did not suit the aviation world, they could change. He offered his pilots what everyone from hockey players to software tycoons to takeover lawyers has been offered on the way to success: an opportunity to transform their relationship to their work.

After leaving Korean Air, Greenberg helped start up a freight airline called Cargo 360, and he took a number of Korean pilots with him. They were all flight engineers, who had been number three, after the captain and first officer, in the strict hierarchy of the original Korean

Air. "These were guys who had performed in the old environment at Korean Air for as much as fifteen to eighteen years," he said. "They had accepted that subservient role. They had been at the bottom of the ladder. We retrained them and put them with Western crew. They've been a great success. They all changed their style. They take initiative. They pull their share of the load. They don't wait for someone to direct them. These are senior people, in their fifties, with a long history in one context, who have been retrained and are now successful doing their job in a Western cockpit. We took them out of their culture and re-normed them."

That is an extraordinarily liberating example. When we understand what it really means to be a good pilot—when we understand how much culture and history and the world outside of the individual matter to professional success—then we don't have to throw up our hands in despair at an airline where pilots crash planes into the sides of mountains. We have a way to make successes out of the unsuccessful.

But first we have to be frank about a subject

that we would all too often rather ignore. In 1994, when Boeing first published safety data showing a clear correlation between a country's plane crashes and its score on Hofstede's Dimensions, the company's researchers practically tied themselves in knots trying not to cause offense. "We're not saying there's anything here, but we think there's something there" is how Boeing's chief engineer for airplane safety put it. Why are we so squeamish? Why is the fact that each of us comes from a culture with its own distinctive mix of strengths and weaknesses, tendencies and predispositions, so difficult to acknowledge? Who we are cannot be separated from where we're from—and when we ignore that fact, planes crash.

14.

Back to the cockpit.

"Captain, the weather radar has helped us a lot." No pilot would say that now. But this was in 1997, before Korean Air took its power distance issues seriously. The captain was tired,

and the engineer's true meaning sailed over the captain's head.

"Yes," the captain says in response. "They are very useful." He isn't listening.

The plane is flying toward the VOR beacon and the VOR is on the side of a mountain. The weather hasn't broken. So the pilots can't see anything. The captain puts the landing gear down and extends the flaps.

At 1:41:48, the captain says, "Wiper on," and the flight engineer turns the wipers on. It's raining now.

At 1:41:59, the first officer asks, "Not in sight?" He's looking for the runway. He can't see it. He's had a sinking feeling in his stomach for some time now. One second later, the Ground Proximity Warning System calls out in its toneless electronic voice, "Five hundred [feet]." The plane is five hundred feet off the ground. The ground in this case is the side of Nimitz Hill. But the crew is confused because they think that the ground means the runway, and how can that be if they can't see the runway? The flight engineer says, "Eh?" in an astonished tone of voice. You can imagine them all thinking furiously, trying to square their assumption of where the plane is with what their instruments are telling them.

At 1:42:19, the first officer says, "Let's make a missed approach." He has finally upgraded from a hint to a crew obligation: he wants to abort the landing. Later, in the crash investigation, it was determined that if he had seized control of the plane in that moment, there would have been enough time to pull up the nose and clear Nimitz Hill. That is what first officers are trained to do when they believe a captain is clearly in the wrong. But it is one thing to learn that in a classroom, and quite another to actually do it in the air, with someone who might rap you with the back of his hand if you make a mistake.

1:42:20. FLIGHT ENGINEER: Not in sight.

With disaster staring them in the face, both the first officer and the engineer have finally spoken up. They want the captain to go around, to pull up and start the landing over again. But it's too late.

1:42:21. First Officer: Not in sight, missed approach.

1:42:22. Flight Engineer: Go around.

1:42:23. Captain: Go around.

1:42:24:05. Ground Proximity Warning System (GPWS): One hundred.

1:42:24:84. GPWS: Fifty.

1:42:25:19. GPWS: Forty.

1:42:25:50. GPWS: Thirty.

1:42:25:78. GPWS: Twenty.

1:42:25:78. [sound of initial impact]

1:42:28:65. [sound of tone]

1:42:28:91. [sound of groans]

1:42:30:54. [sound of tone]

END OF RECORDING

CHAPTER EIGHT

Rice Paddies and Math Tests

"NO ONE WHO CAN RISE BEFORE DAWN THREE HUNDRED SIXTY DAYS A YEAR FAILS TO MAKE HIS FAMILY RICH."

1.

The gateway to the industrial heartland of Southern China runs up through the wide, verdant swath of the Pearl River Delta. The land is covered by a thick, smoggy haze. The freeways are crammed with tractor trailers. Power lines crisscross the landscape. Factories making cameras, computers, watches, umbrellas, and T-shirts stand cheek by jowl with densely packed blocks of apartment buildings and fields of banana and mango trees, sugarcane, papaya, and pineapple destined for the export market. Few landscapes in the world have changed so much in so short a time. A generation ago, the skies would have been clear and the road would have been a two-lane highway. And a generation before that, all you would have seen were rice paddies.

Two hours in, at the headwaters of the Pearl River, lies the city of Guangzhou, and past Guangzhou, remnants of the old China are easier to find. The countryside becomes breathtakingly beautiful, rolling hills dotted with outcroppings of limestone rock against the backdrop of the Nan Ling Mountains. Here and there are the traditional khaki-colored mud-brick huts of the Chinese peasantry. In the small towns, there are open-air markets: chickens and geese in elaborate bamboo baskets, vegetables laid out in rows on the ground, slabs of pork on tables, tobacco being sold in big clumps. And everywhere, there is rice, miles upon miles of it. In the winter season, the paddies are dry and dotted with the stubble of the previous year's crop.

After the crops are planted in early spring, as the humid winds begin to blow, they turn a magical green, and by the time of the first harvest, as the grains emerge on the ends of the rice shoots, the land becomes an unending sea of yellow.

Rice has been cultivated in China for thousands of years. It was from China that the techniques of rice cultivation spread throughout East Asia—Japan, Korea, Singapore, and Taiwan. Year in, year out, as far back as history is recorded, farmers from across Asia have engaged in the same relentless, intricate pattern of agriculture.

Rice paddies are "built," not "opened up" the way a wheat field is. You don't just clear the trees, underbrush, and stones and then plow. Rice fields are carved into mountainsides in an elaborate series of terraces, or painstakingly constructed from marshland and river plains. A rice paddy has to be irrigated, so a complex system of dikes has to be built around the field. Channels must be dug from the nearest water source, and gates built into the dikes so the water flow can be adjusted precisely to cover the right amount of the plant.

The paddy itself, meanwhile, has to have a hard clay floor; otherwise the water will simply seep into the ground. But of course, rice seedlings can't be planted in hard clay, so on top of the clay, there has to be a thick, soft layer of mud. And the claypan, as it's called, has to be carefully engineered so that it will drain properly and also keep the plants submerged at the optimum level. Rice has to be fertilized repeatedly, which is another art. Traditionally, farmers used "night soil" (human manure) and a combination of burned compost, river mud, bean cake, and hemp—and they had to be careful, because too much fertilizer, or the right amount applied at the wrong time, could be as bad as too little.

When the time came to plant, a Chinese farmer would have hundreds of different varieties of rice from which to choose, each one of which offered a slightly different trade-off, say, between yield and how quickly it grew, or how well it did in times of drought, or how it fared in poor soil. A farmer might plant a dozen or more different varieties at one time, adjusting the mix from season to season in order to manage the risk of a crop failure.

He or she (or, more accurately, the whole family, since rice agriculture was a family affair) would plant the seed in a specially prepared seedbed. After a few weeks, the seedlings would be transplanted into the field, in carefully spaced rows six inches apart, and then painstakingly nurtured.

Weeding was done by hand, diligently and unceasingly, because the seedlings could easily be choked by other plant life. Sometimes each rice shoot would be individually groomed with a bamboo comb to clear away insects. All the while, farmers had to check and recheck water levels and make sure the water didn't get too hot in the summer sun. And when the rice ripened, farmers gathered all of their friends and relatives and, in one coordinated burst, harvested it as quickly as possible so they could get a second crop in before the winter dry season began.

Breakfast in South China, at least for those who could afford it, was congee—white rice porridge with lettuce and dace paste and bamboo shoots. Lunch was more congee. Dinner was rice with "toppings." Rice was what you sold at the market to buy the other necessities of life. It was how wealth and status were measured. It dictated almost every working moment of every day. "Rice is life," says the anthropologist Gonçalo Santos, who has studied a traditional South Chinese village. "Without rice, you don't survive. If you want to be anyone in this part of China, you would have to have rice. It made the world go around."

2.

Take a look at the following list of numbers: 4, 8, 5, 3, 9, 7, 6. Read them out loud. Now look away and spend twenty seconds memorizing that sequence before saying them out loud again.

If you speak English, you have about a 50 percent chance of remembering that sequence perfectly. If you're Chinese, though, you're almost certain to get it right every time. Why is that? Because as human beings we store digits in a memory loop that runs for about two seconds. We most easily memorize whatever we can say or read within that two-second span. And Chinese speakers get that list of numbers—4, 8, 5, 3, 9, 7, 6—right almost every time because, unlike English, their language allows them to fit all those seven numbers into two seconds.

That example comes from Stanislas Dehaene's book *The Number Sense.* As Dehaene explains:

> Chinese number words are remarkably brief. Most of them can be uttered in less than one-quarter of a second (for instance, 4 is "si" and 7 "qi"). Their English equivalents—"four," "seven"—are longer: pronouncing them takes about one-third of a second. The memory gap between English and Chinese apparently is entirely due to this difference in length. In languages as diverse as Welsh, Arabic, Chinese, English and Hebrew, there is a reproducible correlation between the time required to pronounce numbers in a given language and the memory span of its speakers. In this domain, the prize for efficacy goes to the Cantonese dia-

lect of Chinese, whose brevity grants residents of Hong Kong a rocketing memory span of about 10 digits.

It turns out that there is also a big difference in how number-naming systems in Western and Asian languages are constructed. In English, we say fourteen, sixteen, seventeen, eighteen, and nineteen, so one might expect that we would also say oneteen, twoteen, threeteen, and fiveteen. But we don't. We use a different form: eleven, twelve, thirteen, and fifteen. Similarly, we have forty and sixty, which sound like the words they are related to (four and six). But we also say fifty and thirty and twenty, which sort of sound like five and three and two, but not really. And, for that matter, for numbers above twenty, we put the "decade" first and the unit number second (twenty-one, twenty-two), whereas for the teens, we do it the other way around (fourteen, seventeen, eighteen). The number system in English is highly irregular. Not so in China, Japan, and Korea. They have a logical counting system. Eleven is ten-one.

Twelve is ten-two. Twenty-four is two-tens-four and so on.

That difference means that Asian children learn to count much faster than American children. Four-year-old Chinese children can count, on average, to forty. American children at that age can count only to fifteen, and most don't reach forty until they're five. By the age of five, in other words, American children are already a *year* behind their Asian counterparts in the most fundamental of math skills.

The regularity of their number system also means that Asian children can perform basic functions, such as addition, far more easily. Ask an English-speaking seven-year-old to add thirty-seven plus twenty-two in her head, and she has to convert the words to numbers (37 + 22). Only then can she do the math: 2 plus 7 is 9 and 30 and 20 is 50, which makes 59. Ask an Asian child to add three-tens-seven and two-tens-two, and then the necessary equation is right there, embedded in the sentence. No number translation is necessary: It's five-tens-nine.

"The Asian system is transparent," says

Karen Fuson, a Northwestern University psychologist who has closely studied Asian-Western differences. "I think that it makes the whole attitude toward math different. Instead of being a rote learning thing, there's a pattern I can figure out. There is an expectation that I can do this. There is an expectation that it's sensible. For fractions, we say three-fifths. The Chinese is literally 'out of five parts, take three.' That's telling you conceptually what a fraction is. It's differentiating the denominator and the numerator."

The much-storied disenchantment with mathematics among Western children starts in the third and fourth grades, and Fuson argues that perhaps a part of that disenchantment is due to the fact that math doesn't seem to make sense; its linguistic structure is clumsy; its basic rules seem arbitrary and complicated.

Asian children, by contrast, don't feel nearly that same bafflement. They can hold more numbers in their heads and do calculations faster, and the way fractions are expressed in their languages corresponds exactly to the way a fraction actually is—and maybe that makes them a little more likely to enjoy math, and maybe because they enjoy math a little more, they try a little harder and take more math classes and are more willing to do their homework, and on and on, in a kind of virtuous circle.

When it comes to math, in other words, Asians have a built-in advantage. But it's an unusual kind of advantage. For years, students from China, South Korea, and Japan—and the children of recent immigrants who are from those countries—have substantially outperformed their Western counterparts at mathematics, and the typical assumption is that it has something to do with a kind of innate Asian proclivity for math.* The psychologist Richard Lynn

* On international comparison tests, students from Japan, South Korea, Hong Kong, Singapore, and Taiwan all score roughly the same in math, around the ninety-eighth percentile. The United States, France, England, Germany, and the other Western industrialized nations cluster at somewhere between the twenty-six and thirty-sixth percentile. That's a big difference.

has even gone so far as to propose an elaborate evolutionary theory involving the Himalayas, really cold weather, premodern hunting practices, brain size, and specialized vowel sounds to explain why Asians have higher IQs.* That's how we think about math. We assume that being good at things like calculus and algebra is a simple function of how smart someone is. But the differences between the number systems in the East and the West suggest something very different—that being good at math may also be rooted in a group's *culture*.

In the case of the Koreans, one kind of

---

* Lynn's claim that Asians have higher IQs has been refuted, convincingly, by a number of other experts, who showed that he based his argument on IQ samples drawn disproportionately from urban, upper-income homes. James Flynn, perhaps the world's leading expert on IQ, has subsequently made a fascinating counterclaim. Asians' IQs, he says, have historically been slightly *lower* than whites' IQs, meaning that their dominance in math has been in spite of their IQ, not because of it. Flynn's argument was outlined in his book *Asian Americans: Achievement Beyond IQ* (1991).

deeply rooted legacy stood in the way of the very modern task of flying an airplane. Here we have another kind of legacy, one that turns out to be perfectly suited for twenty-first-century tasks. Cultural legacies *matter*, and once we've seen the surprising effects of such things as power distance and numbers that can be said in a quarter as opposed to a third of a second, it's hard not to wonder how many other cultural legacies have an impact on our twenty-first-century intellectual tasks. What if coming from a culture shaped by the demands of growing rice also makes you better at math? Could the rice paddy make a difference in the classroom?

3.

The most striking fact about a rice paddy—which can never quite be grasped until you actually stand in the middle of one—is its size. It's *tiny*. The typical rice paddy is about as big as a hotel room. A typical Asian rice farm might be composed of two or three paddies. A village in

China of fifteen hundred people might support itself entirely with 450 acres of land, which in the American Midwest would be the size of a typical family farm. At that scale, with families of five and six people living off a farm the size of two hotel rooms, agriculture changes dramatically.

Historically, Western agriculture is "mechanically" oriented. In the West, if a farmer wanted to become more efficient or increase his yield, he introduced more and more sophisticated equipment, which allowed him to replace human labor with mechanical labor: a threshing machine, a hay baler, a combine harvester, a tractor. He cleared another field and increased his acreage, because now his machinery allowed him to work more land with the same amount of effort. But in Japan or China, farmers didn't have the money to buy equipment—and, in any case, there certainly wasn't any extra land that could easily be converted into new fields. So rice farmers improved their yields by becoming smarter, by being better managers of their own time, and by making better choices. As the anthropologist Francesca Bray puts it, rice agriculture is "skill oriented": if you're willing to weed a bit more diligently, and become more adept at fertilizing, and spend a bit more time monitoring water levels, and do a better job keeping the claypan absolutely level, and make use of every square inch of your rice paddy, you'll harvest a bigger crop. Throughout history, not surprisingly, the people who grow rice have always worked harder than almost any other kind of farmer.

That last statement may seem a little odd, because most of us have a sense that everyone in the premodern world worked really hard. But that simply isn't true. All of us, for example, are descended at some point from hunter-gatherers, and many hunter-gatherers, by all accounts, had a pretty leisurely life. The !Kung bushmen of the Kalahari Desert, in Botswana, who are one of the last remaining practitioners of that way of life, subsist on a rich assortment of fruits, berries, roots, and nuts—in particular the mongongo nut, an incredibly plentiful and protein-rich source of food that lies thick on the ground. They don't grow anything, and it is growing things—preparing, planting, weeding, harvesting, storing—that takes time. Nor do they raise any animals. Occasionally, the male !Kung hunt, but chiefly for sport. All told, !Kung men and women work no more than about twelve to nineteen hours a week, with the balance of the time spent dancing, entertaining, and visiting family and friends. That's, at most, one thousand hours of work a year. (When a bushman was asked once why his people hadn't taken to agriculture, he looked puzzled and said, "Why should we plant, when there are so many mongongo nuts in the world?")

Or consider the life of a peasant in eighteenth-century Europe. Men and women in those days probably worked from dawn to noon two hundred days a year, which works out to about twelve hundred hours of work annually. During harvest or spring planting, the day might be longer. In the winter, much less. In *The Discovery of France,* the historian Graham Robb argues that peasant life in a country like France, even well into the nineteenth century, was essentially brief episodes of work followed by long periods of idleness.

"Ninety-nine percent of all human activity described in this and other accounts [of French country life]," he writes, "took place between late spring and early autumn." In the Pyrenees and the Alps, entire villages would essentially hibernate from the time of the first snow in November until March or April. In more temperate regions of France, where temperatures in the winter rarely fell below freezing, the same pattern held. Robb continues:

> The fields of Flanders were deserted for much of the year. An official report on the Nièvre in 1844 described the strange mutation of the Burgundian day-laborer once the harvest was in and the vine stocks had been burned: "After making the necessary repairs to their tools, these vigorous men will now spend their days in bed, packing their bodies tightly together in order to stay warm and eat less food. They weaken themselves deliberately."
>
> Human hibernation was a physical and economic necessity. Lowering the metabolic rate pre-

> vented hunger from exhausting supplies.... People trudged and dawdled, even in summer.... After the revolution, in Alsace and the Pas-de-Calais, officials complained that wine growers and independent farmers, instead of undertaking "some peaceful and sedentary industry" in the quieter season, "abandon themselves to dumb idleness."

If you were a peasant farmer in Southern China, by contrast, you didn't sleep through the winter. In the short break marked by the dry season, from November through February, you busied yourself with side tasks. You made bamboo baskets or hats and sold them in the market. You repaired the dikes in your rice paddy, and rebuilt your mud hut. You sent one of your sons to work in a nearby village for a relative. You made tofu and dried bean curd and caught snakes (they were a delicacy) and trapped insects. By the time *lahp cheun* (the "turning of the spring") came, you were back in the fields at dawn. Working in a rice field is ten to twenty times more labor-intensive than working on an equivalent-size corn or wheat field. Some estimates put the annual workload of a wet-rice farmer in Asia at *three thousand* hours a year.

4.

Think, for a moment, about what the life of a rice farmer in the Pearl River Delta must have been like. Three thousand hours a year is a staggering amount of time to spend working, particularly if many of those hours involve being bent over in the hot sun, planting and weeding in a rice paddy.

What redeemed the life of a rice farmer, however, was the nature of that work. It was a lot like the garment work done by the Jewish immigrants to New York. It was *meaningful.* First of all, there is a clear relationship in rice farming between effort and reward. The harder you work a rice field, the more it yields. Second, it's complex work. The rice farmer isn't simply planting in the spring and harvesting in the fall. He or she effectively runs a small business, juggling a family workforce, hedging uncertainty through seed selection, building and managing a sophisticated irrigation system, and coordinating the complicated process of harvesting the first crop while simultaneously preparing the second crop.

And, most of all, it's autonomous. The peasants of Europe worked essentially as low-paid slaves of an aristocratic landlord, with little control over their own destinies. But China and Japan never developed that kind of oppressive feudal system, because feudalism simply can't work in a rice economy. Growing rice is too complicated and intricate for a system that requires farmers to be coerced and bullied into going out into the fields each morning. By the fourteenth and fifteenth centuries, landlords in central and Southern China had an almost completely hands-off relationship with their tenants: they would collect a fixed rent and let farmers go about their business.

"The thing about wet-rice farming is, not only do you need phenomenal amounts of labor, but it's very exacting," says the historian Kenneth Pomerantz. "You have to care. It really matters that the field is perfectly leveled before you flood it. Getting it close to level but not quite right makes a big difference in terms of your yield. It really matters that the water is in the fields for just the right amount of time. There's a big difference between lining up the seedlings at exactly the right distance and doing it sloppily. It's not like you put the corn in the ground in mid-March and as long as rain comes by the end of the month, you're okay. You're controlling all the inputs in a very direct way. And when you have something that requires that much care, the overlord has to have a system that gives the actual laborer some set of incentives, where if the harvest comes out well, the farmer gets a bigger share. That's why you get fixed rents, where the landlord says, I get twenty bushels, regardless of the harvest, and if it's really good, you get the extra. It's a crop that doesn't do very well with something like slavery or wage labor. It would just be too easy to leave the gate that controls the irrigation water open a few seconds too long and there goes your field."

The historian David Arkush once compared

Russian and Chinese peasant proverbs, and the differences are striking. "If God does not bring it, the earth will not give it" is a typical Russian proverb. That's the kind of fatalism and pessimism typical of a repressive feudal system, where peasants have no reason to believe in the efficacy of their own work. On the other hand, Arkush writes, Chinese proverbs are striking in their belief that "hard work, shrewd planning and self-reliance or cooperation with a small group will in time bring recompense."

Here are some of the things that penniless peasants would say to one another as they worked three thousand hours a year in the baking heat and humidity of Chinese rice paddies (which, by the way, are filled with leeches):

> "No food without blood and sweat."
>
> "Farmers are busy; farmers are busy; if farmers weren't busy, where would grain to get through the winter come from?"
>
> "In winter, the lazy man freezes to death."
>
> "Don't depend on heaven for food, but on your own two hands carrying the load."

"Useless to ask about the crops, it all depends on hard work and fertilizer."

"If a man works hard, the land will not be lazy."

And, most telling of all: "No one who can rise before dawn three hundred sixty days a year fails to make his family rich." *Rise before dawn? 360 days a year?* For the !Kung leisurely gathering mongongo nuts, or the French peasant sleeping away the winter, or anyone else living in something other than the world of rice cultivation, that proverb would be unthinkable.

This is not, of course, an unfamiliar observation about Asian culture. Go to any Western college campus and you'll find that Asian students have a reputation for being in the library long after everyone else has left. Sometimes people of Asian background get offended when their culture is described this way, because they think that the stereotype is being used as a form of disparagement. But a belief in work ought to be a thing of beauty. Virtually every success story we've seen in this book so far involves someone or some group working harder than their peers. Bill Gates was addicted to his computer as a child. So was Bill Joy. The Beatles put in thousands of hours of practice in Hamburg. Joe Flom ground away for years, perfecting the art of takeovers, before he got his chance. Working really hard is what successful people do, and the genius of the culture formed in the rice paddies is that hard work gave those in the fields a way to find meaning in the midst of great uncertainty and poverty. That lesson has served Asians well in many endeavors but rarely so perfectly as in the case of mathematics.

5.

A few years ago, Alan Schoenfeld, a math professor at Berkeley, made a videotape of a woman named Renee as she was trying to solve a math problem. Renee was in her mid-twenties, with long black hair and round silver glasses. In the tape, she's playing with a software program designed to teach algebra. On the screen are a *y* and an *x* axis. The program asks the user to punch in a set of coordinates and then draws the line from those coordinates on the screen. For example, when she typed in 5 on the *y* axis and 5 on the *x* axis, the computer did this:

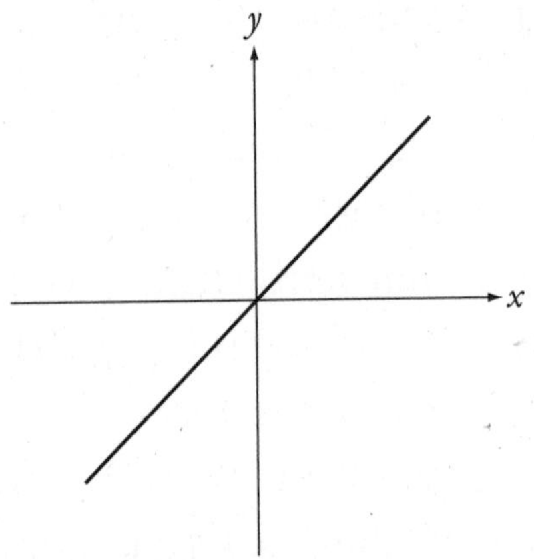

At this point, I'm sure, some vague memory of your middle-school algebra is coming back to you. But rest assured, you don't need to remember any of it to understand the significance of Renee's example. In fact, as you listen to Renee talking in the next few paragraphs, focus not on what she's saying but rather on how she's talking and why she's talking the way she is.

The point of the computer program, which Schoenfeld created, was to teach students about how to calculate the slope of a line. Slope, as I'm sure you remember (or, more accurately, as I'll bet you don't remember; I certainly didn't), is rise over run. The slope of the line in our example is 1, since the rise is 5 and the run is 5.

So there is Renee. She's sitting at the keyboard, and she's trying to figure out what numbers to enter in order to get the computer to draw a line that is absolutely vertical, that is directly superimposed over the *y* axis. Now, those of you who remember your high school math will know that this is, in fact, impossible. A vertical line has an undefined slope. Its rise is infinite: any number on the *y* axis starting at zero and going on forever. It's run on the *x* axis, meanwhile, is zero. Infinity divided by zero is not a number.

But Renee doesn't realize that what she's trying to do can't be done. She is, rather, in the grip of what Schoenfeld calls a "glorious misconception," and the reason Schoenfeld likes to show this particular tape is that it is a perfect demonstration of how this misconception came to be resolved.

Renee was a nurse. She wasn't someone who had been particularly interested in mathematics in the past. But she had somehow gotten hold of the software and was hooked.

"Now, what I want to do is make a straight line with this formula, parallel to the *y* axis," she begins. Schoenfeld is sitting next to her. She looks over at him anxiously. "It's been five years since I did any of this."

She starts to fiddle with the program, typing in different numbers.

"Now if I change the slope that way... minus 1... now what I mean to do is make the line go straight."

As she types in numbers, the line on the screen changes.

"Oops. That's not going to do it."

She looks puzzled.

"What are you trying to do?" Schoenfeld asks.

"What I'm trying to do is make a straight line parallel to the *y* axis. What do I need to do here? I think what I need to do is change this a little bit." She points at the place where the number for the *y* axis is. "That was something I discovered. That when you go from 1 to 2, there was a rather big change. But now if you get way up there you have to keep changing."

This is Renee's glorious misconception. She's noticed the higher she makes the *y* axis coordinate, the steeper the line gets. So she thinks the key to making a vertical line is just making the *y* axis coordinate large enough.

"I guess 12 or even 13 could do it. Maybe even as much as 15."

She frowns. She and Schoenfeld go back and forth. She asks him questions. He prods her gently in the right direction. She keeps trying and trying, one approach after another.

At one point, she types in 20. The line gets a little bit steeper.

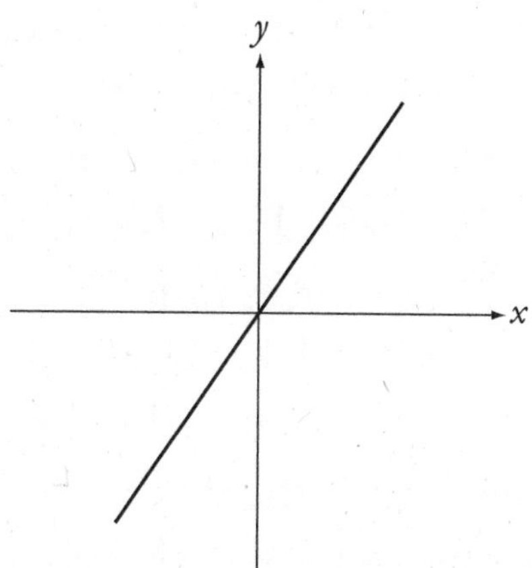

She types in 40. The line gets steeper still.

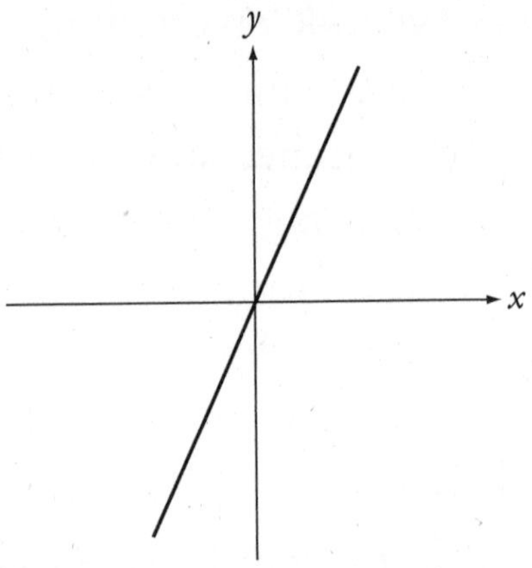

"I see that there is a relationship there. But as to why, it doesn't seem to make sense to me.... What if I do 80? If 40 gets me halfway, then 80 should get me all the way to the *y* axis. So let's just see what happens."

She types in 80. The line is steeper. But it's still not totally vertical.

"Ohhh. It's infinity, isn't it? It's never going to get there." Renee is close. But then she reverts to her original misconception.

"So what do I need? 100? Every time you double the number, you get halfway to the *y* axis. But it never gets there..."

She types in 100.

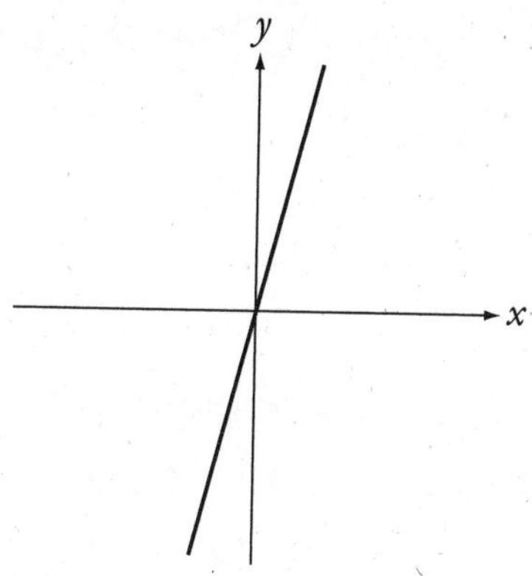

"It's closer. But not quite there yet."

She starts to think out loud. It's obvious she's on the verge of figuring something out. "Well, I knew this, though . . . but . . . I knew that. For each one up, it goes that many over. I'm still somewhat confused as to why . . ."

She pauses, squinting at the screen.

"I'm getting confused. It's a tenth of the way to the one. But I don't want it to be . . ."

And then she sees it.

"Oh! It's any number up, and zero over. It's any number divided by zero!" Her face lights up. "A vertical line is anything divided by zero—and that's an undefined number. Ohhh. Okay. Now I see. The slope of a vertical line is undefined. Ahhhh. That means something now. I won't forget that!"

6.

Over the course of his career, Schoenfeld has videotaped countless students as they worked on math problems. But the Renee tape is one of his favorites because of how beautifully it illustrates what he considers to be the secret to learning mathematics. *Twenty-two minutes* pass from the moment Renee begins playing with the computer program to the moment she says, "Ahhhh. That means something now." That's a *long* time. "This is eighth-grade mathematics," Schoenfeld said. "If I put the average eighth grader in the same position as Renee, I'm guessing that after the first few attempts, they would have said, 'I don't get it. I need you to explain it.'" Schoenfeld once asked a group of high school students how long they would work on a homework question before they concluded it was too hard for them ever to solve. Their answers ranged from thirty seconds to five minutes, with the average answer two minutes.

But Renee persists. She experiments. She goes back over the same issues time and again. She thinks out loud. She keeps going and going. She simply won't give up. She knows on some vague level that there is something wrong with her theory about how to draw a vertical line, and she won't stop until she's absolutely sure she has it right.

Renee wasn't a math natural. Abstract concepts like "slope" and "undefined" clearly didn't come easily to her. But Schoenfeld could not have found her more impressive.

"There's a will to make sense that drives what she does," Schoenfeld says. "She wouldn't accept a superficial 'Yeah, you're right' and walk away. That's not who she is. And that's really unusual." He rewound the tape and pointed to a moment when Renee reacted with genuine surprise to something on the screen.

"Look," he said. "She does a double take. Many students would just let that fly by. Instead, she thought, 'That doesn't jibe with whatever I'm thinking. I don't get it. That's important. I want an explanation.' And when she finally gets the explanation, she says, 'Yeah, that fits.' "

At Berkeley, Schoenfeld teaches a course on problem solving, the entire point of which, he says, is to get his students to unlearn the mathematical habits they picked up on the way to university. "I pick a problem that I don't know how to solve," he says. "I tell my students, 'You're going to have a two-week take-home exam. I know your habits. You're going to do nothing for the first week and start it next week, and I want to warn you now: If you only spend one week on this, you're not going to solve it. If, on the other hand, you start working the day I give you the midterm, you'll be frustrated. You'll come to me and say, 'It's impossible.' I'll tell you, Keep working, and by week two, you'll find you'll make significant progress."

We sometimes think of being good at mathematics as an innate ability. You either have "it" or you don't. But to Schoenfeld, it's not so much ability as *attitude*. You master mathematics if you are willing to try. That's what Schoenfeld attempts to teach his students. Success is a function of persistence and doggedness and the willingness to work hard for twenty-two minutes to make sense of something that most people would give up on after thirty seconds. Put a bunch of Renees in a classroom, and give them the space and time to explore mathematics for themselves, and you could go a long way. Or imagine a country where Renee's doggedness is not the exception, but a cultural trait, embedded as deeply as the culture of honor in the Cumberland Plateau. Now that would be a country good at math.

7.

Every four years, an international group of educators administers a comprehensive mathematics and science test to elementary and junior high students around the world. It's the TIMSS (the same test you read about earlier, in the discussion of differences between fourth graders born near the beginning of a school cutoff date and those born near the end of the date), and the point of the TIMSS is to compare the educational achievement of one country with another's.

When students sit down to take the TIMSS exam, they also have to fill out a questionnaire.

It asks them all kinds of things, such as what their parents' level of education is, and what their views about math are, and what their friends are like. It's not a trivial exercise. It's about 120 questions long. In fact, it is so tedious and demanding that many students leave as many as ten or twenty questions blank.

Now, here's the interesting part. As it turns out, the average number of items answered on that questionnaire varies from country to country. It is possible, in fact, to rank all the participating countries according to how many items their students answer on the questionnaire. Now, what do you think happens if you compare the questionnaire rankings with the math rankings on the TIMSS? *They are exactly the same.* In other words, countries whose students are willing to concentrate and sit still long enough and focus on answering every single question in an endless questionnaire are the same countries whose students do the best job of solving math problems.

The person who discovered this fact is an educational researcher at the University of Pennsylvania named Erling Boe, and he stumbled across it by accident. "It came out of the blue," he says. Boe hasn't even been able to publish his findings in a scientific journal, because, he says, it's just a bit too weird. Remember, he's not saying that the ability to finish the questionnaire and the ability to excel on the math test are related. He's saying that they are *the same:* if you compare the two rankings, they are identical.

Think about this another way. Imagine that every year, there was a Math Olympics in some fabulous city in the world. And every country in the world sent its own team of one thousand eighth graders. Boe's point is that we could predict precisely the order in which every country would finish in the Math Olympics *without asking a single math question.* All we would have to do is give them some task measuring how hard they were willing to work. In fact, we wouldn't even have to give them a task. We should be able to predict which countries are best at math simply by looking at which national cultures place the highest emphasis on effort and hard work.

So, which places are at the top of both lists? The answer shouldn't surprise you: Singapore,

South Korea, China (Taiwan), Hong Kong, and Japan. What those five have in common, of course, is that they are all cultures shaped by the tradition of wet-rice agriculture and meaningful work.* They are the kinds of places where, for

---

* Two small points. Mainland China isn't on this list because China doesn't yet take part in the TIMSS study. But the fact that Taiwan and Hong Kong rank so highly suggests that the mainland would probably also do really well.

Second, and perhaps more important, what happens in the north of China, which isn't a wet-rice agriculture society but historically a wheat-growing culture, much like Western Europe? Are they good at math too? The short answer is that we don't know. The psychologist James Flynn points out, though, that the overwhelming majority of Chinese immigrants to the West—the people who have done so well in math here—are from South China. The Chinese students graduating at the top of their class at MIT are the descendants, chiefly, of people from the Pearl River Delta. He also points out that the lowest-achieving Chinese Americans are the so-called Sze Yap people, who come from the edges of the Delta, "where soil was less fertile and agriculture less intense."

hundreds of years, penniless peasants, slaving away in the rice paddies three thousand hours a year, said things to one another like "No one who can rise before dawn three hundred sixty days a year fails to make his family rich."*

* There is actually a significant scientific literature measuring Asian "persistence." In a typical study, Priscilla Blinco gave large groups of Japanese and American first graders a very difficult puzzle and measured how long they worked at it before they gave up. The American children lasted, on average, 9.47 minutes. The Japanese children lasted 13.93 minutes, roughly 40 percent longer.

CHAPTER NINE

Marita's Bargain

"ALL MY FRIENDS NOW ARE FROM KIPP."

1.

In the mid-1990s, an experimental public school called the KIPP Academy opened on the fourth floor of Lou Gehrig Junior High School in New York City.* Lou Gehrig is in the seventh school district, otherwise known as the South Bronx, one of the poorest neighborhoods

* KIPP stands for "Knowledge Is Power Program."

in New York City. It is a squat, gray 1960s-era building across the street from a bleak-looking group of high-rises. A few blocks over is Grand Concourse, the borough's main thoroughfare. These are not streets that you'd happily walk down, alone, after dark.

KIPP is a middle school. Classes are large: the fifth grade has two sections of thirty-five students each. There are no entrance exams or admissions requirements. Students are chosen by lottery, with any fourth grader living in the Bronx eligible to apply. Roughly half of the students are African American; the rest are Hispanic. Three-quarters of the children come from single-parent homes. Ninety percent qualify for "free or reduced lunch," which is to say that their families earn so little that the federal government chips in so the children can eat properly at lunchtime.

KIPP Academy seems like the kind of school in the kind of neighborhood with the kind of student that would make educators despair—except that the minute you enter the building, it's clear that something is different.

The students walk quietly down the hallways in single file. In the classroom, they are taught to turn and address anyone talking to them in a protocol known as "SSLANT": smile, sit up, listen, ask questions, nod when being spoken to, and track with your eyes. On the walls of the school's corridors are hundreds of pennants from the colleges that KIPP graduates have gone on to attend. Last year, hundreds of families from across the Bronx entered the lottery for KIPP's two fifth-grade classes. It is no exaggeration to say that just over ten years into its existence, KIPP has become one of the most desirable public schools in New York City.

What KIPP is most famous for is mathematics. In the South Bronx, only about 16 percent of all middle school students are performing at or above their grade level in math. But at KIPP, by the end of fifth grade, many of the students call math their favorite subject. In seventh grade, KIPP students start *high school* algebra. By the end of eighth grade, 84 percent of the students are performing at or above their grade level, which is to say that this motley group of randomly chosen lower-income kids from dingy apartments in one of the country's worst neighborhoods—whose parents, in an overwhelming number of cases, never set foot in a college—do as well in mathematics as the privileged eighth graders of American's wealthy suburbs. "Our kids' reading is on point," said David Levin, who founded KIPP with a fellow teacher, Michael Feinberg, in 1994. "They struggle a little bit with writing skills. But when they leave here, they rock in math."

There are now more than fifty KIPP schools across the United States, with more on the way. The KIPP program represents one of the most promising new educational philosophies in the United States. But its success is best understood not in terms of its curriculum, its teachers, its resources, or some kind of institutional innovation. KIPP is, rather, an organization that has succeeded by taking the idea of cultural legacies seriously.

2.

In the early nineteenth century, a group of reformers set out to establish a system of public education in the United States. What passed for public school at the time was a haphazard assortment of locally run one-room schoolhouses and overcrowded urban classrooms scattered around the country. In rural areas, schools closed in the spring and fall and ran all summer long, so that children could help out in the busy planting and harvesting seasons. In the city, many schools mirrored the long and chaotic schedules of the children's working-class parents. The reformers wanted to make sure that all children went to school and that public school was comprehensive, meaning that all children got enough schooling to learn how to read and write and do basic arithmetic and function as productive citizens.

But as the historian Kenneth Gold has pointed out, the early educational reformers were also tremendously concerned that children not get *too much* schooling. In 1871, for example, the US commissioner of education published a report by Edward Jarvis on the "Relation of Education to Insanity." Jarvis had studied 1,741 cases of insanity and concluded that "over-study" was responsible for 205 of them. "Education lays the foundation of a large portion of the causes of mental disorder," Jarvis wrote. Similarly, the pioneer of public education in Massachusetts, Horace Mann, believed that working students too hard would create a "most pernicious influence upon character and habits. . . . Not infrequently is health itself destroyed by over-stimulating the mind." In the education journals of the day, there were constant worries about overtaxing students or blunting their natural abilities through too much schoolwork.

The reformers, Gold writes:

> strove for ways to reduce time spent studying, because long periods of respite could save the mind from injury. Hence the elimination of Saturday classes, the shortening of the school day, and the lengthening of vacation—all of which occurred over the course of the nineteenth century. Teachers were cautioned that "when [students] are required

> to study, their bodies should not be exhausted by long confinement, nor their minds bewildered by prolonged application." Rest also presented particular opportunities for strengthening cognitive and analytical skills. As one contributor to the *Massachusetts Teacher* suggested, "it is when thus relieved from the state of tension belonging to actual study that boys and girls, as well as men and women, acquire the habit of thought and reflection, and of forming their own conclusions, independently of what they are taught and the authority of others."

This idea—that effort must be balanced by rest—could not be more different from Asian notions about study and work, of course. But then again, the Asian worldview was shaped by the rice paddy. In the Pearl River Delta, the rice farmer planted two and sometimes three crops a year. The land was fallow only briefly. In fact, one of the singular features of rice cultivation is that because of the nutrients carried by the water used in irrigation, the more a plot of land is cultivated, the more fertile it gets.

But in Western agriculture, the opposite is true. Unless a wheat- or cornfield is left fallow every few years, the soil becomes exhausted. Every winter, fields are empty. The hard labor of spring planting and fall harvesting is followed, like clockwork, by the slower pace of summer and winter. This is the logic the reformers applied to the cultivation of young minds. We formulate new ideas by analogy, working from what we know toward what we don't know, and what the reformers knew were the rhythms of the agricultural seasons. A mind must be cultivated. But not too much, lest it be exhausted. And what was the remedy for the dangers of exhaustion? The long summer vacation—a peculiar and distinctive American legacy that has had profound consequences for the learning patterns of the students of the present day.

3.

Summer vacation is a topic seldom mentioned in American educational debates. It is considered a permanent and inviolate feature of school life, like high school football or the senior prom. But take a look at the following sets of elementary school test-score results, and see if your faith in the value of long summer holidays isn't profoundly shaken.

These numbers come from research led by the Johns Hopkins University sociologist Karl Alexander. Alexander tracked the progress of 650 first graders from the Baltimore public school system, looking at how they scored on a widely used math- and reading-skills exam called the California Achievement Test. These are reading scores for the first five years of elementary school, broken down by socioeconomic class—low, middle, and high.

Class	1st Grade	2nd Grade	3rd Grade	4th Grade	5th Grade
Low	329	375	397	433	461
Middle	348	388	425	467	497
High	361	418	460	506	534

Look at the first column. The students start in first grade with meaningful, but not overwhelming, differences in their knowledge and ability. The first graders from the wealthiest homes have a 32-point advantage over the first graders from the poorest homes—and by the way, first graders from poor homes in Baltimore are *really* poor. Now look at the fifth-grade column. By that point, four years later, the initially modest gap between rich and poor has more than doubled.

This "achievement gap" is a phenomenon that has been observed over and over again, and it typically provokes one of two responses. The first response is that disadvantaged kids simply don't have the same inherent ability to learn as children from more privileged backgrounds. They're not as smart. The second, slightly more optimistic conclusion is that, in some way, our schools are failing poor children: we simply aren't doing a good enough job of teaching them the skills they need. But here's where Alexander's study gets interesting, because it turns out that neither of those explanations rings true.

The city of Baltimore didn't give its kids the

California Achievement Test just at the end of every school year, in June. It gave them the test in September too, just after summer vacation ended. What Alexander realized is that the second set of test results allowed him to do a slightly different analysis. If he looked at the difference between the score a student got at the beginning of the school year, in September, and the score he or she got the following June, he could measure—precisely—how much that student learned over the school year. And if he looked at the difference between a student's score in June and then in the following September, he could see how much that student learned over the course of the summer. In other words, he could figure out—at least in part—how much of the achievement gap is the result of things that happen during the school year, and how much it has to do with what happens during summer vacation.

Let's start with the school-year gains. This table shows how many points students' test scores rose from the time they started classes in September to the time they stopped in June.

The "Total" column represents their cumulative classroom learning from all five years of elementary school.

Class	1st Grade	2nd Grade	3rd Grade	4th Grade	5th Grade	Total
Low	55	46	30	33	25	189
Middle	69	43	34	41	27	214
High	60	39	34	28	23	184

Here is a completely different story from the one suggested by the first table. The first set of test results made it look like lower-income kids were somehow failing in the classroom. But here we see plainly that isn't true. Look at the "Total" column. Over the course of five years of elementary school, poor kids "out-learn" the wealthiest kids 189 points to 184 points. They lag behind the middle-class kids by only a modest amount, and, in fact, in one year, second grade, they learn more than the middle- or upper-class kids.

Next, let's see what happens if we look just at how reading scores change during summer vacation.

Class	After 1st	After 2nd	After 3rd	After 4th	Total
Low	–3.67	–1.70	2.74	2.89	0.26
Middle	–3.11	4.18	3.68	2.34	7.09
High	15.38	9.22	14.51	13.38	52.49

Do you see the difference? Look at the first column, which measures what happens over the summer after first grade. The wealthiest kids come back in September and their reading scores have jumped more than 15 points. The poorest kids come back from the holidays and their reading scores have *dropped* almost 4 points. Poor kids may out-learn rich kids during the school year. But during the summer, they fall far behind.

Now take a look at the last column, which totals up all the summer gains from first grade to fifth grade. The reading scores of the poor kids go up by .26 points. *When it comes to reading skills, poor kids learn nothing when school is not in session.* The reading scores of the rich kids, by contrast, go up by a whopping 52.49 points. Virtually all of the advantage that wealthy students have over poor students is the result of differences in the way privileged kids learn while they are *not* in school.

What are we seeing here? One very real possibility is that these are the educational consequences of the differences in parenting styles that we talked about in the Chris Langan chapter. Think back to Alex Williams, the nine-year-old whom Annette Lareau studied. His parents believe in concerted cultivation. He gets taken to museums and gets enrolled in special programs and goes to summer camp, where he takes classes. When he's bored at home, there are plenty of books to read, and his parents see it as their responsibility to keep him actively engaged in the world around him. It's not hard to see how Alex would get better at reading and math over the summer.

But not Katie Brindle, the little girl from the other side of the tracks. There's no money to send her to summer camp. She's not getting driven by her mom to special classes, and there aren't books lying around her house that she can read if she gets bored. There's probably just a television. She may still have a wonderful vacation, making new friends, playing outside, going to the movies, having the kind of carefree summer days that we all dream about. None of those things, though, will improve her math and reading skills, and every carefree summer day she spends puts her further and further behind Alex. Alex isn't necessarily smarter than Katie. He's just out-learning her: he's putting in a few solid months of learning during the summer while she watches television and plays outside.

What Alexander's work suggests is that the way in which education has been discussed in the United States is backwards. An enormous amount of time is spent talking about reducing class size, rewriting curricula, buying every student a shiny new laptop, and increasing school funding—all of which assumes that there is something fundamentally wrong with the job schools are doing. But look back at the second table, which shows what happens between September and June. Schools *work.* The only problem with school, for the kids who aren't achieving, is that there isn't enough of it.

Alexander, in fact, has done a very simple calculation to demonstrate what would happen if the children of Baltimore went to school year-round. The answer is that poor kids and wealthy kids would, by the end of elementary school, be doing math and reading at almost the same level.

Suddenly the causes of Asian math superiority become even more obvious. Students in Asian schools don't have long summer vacations. Why would they? Cultures that believe that the route to success lies in rising before dawn 360 days a year are scarcely going to give their children three straight months off in the summer. The school year in the United States is, on average, 180 days long. The South Korean school year is 220 days long. The Japanese school year is 243 days long.

One of the questions asked of test takers on a recent math test given to students around the world was how many of the algebra, calculus, and geometry questions covered subject matter that they had previously learned in class. For Japanese twelfth graders, the answer was 92 percent. That's the value of going to school 243 days a year. You have the time to learn everything that needs to be learned—and you have less time to unlearn it. For American twelfth graders, the comparable figure was 54 percent. For its poorest students, America doesn't have a school problem. It has a summer vacation problem, and that's the problem the KIPP schools set out to solve. They decided to bring the lessons of the rice paddy to the American inner city.

4.

"They start school at seven twenty-five," says David Levin of the students at the Bronx KIPP Academy. "They all do a course called thinking skills until seven fifty-five. They do ninety minutes of English, ninety minutes of math every day, except in fifth grade, where they do two hours of math a day. An hour of science, an hour of social science, an hour of music at least twice a week, and then you have an hour and fifteen minutes of orchestra on top of that. Everyone does orchestra. The day goes from seven twenty-five until five p.m. After five, there are homework clubs, detention, sports teams. There are kids here from seven twenty-five until seven p.m. If you take an average day, and you take out lunch and recess, our kids are spending fifty to sixty percent more time learning than the traditional public school student."

Levin was standing in the school's main hallway. It was lunchtime and the students were trooping by quietly in orderly lines, all of them in their KIPP Academy shirts. Levin stopped a girl whose shirttail was out. "Do me a favor, when you get a chance," he called out, miming a tucking-in movement. He continued: "Saturdays they come in nine to one. In the summer, it's eight to two." By summer, Levin was referring to the fact that KIPP students do three extra weeks of school, in July. These are, after all, precisely the kind of lower-income kids who Alexander identified as losing ground over the long summer vacation, so KIPP's response is simply to not have a long summer vacation.

"The beginning is hard," he went on. "By

the end of the day they're restless. Part of it is endurance, part of it is motivation. Part of it is incentives and rewards and fun stuff. Part of it is good old-fashioned discipline. You throw all of that into the stew. We talk a lot here about grit and self-control. The kids know what those words mean."

Levin walked down the hall to an eighth-grade math class and stood quietly in the back. A student named Aaron was at the front of the class, working his way through a problem from the page of thinking-skills exercises that all KIPP students are required to do each morning. The teacher, a ponytailed man in his thirties named Frank Corcoran, sat in a chair to the side, only occasionally jumping in to guide the discussion. It was the kind of scene repeated every day in American classrooms—with one difference. Aaron was up at the front, working on that single problem, for *twenty* minutes—methodically, carefully, with the participation of the class, working his way through not just the answer but also the question of whether there was more than one way to get the answer. It was

Renee painstakingly figuring out the concept of undefined slope all over again.

"What that extra time does is allow for a more relaxed atmosphere," Corcoran said, after the class was over. "I find that the problem with math education is the sink-or-swim approach. Everything is rapid fire, and the kids who get it first are the ones who are rewarded. So there comes to be a feeling that there are people who can do math and there are people who aren't math people. I think that extended amount of time gives you the chance as a teacher to explain things, and more time for the kids to sit and digest everything that's going on—to review, to do things at a much slower pace. It seems counterintuitive but we do things at a slower pace and as a result we get through a lot more. There's a lot more retention, better understanding of the material. It lets me be a little bit more relaxed. We have time to have games. Kids can ask any questions they want, and if I'm explaining something, I don't feel pressed for time. I can go back over material and not feel time pressure." The extra time gave Corcoran the chance to make mathematics *meaningful:* to let his students see the clear relationship between effort and reward.

On the walls of the classroom were dozens of certificates from the New York State Regents exam, testifying to first-class honors for Corcoran's students. "We had a girl in this class," Corcoran said. "She was a horrible math student in fifth grade. She cried every Saturday when we did remedial stuff. Huge tears and tears." At the memory, Corcoran got a little emotional himself. He looked down. "She just e-mailed us a couple weeks ago. She's in college now. She's an accounting major."

5.

The story of the miracle school that transforms losers into winners is, of course, all too familiar. It's the stuff of inspirational books and sentimental Hollywood movies. But the reality of places like KIPP is a good deal less glamorous than that. To get a sense of what 50 to 60 percent more learning time means, listen to the typical day in the life of a KIPP student.

The student's name is Marita. She's an only child who lives in a single-parent home. Her mother never went to college. The two of them share a one-bedroom apartment in the Bronx. Marita used to go to a parochial school down the street from her home, until her mother heard of KIPP. "When I was in fourth grade, me and one of my other friends, Tanya, we both applied to KIPP," Marita said. "I remember Miss Owens. She interviewed me, and the way she was saying made it sound so hard I thought I was going to prison. I almost started crying. And she was like, If you don't want to sign this, you don't have to sign this. But then my mom was right there, so I signed it."

With that, her life changed. (Keep in mind, while reading what follows, that Marita is twelve years old.)

"I wake up at five-forty-five a.m. to get a head start," she says. "I brush my teeth, shower. I get some breakfast at school, if I am running late. Usually get yelled at because I am taking too long. I meet my friends Diana and Steven at the bus stop, and we get the number one bus."

A 5:45 wakeup is fairly typical of KIPP students, especially given the long bus and subway commutes that many have to get to school. Levin, at one point, went into a seventh-grade music class with seventy kids in it and asked for a show of hands on when the students woke up. A handful said they woke up after six. Three quarters said they woke up before six. And almost half said they woke up before 5:30. One classmate of Marita's, a boy named José, said he sometimes wakes up at three or four a.m., finishes his homework from the night before, and then "goes back to sleep for a bit."

Marita went on:

> I leave school at five p.m., and if I don't lollygag around, then I will get home around five-thirty. Then I say hi to my mom really quickly and start my homework. And if it's not a lot of homework that day, it will take me two to three hours, and I'll be done around nine p.m. Or if we have

essays, then I will be done like ten p.m., or ten-thirty p.m.

Sometimes my mom makes me break for dinner. I tell her I want to go straight through, but she says I have to eat. So around eight, she makes me break for dinner for, like, a half hour, and then I get back to work. Then, usually after that, my mom wants to hear about school, but I have to make it quick because I have to get in bed by eleven p.m. So I get all my stuff ready, and then I get into bed. I tell her all about the day and what happened, and by the time we are finished, she is on the brink of sleeping, so that's probably around eleven-fifteen. Then I go to sleep, and the next morning we do it all over again. We are in the same room. But it's a huge bedroom and you can split it into two, and we have beds on other sides. Me and my mom are very close.

She spoke in the matter-of-fact way of children who have no way of knowing how unusual their situation is. She had the hours of a lawyer trying to make partner, or of a medical resident. All that was missing were the dark circles under her eyes and a steaming cup of coffee, except that she was too young for either.

"Sometimes I don't go to sleep when I'm supposed to," Marita continued. "I go to sleep at, like, twelve o'clock, and the next afternoon, it will hit me. And I will doze off in class. But then I have to wake up because I have to get the information. I remember I was in one class, and I was dozing off and the teacher saw me and said, 'Can I talk to you after class?' And he asked me, 'Why were you dozing off?' And I told him I went to sleep late. And he was, like, 'You need to go to sleep earlier.' "

6.

Marita's life is not the life of a typical twelve-year-old. Nor is it what we would necessarily wish for a twelve-year-old. Children, we like to believe, should have time to play and dream and sleep. Marita has responsibilities. What is being asked of her is the same thing that was asked of the Korean pilots. To become a success at what they did, they had to shed some part of their own identity, because the deep respect for authority that runs throughout Korean culture simply does not work in the cockpit. Marita has had to do the same because the cultural legacy she had been given does not match her circumstances either—not when middle- and upper-middle-class families are using weekends and summer vacation to push their children ahead. Her community does not give her what she needs. So what does she have to do? Give up her evenings and weekends and friends—all the elements of her old world—and replace then with KIPP.

Here is Marita again, in a passage that is little short of heartbreaking:

> Well, when we first started fifth grade, I used to have contact with one of the girls from my old school, and whenever I left school on Friday, I would go to her house and stay there until my mom would get home from work. So I would be at her house and I would be doing my homework. She would never have any homework. And she would say, "Oh, my God, you stay there late." Then she

> said she wanted to go to KIPP, but then she would say that KIPP is too hard and she didn't want to do it. And I would say, "Everyone says that KIPP is hard, but once you get the hang of it, it's not really that hard." She told me, "It's because you are smart." And I said, "No, every one of us is smart." And she was so discouraged because we stayed until five and we had a lot of homework, and I told her that us having a lot of homework helps us do better in class. And she told me she didn't want to hear the whole speech. All my friends now are from KIPP.

Is this a lot to ask of a child? It is. But think of things from Marita's perspective. She has made a bargain with her school. She will get up at five-forty-five in the morning, go in on Saturdays, and do homework until eleven at night. In return, KIPP promises that it will take kids like her who are stuck in poverty and give them a chance to get out. It will get 84 percent of them up to or above their grade level in mathematics. On the strength of that performance, 90 percent of KIPP students get scholarships to private or parochial high schools instead of having to attend their own desultory high schools in the Bronx. And on the strength of that high school experience, more than 80 percent of KIPP graduates will go on to college, in many cases being the first in their family to do so.

How could that be a bad bargain? Everything we have learned in *Outliers* says that success follows a predictable course. It is not the brightest who succeed. If it were, Chris Langan would be up there with Einstein. Nor is success simply the sum of the decisions and efforts we make on our own behalf. It is, rather, a gift. Outliers are those who have been given opportunities—and who have had the strength and presence of mind to seize them. For hockey and soccer players born in January, it's a better shot at making the all-star team. For the Beatles, it was Hamburg. For Bill Gates, the lucky break was being born at the right time and getting the gift of a computer terminal in junior high. Joe Flom and the founders of Wachtell, Lipton, Rosen and Katz got multiple breaks. They were born at the right time with the right parents and the right ethnicity, which allowed them to practice takeover law for twenty years before the rest of the legal world caught on. And what Korean Air did, when it finally turned its operations around, was give its pilots the opportunity to escape the constraints of their cultural legacy.

The lesson here is very simple. But it is striking how often it is overlooked. We are so caught in the myths of the best and the brightest and the self-made that we think outliers spring naturally from the earth. We look at the young Bill Gates and marvel that our world allowed that thirteen-year-old to become a fabulously successful entrepreneur. But that's the wrong lesson. Our world only allowed one thirteen-year-old unlimited access to a time-sharing terminal in 1968. If a million teenagers had been given the same opportunity, how many more Microsofts would we have today? To build a better world we need to replace the patchwork of lucky breaks and arbitrary advantages that today determine success—the fortunate birth dates and the happy accidents of history—with a society that provides opportunities for all. If Canada had a second hockey league for those children born in the last half of the year, it would today have *twice* as many adult hockey stars. Now multiply that sudden flowering of talent by every field and profession. The world could be so much richer than the world we have settled for.

Marita doesn't need a brand-new school with acres of playing fields and gleaming facilities. She doesn't need a laptop, a smaller class, a teacher with a PhD, or a bigger apartment. She doesn't need a higher IQ or a mind as quick as Chris Langan's. All those things would be nice, of course. But they miss the point. Marita just needed a *chance.* And look at the chance she was given! Someone brought a little bit of the rice paddy to the South Bronx and explained to her the miracle of meaningful work.

EPILOGUE

A Jamaican Story

"IF A PROGENY OF YOUNG COLORED CHILDREN IS BROUGHT FORTH, THESE ARE EMANCIPATED."

1.

On September 9, 1931, a young woman named Daisy Nation gave birth to twin girls. She and her husband, Donald, were schoolteachers in a tiny village called Harewood, in the central Jamaican parish of Saint Catherine's. They named their daughters Faith and Joyce. When Donald was told that he had fathered twins, he sank down on his knees and surrendered responsibility for their lives over to God.

The Nations lived in a small cottage on the grounds of Harewood's Anglican church. The schoolhouse was next door, a long, single-room barn of a building raised on concrete stilts. On some days, there might be as many as three hundred children in the room, and on others, less than two dozen. The children would read out loud or recite their times tables. Writing was done on slates. Whenever possible, the classes would move outside, under the mango trees. If the children were out of control, Donald Nation would walk from one end of the room to the other, waving a strap from left to right as the children scrambled back to their places.

He was an imposing man, quiet and dignified, and a great lover of books. In his small library were works of poetry and philosophy and novels by such writers as Somerset Maugham. Every day he would read the newspaper closely, following the course of the events around the word. In the evening, his best friend, Archdeacon Hay, the Anglican pastor who lived on the other side of the hill, would come over and sit on Donald's veranda, and together they would expound on the problems of Jamaica. Donald's wife, Daisy, was from the parish of Saint Elizabeth. Her maiden name was Ford, and her father had owned a small grocery store. She was one of three sisters, and she was renowned for her beauty.

At the age of eleven, the twins won scholarships to a boarding school called Saint Hilda's near the north coast. It was an old Anglican private school, established for the daughters of English clergy, property owners, and overseers. From Saint Hilda's they applied and were accepted to University College, in London. Not long afterward, Joyce went to a twenty-first-birthday party for a young English mathematician named Graham. He stood up to recite a poem and forgot his lines, and Joyce became embarrassed for him—even though it made no sense for her to feel embarrassed, because she did not know him at all. Joyce and Graham fell in love and got married. They moved to Canada. Graham was a math professor. Joyce became a successful writer and a family therapist. They had three sons and built a beautiful house on a hill, off in the countryside. Graham's last name is Gladwell. He is my father, and Joyce Gladwell is my mother.

2.

That is the story of my mother's path to success—and it isn't true. It's not a lie in the sense that the facts were made up. But it is false in the way that telling the story of Bill Gates without mentioning the computer at Lakeside is false, or accounting for Asian math prowess without going back to the rice paddies is false. It leaves out my mother's many opportunities and the importance of her cultural legacy.

In 1935, for example, when my mother and her sister were four, a historian named William M. MacMillan visited Jamaica. He was a professor at the University of Witwatersrand in

Johannesburg, South Africa. MacMillan was a man before his time: he was deeply concerned with the social problems of South Africa's black population, and he came to the Caribbean to make the same argument he had made back home in South Africa.

Chief among MacMillan's concerns was Jamaica's educational system. Formal schooling—if you could call what happened in the wooden barn next door to my grandparents' house "formal schooling"—went only to fourteen years of age. Jamaica had no public high schools or universities. Those with academic inclinations took extra classes with the head teacher in their teenage years and with luck made it into teachers' college. Those with broader ambitions had to somehow find their way into a private school, and from there to a university in the United States or England.

But scholarships were few and far between, and the cost of private schooling was prohibitive for all but a privileged few. The "bridge from the primary schools" to high school, MacMillan later wrote, in a blistering critique of

England's treatment of its colonies entitled *Warning from the West Indies,* "is narrow and insecure." The school system did nothing for the "humblest" classes. He went on: "If anything these schools are a factor deepening and sharpening social distinctions." If the government did not give its people opportunities, he warned, there would be trouble.

A year after MacMillan published his book, a wave of riots and unrest swept the Caribbean. Fourteen people were killed and fifty-nine injured in Trinidad. Fourteen were killed and forty-seven injured in Barbados. In Jamaica, a series of violent strikes shut down the country, and a state of emergency was declared. Panicked, the British government took MacMillan's prescriptions to heart and, among other reforms, proposed a series of "all-island" scholarships for academically minded students to go to private high schools. The scholarships began in 1941. My mother and her twin sister sat for the exam the following year. That is how they got a high school education; had they been born two or three or four years earlier, they might never have gotten a full education. My mother owes the course her life took to the timing of her birth, to the rioters of 1937, and to W. M. MacMillan.

I described Daisy Nation, my grandmother, as "renowned for her beauty." But the truth is that was a careless and condescending way to describe her. She was a force. The fact that my mother and her sister left Harewood for Saint Hilda's was my grandmother's doing. My grandfather may have been an imposing and learned man, but he was an idealist and a dreamer. He buried himself in his books. If he had ambitions for his daughters, he did not have the foresight and energy to make them real. My grandmother did. Saint Hilda's was her idea: some of the wealthier families in the area sent their daughters there, and she saw what a good school meant. Her daughters did not play with the other children of the village. They read. Latin and algebra were necessary for high school, so she had her daughters tutored by Archdeacon Hay.

"If you'd asked her about her goals for her children, she would have said she wanted us out of there," my mother recalls. "She didn't feel that the Jamaican context offered enough. And if the opportunity was there to go on, and you were able to take it, then to her the sky was the limit."

When the results came back from the scholarship exam, only my aunt was awarded a scholarship. My mother was not. That's another fact that my first history was careless about. My mother remembers her parents standing in the doorway, talking to each other. "We have no more money." They had paid the tuition for the first term and bought the uniforms and had exhausted their savings. What would they do when the second-term fees for my mother came due? But then again, they couldn't send one daughter and not the other. My grandmother was steadfast. She sent both—and prayed—and at the end of the first term, it turned out that one of the other girls at the school had won two scholarships, so the second was given to my mother.

When it came time to go to university, my aunt, the academic twin, won what was called a Centenary Scholarship. The "Centenary" was a reference to the fact that the scholarship was established one hundred years after the abolition of slavery in Jamaica. It was reserved for the graduates of public elementary schools, and, in a measure of how deeply the British felt about honoring the memory of abolition, there was a total of one Centenary scholarship awarded every year for the whole island, with the prize going to the top girl and the top boy in alternating years. The year my aunt applied was one of the "girl" years. She was lucky. My mother was not. My mother was faced with the cost of passage to England, room and board and living expenses, and tuition at the University of London. To get a sense of how daunting that figure was, the value of the Centenary scholarship my aunt won was probably as much as the sum of my grandparents' annual salaries. There were no student loan programs, no banks with lines of credit for schoolteachers out in the countryside. "If I'd asked my father," my mother says, "he would have replied, 'We have no money.' "

What did Daisy do? She went to the Chinese shopkeeper in a neighboring town. Jamaica has a very large Chinese population that since the nineteenth century has dominated the commercial life of the island. In Jamaican parlance, a store is not a store, it is a "Chinee-shop." Daisy went to the "Chinee-shop," to Mr. Chance, and borrowed the money. No one knows how much she borrowed, although it must have been an enormous sum. And no one knows why Mr. Chance lent it to Daisy, except of course that she was Daisy Nation, and she paid her bills promptly and had taught the Chance children at Harewood School. It was not always easy to be a Chinese child in a Jamaican schoolyard. The Jamaican children would taunt the Chinese children. *"Chinee nyan [eat] dog."* Daisy was a kindly and beloved figure, an oasis amid that hostility. Mr. Chance may have felt in her debt.

"Did she tell me what she was doing? I didn't even ask her," my mother remembers. "It just occurred. I just applied to university and got in. I acted completely on faith that I could rely on my mother, without even realizing that I was relying on my mother."

Joyce Gladwell owes her college education first to W. M. MacMillan, and then to the student at Saint Hilda's who gave up her scholarship, and then to Mr. Chance, and then, most of all, to Daisy Nation.

3.

Daisy Nation was from the northwestern end of Jamaica. Her great-grandfather was William Ford. He was from Ireland, and he arrived in Jamaica in 1784 having bought a coffee plantation. Not long after his arrival, he bought a slave woman and took her as his concubine. He noticed her on the docks at Alligator Pond, a fishing village on the south coast. She was an Igbo tribeswoman from West Africa. They had a son, whom they named John. He was, in the language of the day, a "mulatto"; he was colored—and all of the Fords from that point on fell into Jamaica's colored class.

In the American South during that same period, it would have been highly unusual for a white landowner to have such a public relationship with a slave. Sexual relations between whites and blacks were considered morally repugnant. Laws were passed prohibiting miscegenation, the last of which were not struck down by the US Supreme Court until 1967. A plantation owner who lived openly with a slave woman would have been socially ostracized, and any offspring from the union of black and white would have been left in slavery.

In Jamaica, attitudes were very different. The Caribbean in those years was little more than a massive slave colony. Blacks outnumbered whites by a ratio of more than ten to one. There were few, if any, marriageable white women, and as a result, the overwhelming majority of white men in the West Indies had black or brown mistresses. One British plantation owner in Jamaica who famously kept a precise diary of his sexual exploits slept with 138 different women in his thirty-seven years on the island, almost all of them slaves and, one suspects, not all of them willing partners. And whites saw mulattoes—the children of those relationships—as potential allies, a buffer between them and the enormous numbers of slaves on the island. Mulatto women were prized as mistresses, and their children, one shade lighter in turn, moved still further up the social and economic ladder. Mulattoes rarely worked in the fields. They lived the much easier life of working in the "house." They were the ones most likely to be freed. So many mulatto mistresses were left substantial fortunes in the wills of white property owners that the Jamaica legislature once passed a law capping bequests at two thousand pounds (which, at the time, was an enormous sum).

"When a European arrives in the West Indies and gets settled or set down for any length of time, he finds it necessary to provide himself with a housekeeper or mistress," one eighteenth-century observer wrote. "The choice he has an opportunity of making is various, a black, a tawney, a mulatto or a mestee, one of which can be purchased for 100 or 150 sterling. . . . If a progeny of young colored children is brought forth, these are emancipated, and mostly sent by those fathers who can afford it, at the age of three or four years, to be educated in England."

This is the world Daisy's grandfather John was born into. He was one generation removed from a slave ship, living in a country best described as an African penal colony, and he was a free man, with every benefit of education. He married another mulatto, a woman who was half European and half Arawak, which is the Indian tribe indigenous to Jamaica, and had seven children.

"These people—the coloreds—had a lot of status," the Jamaican sociologist Orlando Patterson says. "By eighteen twenty-six, they had full civil liberties. In fact, they achieve full civil liberties at the same time as the Jews do in Jamaica. They could vote. Do anything a white person could do—and this is within the context of what was still a slave society.

"Ideally, they would try to be artisans.

Remember, Jamaica has sugar plantations, which are very different from the cotton plantations you find in the American South. Cotton is a predominantly agricultural pursuit. You are picking this stuff, and almost all of the processing was done in Lancashire, or the North. Sugar is an agro-industrial complex. You have to have the factory right there, because sugar starts losing sucrose within hours of being picked. You had no choice but to have the sugar mill right there, and sugar mills require a wide range of occupations. The coopers. The boiler men. The carpenters—and a lot of those jobs were filled by colored people."

It was also the case that Jamaica's English elite, unlike their counterparts in the United States, had little interest in the grand project of nation building. They wanted to make their money and go back to England. They had no desire to stay in what they considered a hostile land. So the task of building a new society—with the many opportunities it embodied—fell to the coloreds as well.

"By eighteen fifty, the mayor of Kingston

[the Jamaican capital] was a colored person," Patterson went on. "And so was the founder of the *Daily Gleaner* [Jamaica's major newspaper]. These were colored people, and from very early on, they came to dominate the professional classes. The whites were involved in business or the plantation. The people who became doctors and lawyers were these colored people. These were the people running the schools. The bishop of Kingston was a classic brown man. They weren't the economic elite. But they were the cultural elite."

The chart below shows a breakdown of two categories of Jamaican professionals—lawyers and members of parliament—in the early 1950s. The categorization is by skin tone. "White and light" refers to people who are either entirely white or, more likely, who have some black heritage that is no longer readily apparent. "Olive" is one step below that, and "light brown" one step below olive (although the difference between those two shades might not be readily apparent to anyone but a Jamaican). The fact to keep in mind is that in the 1950s "blacks" made up about 80 percent of the Jamaican population, outnumbering coloreds five to one.

Ethnicity	**Lawyers (percentage)**	**Members of Parliament (percentage)**
Chinese	3.1	
East Indians	—	
Jews	7.1	
Syrians	—	
White and light	38.8	10
Olive	10.2	13
Light brown	17.3	19
Dark brown	10.2	39
Black	5.1	10
Unknown	8.2	

Look at the extraordinary advantage that their little bit of whiteness gave the colored minority. Having an ancestor who worked in the house and not in the fields, who got full civil rights in 1826, who was valued instead of enslaved, who got a shot at meaningful work instead of being consigned to the sugarcane fields, made all the difference in occupational success two and three generations later.

Daisy Ford's ambition for her daughters did not come from nowhere, in other words. She was the inheritor of a legacy of privilege. Her older brother Rufus, with whom she went to live as a child, was a teacher and a man of learning. Her brother Carlos went to Cuba and then came back to Jamaica and opened a garment factory. Her father, Charles Ford, was a produce wholesaler. Her mother, Ann, was a Powell, another educated, upwardly mobile colored family—and the same Powells who would two generations later produce Colin Powell. Her uncle Henry owned property. Her grandfather John—the son of William Ford and his African concubine—became a preacher. No less than three members of the extended Ford family ended up winning Rhodes Scholarships. If my mother owed W. M. MacMillan and the rioters of 1937 and Mr. Chance and her mother, Daisy Ford, then Daisy owed Rufus and Carlos and Ann and Charles and John.

4.

My grandmother was a remarkable woman. But it is important to remember that the steady upward path upon which the Fords embarked began with a morally complicated act: William Ford looked upon my great-great-great-grandmother with desire at a slave market in Alligator Pond and purchased her.

The slaves who were not so chosen had short and unhappy lives. In Jamaica, the plantation owners felt it made the most sense to extract the maximum possible effort from their human property while the property was still young — to work their slaves until they were either useless or dead — and then simply buy another round at the market. They had no trouble with the philosophical contradiction of cherishing the children they had with a slave and simultaneously thinking of slaves as property. William Thistlewood, the plantation owner who cataloged his sexual exploits, had a lifelong relationship with a slave named Phibbah, whom, by all accounts, he adored, and who bore him a son. But to his "field" slaves, he was a monster, whose preferred punishment for those who tried to run away was what he called "Derby's dose." The runaway would be beaten, and salt pickle, lime juice, and bird pepper would be rubbed into his or her open wounds. Another slave would defecate into the mouth of the miscreant, who would then be gagged for four to five hours.

It is not surprising, then, that the brown-skinned classes of Jamaica came to fetishize their lightness. It was their great advantage. They scrutinized the shade of one another's skin and played the color game as ruthlessly in the end as the whites did. "If, as often happens, children are of different shades of color in a family," the Jamaican sociologist Fernando Henriques once wrote:

> the most lightly colored will be favored at the expense of the others. In adolescence, and until marriage, the darker members of the family will be kept out of the way when the friends of the fair or fairer members of the family are being entertained.

> The fair child is regarded as raising the color of the family and nothing must be put in the way of its success, that is in the way of a marriage which will still further raise the color status of the family. A fair person will try to sever social relations he may have with darker relatives... the darker members of a Negro family will encourage the efforts of a very fair relative to "pass" for White. The practices of intra-family relations lay the foundation for the public manifestation of color prejudice.

My family was not immune to this. Daisy was inordinately proud of the fact her husband was lighter than she was. But that same prejudice was then turned on her: "Daisy's nice, you know," her mother-in-law would say, "but she's too dark."

One of my mother's relatives (I'll call her Aunt Joan) was also well up the color totem pole. She was "white and light." But her husband was what in Jamaica is called an "Injun"—a man with a dark complexion and straight, fine black hair—and their daughters were dark like their father. One day, after her husband had died, she was traveling on a train to visit her daughter, and she met and took an interest in a light-skinned man in the same railway car. What happened next is something that Aunt Joan told only my mother, years later, with the greatest of shame. When she got off the train, she walked right by her daughter, disowning her own flesh and blood, because she did not want a man so light-skinned and desirable to know that she had borne a daughter so dark.

In the 1960s, my mother wrote a book about her experiences. It was entitled *Brown Face, Big Master,* the "brown face" referring to herself, and the "big master" referring, in the Jamaican dialect, to God. At one point, she describes a time just after my parents were married when they were living in London and my eldest brother was still a baby. They were looking for an apartment, and after a long search, my father found one in a London suburb. On the day after they moved in, however, the landlady ordered them out. "You didn't tell me your wife was Jamaican," she told my father in a rage.

In her book, my mother describes her long struggle to make sense of this humiliation, to reconcile her experience with her faith. In the end, she was forced to acknowledge that anger was not an option and that as a colored Jamaican whose family had benefited for generations from the hierarchy of race, she could hardly reproach another for the impulse to divide people by the shade of their skin:

> I complained to God in so many words: "Here I was, the wounded representative of the negro race in our struggle to be accounted free and equal with the dominating whites!" And God was amused; my prayer did not ring true with Him. I would try again. And then God said, "Have you not done the same thing? Remember this one and that one, people whom you have slighted or avoided or treated less considerately than others because they were different superficially, and you were ashamed to be identified with them. Have you not been glad that you are not more colored than you are? Grateful that you are not black?"

> My anger and hate against the landlady melted. I was no better than she was, nor worse for that matter.... We were both guilty of the sin of self-regard, the pride and the exclusiveness by which we cut some people off from ourselves.

It is not easy to be so honest about where we're from. It would be simpler for my mother to portray her success as a straightforward triumph over victimhood, just as it would be simpler to look at Joe Flom and call him the greatest lawyer ever—even though his individual achievements are so impossibly intertwined with his ethnicity, his generation, the particulars of the garment industry, and the peculiar biases of the downtown law firms. Bill Gates could accept the title of genius, and leave it at that. It takes no small degree of humility for him to look back on his life and say, "I was very lucky." And he was. The Mothers' Club of Lakeside Academy bought him a computer in 1968. It is impossible for a hockey player, or Bill Joy, or Robert Oppenheimer, or any other outlier for that matter, to look down from their lofty perch and say with truthfulness, "I did this, all by myself." Superstar lawyers and math whizzes and software entrepreneurs appear at first blush to lie outside ordinary experience. But they don't. They are products of history and community, of opportunity and legacy. Their success is not exceptional or mysterious. It is grounded in a web of advantages and inheritances, some deserved, some not, some earned, some just plain lucky—but all critical to making them who they are. The outlier, in the end, is not an outlier at all.

My great-great-great-grandmother was bought at Alligator Pond. That act, in turn, gave her son, John Ford, the privilege of a skin color that spared him a life of slavery. The culture of possibility that Daisy Ford embraced and put to use so brilliantly on behalf of her daughters was passed on to her by the peculiarities of the West Indian social structure. And my mother's education was the product of the riots of 1937 and the industriousness of Mr. Chance. These were history's gifts to my family—and if the resources of that grocer, the fruits of those riots, the possibilities of that culture, and the privileges of that skin tone had been extended to others, how many more would now live a life of fulfillment, in a beautiful house high on a hill?

Notes

INTRODUCTION

John G. Bruhn and Stewart Wolf have published two books on their work in Roseto: *The Roseto Story* (Norman: University of Oklahoma Press, 1979) and *The Power of Clan: The Influence of Human Relationships on Heart Disease* (New Brunswick, N.J.: Transaction Publishers, 1993). For a comparison of Roseto Valfortore, Italy, and Roseto, Pennsylvania, USA, see Carla Bianco, *The Two Rosetos* (Bloomington: Indiana University Press, 1974). Roseto might be unique among small Pennsylvania towns in the degree of academic interest it has attracted.

ONE: THE MATTHEW EFFECT

Jeb Bush's fantasies about being a self-made man are detailed in S. V. Dáte's *Jeb: America's Next Bush* (New York: Jeremy P. Tarcher/Penguin, 2007), esp. pages 80–81. Dáte writes: "In both his 1994 and 1998 runs, Jeb made it clear: not only was he not apologizing for his background, he was proud of where he was financially, and certain that it was the result of his own pluck and work ethic. 'I've worked real hard for what I've achieved and I'm quite proud of it,' he told the *St. Petersburg Times* in 1993. 'I have no sense of guilt, no sense of wrongdoing.'

"The attitude was much the same as he had expressed on CNN's *Larry King Live* in 1992: 'I think, overall, it's a disadvantage,' he said of being the president's son when it came to his business opportunities. 'Because you're restricted in what you can do.'

"This thinking cannot be described as anything other than delusional."

The Lethbridge Broncos, who were playing the day that Paula and Roger Barnsley first noticed the relative-age effect, were a junior ice hockey team in the Western Hockey League from 1974 until 1986. They won the WHL Championship in 1982–83, and three years later were brought back to Swift Current in Saskatchewan. See http://en.wikipedia.org/wiki/Lethbridge_Broncos.

For an overview of the relative-age effect, see Jochen Musch and Simon Grondin, "Unequal Competition as an Impediment to Personal Development: A Review of the Relative Age Effect in Sport," published in *Developmental Review* 21, no. 2 (2001): 147–167.

Roger Barnsley and A. H. Thompson have put their study on a Web site, http://www.socialproblemindex.ualberta.ca/relage.htm.

Self-fulfilling prophecies can be traced back to ancient Greek and Indian literature, but the term itself was coined by Robert K. Merton in *Social Theory and Social Structure* (New York: Free Press, 1968).

Barnsley and his team branched out into other sports. See R. Barnsley, A. H. Thompson, and Philipe Legault,

"Family Planning: Football Style. The Relative Age Effect in Football," published in the *International Review for the Sociology of Sport* 27, no. 1 (1992): 77–88.

The statistics for the relative-age effect in baseball come from Greg Spira, in *Slate* magazine, http://www.slate.com/id/2188866/.

A. Dudink, at the University of Amsterdam, showed how the cutoff date for English Premier League soccer creates the same age hierarchy as is seen in Canadian hockey. See "Birth Date and Sporting Success," *Nature* 368 (1994): 592.

Interestingly, in Belgium, the cutoff date for soccer used to be August 1, and back then, almost a quarter of their top players were born in August and September. But then the Belgian soccer federation switched to January 1, and sure enough, within a few years, there were almost no elite soccer players born in December, and an overwhelming number born in January. For more, see Werner F. Helsen, Janet L. Starkes, and Jan van Winckel, "Effects of a Change in Selection Year on Success in Male Soccer Players," *American Journal of Human Biology* 12, no. 6 (2000): 729–735.

Kelly Bedard and Elizabeth Dhuey's data comes from "The Persistence of Early Childhood Maturity: International Evidence of Long-Run Age Effects," published in the *Quarterly Journal of Economics* 121, no. 4 (2006): 1437–1472.

TWO: THE 10,000-HOUR RULE

Much of the discussion of Bill Joy's history comes from Andrew Leonard's *Salon* article, "BSD Unix: Power to the People, from the Code," May 16, 2000, http://archive.salon.com/tech/fsp/2000/05/16/chapter_2_part_one/index.html.

For a history of the University of Michigan Computer Center, see "A Career Interview with Bernie Galler," professor emeritus in the Electrical Engineering and Computer Science department at the school, *IEEE Annals of the History of Computing* 23, no. 4 (2001): 107–112.

One of (many) wonderful articles by Ericsson and his colleagues about the ten-thousand-hour rule is K. Anders Ericsson, Ralf Th. Krampe, and Clemens Tesch-Römer, "The Role of Deliberate Practice in the Acquisition of Expert Performance," *Psychological Review* 100, no. 3 (1993): 363–406.

Daniel J. Levitin talks about the ten thousand hours it takes to get mastery in *This Is Your Brain on Music: The Science of a Human Obsession* (New York: Dutton, 2006), p. 197.

Mozart's development as a prodigy is discussed in Michael J. A. Howe's *Genius Explained* (Cambridge: Cambridge University Press, 1999), p. 3.

Harold Schonberg is quoted in John R. Hayes, *Thinking and Learning Skills.* Vol. 2: *Research and Open Questions,* ed. Susan F. Chipman, Judith W. Segal, and Robert Glaser (Hillsdale, N.J.:Lawrence Erlbaum Associates, 1985).

For chess's exception to the rule, grandmaster Bobby Fischer, see Neil Charness, Ralf Th. Krampe, and Ulrich Mayr in their essay "The Role of Practice and Coaching in Entrepreneurial Skill Domains: An International Comparison of Life-Span Chess Skill Acquisition," in *The Road to Excellence: The Acquisition of Expert Performance in the Arts and Sciences, Sports and Games,* ed. K. Anders Ericsson (Hillsdale, N.J.: Lawrence Erlbaum Associates, 1996), pp. 51–126, esp. p. 73.

To read more about the time-sharing revolution, see Stephen Manes and Paul Andrews's *Gates: How Microsoft's Mogul Reinvented an Industry—And Made Himself the Richest Man in America* (New York: Touchstone, 1994), p. 26.

Philip Norman wrote the Beatles' biography *Shout!* (New York: Fireside, 2003).

John Lennon and George Harrison's reminiscences about the band's beginning in Hamburg come from *Hamburg Days* by George Harrison, Astrid Kirchherr, and Klaus Voorman (Surrey: Genesis Publications, 1999). The quotation is from page 122.

Robert W. Weisberg discusses the Beatles—and computes the hours they spent practicing—in "Creativity and Knowledge: A Challenge to Theories" in *Handbook of Creativity,* ed. Robert J. Sternberg (Cambridge: Cambridge University Press, 1999): 226–250.

The complete list of the richest people in history can be found at http://en.wikipedia.org/wiki/Wealthy_historical_figures_2008.

The reference to C. Wright Mills in the footnote comes from *The American Business Elite: A Collective Portrait,* published in the *Journal of Economic History* 5 (December 1945): 20–44.

Steve Jobs's pursuit of Bill Hewlett is described in Lee Butcher's *Accidental Millionaire: The Rise and Fall of Steve Jobs at Apple Computer* (New York: Paragon House, 1987).

THREE: THE TROUBLE WITH GENIUSES, PART 1

The episode of *1 vs. 100* featuring Chris Langan aired January 25, 2008.

Leta Hollingworth, who is mentioned in the footnote, published her account of "L" in *Children Above 180 IQ* (New York: World Books, 1942).

Among other excellent sources on the life and times of Lewis Terman are Henry L. Minton, "Charting Life History: Lewis M. Terman's Study of the Gifted" in *The Rise of Experimentation in American Psychology,* ed. Jill G. Morawski (New Haven: Yale University Press, 1988); Joel N. Shurkin, *Terman's Kids* (New York: Little, Brown, 1992); and May Seagoe, *Terman and the Gifted* (Los Altos: Kauffman, 1975). The discussion of Henry Cowell comes from Seagoe.

Liam Hudson's discussion of the limitations of IQ tests can be found in *Contrary Imaginations: A Psychological*

Study of the English Schoolboy (Middlesex: Penguin Books, 1967). Hudson is an absolute delight to read.

The Michigan Law School study "Michigan's Minority Graduates in Practice: The River Runs Through Law School," written by Richard O. Lempert, David L. Chambers, and Terry K. Adams, appears in *Law and Social Inquiry* 25, no. 2 (2000).

Pitirim Sorokin's rebuttal to Terman was published in *Fads and Foibles in Modern Sociology and Related Sciences* (Chicago: Henry Regnery, 1956).

FOUR: THE TROUBLE WITH GENIUSES, PART 2

Kai Bird and Martin J. Sherwin, *American Prometheus: The Triumph and Tragedy of J. Robert Oppenheimer* (New York: Knopf, 2005).

Robert J. Sternberg has written widely on practical intelligence and similar subjects. For a good, nonacademic account, see *Successful Intelligence: How Practical and Creative Intelligence Determine Success in Life* (New York: Plume, 1997).

As should be obvious, I loved Annette Lareau's book. It is well worth reading, as I have only begun to outline her argument from *Unequal Childhoods: Class, Race, and Family Life* (Berkeley: University of California Press, 2003).

Another excellent discussion of the difficulties in focusing solely on IQ is Stephen J. Ceci's *On Intelligence: A*

Bioecological Treatise on Intellectual Development (Cambridge, Mass.: Harvard University Press, 1996).

For a gentle but critical assessment of Terman's study, see "The Vanishing Genius: Lewis Terman and the Stanford Study" by Gretchen Kreuter. It was published in the *History of Education Quarterly* 2, no. 1 (March 1962): 6–18.

FIVE: THE THREE LESSONS OF JOE FLOM

The definitive history of Skadden, Arps and the takeover culture was written by Lincoln Caplan, *Skadden: Power, Money, and the Rise of a Legal Empire* (New York: Farrar, Straus, and Giroux, 1993).

Alexander Bickel's obituary ran in the *New York Times* on November 8, 1974. The transcript of his interview is from the American Jewish Committee's oral history project, which is archived at the New York Public Library.

Erwin O. Smigel writes about New York's old white-shoe law firms in *The Wall Street Lawyer: Professional Organization Man?* (Bloomington: Indiana University Press, 1969). Their particular employee preferences are listed on page 37.

Louis Auchincloss has written more about the changes that took place in the old-line law firms of Manhattan in the postwar years than anyone. The quotation is from his book *The Scarlet Letters* (New York: Houghton Mifflin, 2003), p. 153.

The economic annihilation faced by lawyers at the lower end of the social spectrum during the Depression is explored in Jerold S. Auerbach's *Unequal Justice: Lawyers and Social Change in Modern America* (Oxford: Oxford University Press, 1976), p. 159.

Statistics on the fluctuating birth rate in America during the twentieth century can be found at http://www.infoplease.com/ipa/A0005067.html.

The impact of the "demographic trough" is explored in Richard A. Easterlin's *Birth and Fortune: The Impact of Numbers on Personal Welfare* (Chicago: University of Chicago Press, 1987). H. Scott Gordon's paean to the circumstances of children born during a trough is from p. 4 of his presidential address to the Western Economic Association at the annual meeting in Anaheim, California, in June of 1977, "On Being Demographically Lucky: The Optimum Time to Be Born." It is quoted on page 31.

For a definitive account of the rise of Jewish lawyers, see Eli Wald, "The Rise and Fall of the WASP and Jewish Law Firms," *Stanford Law Review* 60, no. 6 (2008): 1803.

The story of the Borgenichts was told by Louis to Harold H. Friedman and published as *The Happiest Man: The Life of Louis Borgenicht* (New York: G. P. Putnam's Sons, 1942).

For more on the various occupations of nineteenth- and twentieth- century immigrants to America, read Thomas Kessner's *The Golden Door: Italian and Jewish Immigrant Mobility in New York City 1880–1915* (New York: Oxford University Press, 1977).

Stephen Steinberg's *The Ethnic Myth: Race, Ethnicity, and Class in America* (Boston: Beacon Press, 1982) includes a brilliant chapter on Jewish immigrants to New York, to which I am heavily indebted.

Louise Farkas's research was part of her master's thesis at Queen's college: Louise Farkas, "Occupational Genealogies of Jews in Eastern Europe and America, 1880–1924 (New York: Queens College Spring Thesis, 1982).

SIX: HARLAN, KENTUCKY

Harry M. Caudill wrote about Kentucky, its beauty and its troubles, in *Night Comes to the Cumberlands: A Biography of a Depressed Area* (Boston: Little, Brown, 1962).

The impact of coal mining on Harlan County is examined in "Social Disorganization and Reorganization in Harlan County, Kentucky," by Paul Frederick Cressey in *American Sociological Review* 14, no. 3 (June 1949): 389–394.

The bloody and complicated Turner-Howard feud is described, along with other Kentucky feuds, in John Ed Pearce's marvelously entertaining *Days of Darkness: The Feuds of Eastern Kentucky* (Lexington: University Press of Kentucky, 1994), p. 11.

The same clashes are assessed from an anthropological perspective by Keith F. Otterbein in "Five Feuds: An Analysis of Homicides in Eastern Kentucky in the Late Nineteenth

Century," *American Anthropologist* 102, no. 2 (June 2000): 231–243.

J. K. Campbell's essay "Honour and the Devil" appeared in J. G. Peristiany (ed.), *Honour and Shame: The Values of Mediterranean Society* (Chicago: University of Chicago Press, 1966).

The Scotch-Irish ancestry of the southern backcountry, as well as a phonetic guide to Scotch-Irish speech, can be found in David Hackett Fischer's monumental study of early American history, *Albion's Seed: Four British Folkways in America* (Oxford: Oxford University Press, 1989), p. 652.

The high murder rate in the South, and the specific nature of these murders, is discussed by John Shelton Reed in *One South: An Ethnic Approach to Regional Culture* (Baton Rouge: Louisiana State University Press, 1982). See, particularly, chapter 11, "Below the Smith and Wesson Line."

For more on the historical causes of the southern temperament and the insult experiment at the University of Michigan, see *Culture of Honor: The Psychology of Violence in the South,* by Richard E. Nisbett and Dov Cohen (Boulder, Colo.: Westview Press, Inc., 1996).

Raymond D. Gastil's study on the correlation between "southernness" and the US murder rate, "Homicide and a Regional Culture of Violence," was published in the *American Sociological Review* 36 (1971): 412–427.

Cohen, with Joseph Vandello, Sylvia Puente, and Adrian

Rantilla, worked on another study about the American North-South cultural divide: "'When You Call Me That, Smile!' How Norms for Politeness, Interaction Styles, and Aggression Work Together in Southern Culture," *Social Psychology Quarterly* 62, no. 3 (1999): 257–275.

SEVEN: THE ETHNIC THEORY OF PLANE CRASHES

The National Transportation Safety Board, the federal agency that investigates civil aviation accidents, published an Aircraft Accident Report on the Korean Air 801 crash: NTSB/AAR-00/01.

The footnote about Three Mile Island draws heavily on the analysis of Charles Perrow's classic *Normal Accidents: Living with High Risk Technologies* (New York: Basic Books, 1984).

The seven-errors-per-accident statistic was calculated by the National Transportation Safety Board in a safety study titled "A Review of Flightcrew-Involved Major Accidents of U.S. Air Carriers, 1978 Through 1990" (Safety Study NTSB/SS-94/01, 1994).

The agonizing dialogue and analysis of the Avianca 052 crash can be found in the National Transportation Safety Board Accident Report AAR-91/04.

Ute Fischer and Judith Orasanu's study of mitigation in the cockpit, "Cultural Diversity and Crew Communication," was presented at the fiftieth Astronautical Congress in Amsterdam, October 1999. It was published by the American Institute of Aeronautics and Astronautics.

Dialogue between the fated Air Florida captain and first officer is quoted in a second study by Fischer and Orasanu, "Error-Challenging Strategies: Their Role in Preventing and Correcting Errors," produced as part of the International Ergonomics Association fourteenth Triennial Congress and Human Factors and Ergonomics Society Forty-second Annual Meeting in San Diego, California, August 2000.

The unconscious impact of nationality on behavior was formally calculated by Geert Hofstede and outlined in *Culture's Consequences: Comparing Values, Behaviors, Institutions, and Organizations Across Nations* (Thousand Oaks, Calif.: Sage Publications, 2001). The study of French and German manufacturing plants that he quotes on page 102 was done by M. Brossard and M. Maurice, "Existe-t-il un modèle universel des structures d'organisation?," *Sociologie du Travail* 16, no. 4 (1974): 482–495.

The application of Hofstede's Dimensions to airline pilots was carried out by Robert L. Helmreich and Ashleigh Merritt in "Culture in the Cockpit: Do Hofstede's Dimensions Replicate?," *Journal of Cross-Cultural Psychology* 31, no. 3 (May 2000): 283–301.

Robert L. Helmreich's cultural analysis of the Avianca crash is called "Anatomy of a System Accident: The Crash of Avianca Flight 052," *International Journal of Aviation Psychology* 4, no. 3 (1994): 265–284.

The linguistic indirectness of Korean speech as compared with American was observed by Ho-min Sohn at the University of Hawaii in his paper "Intercultural Communication in Cognitive Values: Americans and Koreans," published in *Language and Linguistics* 9 (1993): 93–136.

EIGHT: RICE PADDIES AND MATH TESTS

To read more on the history and intricacies of rice cultivation, see Francesca Bray's *The Rice Economies: Technology and Development in Asian Societies* (Berkeley: University of California Press, 1994).

The logic of Asian numerals compared with their Western counterparts is discussed in Stanislas Dehaene in *The Number Sense: How the Mind Creates Mathematics* (Oxford: Oxford University Press, 1997).

Graham Robb, *The Discovery of France* (New York: W. W. Norton, 2007).

The surprisingly secure and leisurely life of the !Kung is detailed in chapter 4 of *Man the Hunter,* ed. Richard B. Lee and Irven DeVore, with help from Jill Nash-Mitchell (New York: Aldine, 1968).

The working year of European peasantry was calculated by Antoine Lavoisier and quoted by B. H. Slicher van Bath in *The Agrarian History of Western Europe, A.D. 500–1850,* trans. Olive Ordish (New York: St. Martin's, 1963).

Activities	Days	Percentage
Ploughing and sowing	12	5.8
Cereal harvest	28	13.6
Haymaking and carting	24	11.7
Threshing	130	63.1
Other work	12	5.8
Total	206	100.0

The fatalism of Russian peasant proverbs is contrasted with the self-reliance of Chinese ones by R. David Arkush in "*If Man Works Hard the Land Will Not Be Lazy*—Entrepreneurial Values in North Chinese Peasant Proverbs," *Modern China* 10, no. 4 (October 1984): 461–479.

The correlation between students' national average scores in TIMSS and their persistence in answering the student survey attached to the test has been evaluated in "Predictors of National Differences in Mathematics and Science Achievement of Eighth Grade Students: Data from TIMSS for the Six-Nation Educational Research Program," by Erling E. Boe, Henry May, Gema Barkanic, and Robert F. Boruch at the Center for Research and Evaluation in Social Policy, Graduate School of Education, University of Pennsylvania. It was revised February 28, 2002. The graph showing the results can be seen on page 9.

Results of the TIMSS tests throughout the years can be found on the National Center for Education Statistics Web site, http://nces.ed.gov/timss/.

Priscilla Blinco's study is entitled "Task Persistence in Japanese Elementary Schools" and can be found in Edward

Beauchamp, ed., *Windows on Japanese Education* (New York: Greenwood Press, 1991).

NINE: MARITA'S BARGAIN

An article in the *New York Times Magazine* by Paul Tough, "What It Takes to Make a Student" (November 26, 2006), examines the impact of the government's No Child Left Behind policy, the reasons for the education gap, and the impact of charter schools such as KIPP.

Kenneth M. Gold, *School's In: The History of Summer Education in American Public Schools* (New York: Peter Lang, 2002), is an unexpectedly fascinating account of the roots of the American school year.

Karl L. Alexander, Doris R. Entwisle, and Linda S. Olson's study on the impact of summer vacation is called "Schools, Achievement, and Inequality: A Seasonal Perspective," published in *Education Evaluation and Policy Analysis* 23, no. 2 (Summer 2001): 171–191.

Much of the cross-national data comes from Michael J. Barrett's "The Case for More School Days," published in the *Atlantic Monthly* in November 1990, p. 78.

EPILOGUE: A JAMAICAN STORY

William M. MacMillan details how his fears came to pass in the preface to the second edition of *Warning from the*

West Indies: A Tract for Africa and the Empire (U.K.: Penguin Books, 1938).

The sexual exploits and horrific punishments of Jamaica's white ruling class are detailed by Trevor Burnard in *Mastery, Tyranny and Desire: Thomas Thistlewood and His Slaves in the Anglo-Jamaican World* (Chapel Hill: University of North Carolina Press, 2004).

The intermediary color class in the West Indies, not seen in the American South, is described by Donald L. Horowitz in "Color Differentiation in the American Systems of Slavery," *Journal of Interdisciplinary History* 3, no. 3 (Winter 1973): 509–541.

Population and employment statistics among the different-colored classes in 1950s Jamaica are taken from Leonard Broom's essay "The Social Differentiation of Jamaica," *American Sociological Review* 19, no. 2 (April 1954): 115–125.

Divisions of color within families are explored by Fernando Henriques in "Colour Values in Jamaican Society," *British Journal of Sociology* 2, no. 2 (June 1951): 115–121.

Joyce Gladwell's experiences as a black woman in the UK are from *Brown Face, Big Master* (London: Inter-Varsity Press, 1969). It is a wonderful book. I recommend it highly—although, as you can imagine, I could be a bit biased.

Acknowledgments

I'm happy to say that *Outliers* conforms to its own thesis. It was very much a collective effort. I was inspired, as I seem to always be, by the work of Richard Nisbett. It was reading the *Culture of Honor* that set in motion a lot of the thinking that led to this book. Thank you, Professor Nisbett.

As always, I prevailed upon my friends to critique various drafts of the manuscript. Happily, they complied, and *Outliers* is infinitely better as a result. Many thanks to Jacob Weisberg, Terry Martin, Robert McCrum, Sarah Lyall, Charles Randolph, Tali Farhadian, Zoe Rosenfeld, and Bruce Headlam. Stacey Kalish and Sarah Kessler did yeoman's work in research and fact-checking. Suzy Hansen performed her usual editorial magic. David Remnick graciously gave me time off from my duties at *The New Yorker* to complete this book. Thank you, as always, David. Henry Finder, my editor at *The New Yorker,* saved me from myself and reminded me how to think, as he always does. I have worked with Henry for so long that I now have what I like to call the "internal Finder," which is a self-correcting voice inside my head that gives me the benefit of Henry's wisdom even when he is not there. Both Finders—internal and external—were invaluable.

Bill Phillips and I have been two for two so far, and I'm very grateful I was able to enlist his Midas touch once more. Thank you, Bill. Here's hoping we go three for three. Will Goodlad and Stefan McGrath at Penguin in England, and Michael Pietsch and—especially—Geoff Shandler at Little, Brown saw this manuscript through, from start to finish. Thanks to the rest of the team at Little, Brown as well: Heather Fain and Heather Rizzo and Junie Dahn. My fellow Canadian Pamela Marshall is a word wizard. I cannot imagine publishing a book without her.

Two final words of appreciation. Tina Bennett, my agent, has been with me from the very beginning. She is insightful and thoughtful and encouraging and unfailingly wise, and when I think of what she has done for me, I feel as lucky as a hockey player born on January 1.

I owe thanks most of all, though, to my parents, Graham and Joyce. This is a book about the meaning of work, and I learned that work can be meaningful from my father. Everything he does—from his most complex academic mathematics to digging in the garden—he tackles with joy and resolve and enthusiasm. My earliest memories of my father are of seeing him work at his desk and realizing that he was happy. I did not know it then, but that was one of the most precious gifts a father can give his child. My mother, for her part, taught me how to express myself; she taught me that there is beauty in saying something clearly and simply.

She read every word of this book and tried to hold me to that standard. My grandmother Daisy, to whom *Outliers* is dedicated, gave my mother the gift of opportunity. My mother has done the same for me.

MALCOLM GLADWELL is the author of the #1 international bestsellers *The Tipping Point* and *Blink*. He is a staff writer for *The New Yorker* and was formerly a business and science reporter at the *Washington Post*. For more information about Malcolm Gladwell, visit his Web site at www.gladwell.com.